THE GREAT
BEANIE
BABY
BUBBLE

THE GREAT
BEANIE
BABY

BUBBLE

MASS DELUSION AND
THE DARK SIDE OF CUTE

ZAC BISSONNETTE

WITHDRAWN

PORTFOLIO / PENGUIN

PORTFOLIO / PENGUIN
Published by the Penguin Group
Penguin Group (USA) LLC
375 Hudson Street
New York, New York 10014

USA | Canada | UK | Ireland | Australia | New Zealand | India | South Africa | China
penguin.com
A Penguin Random House Company

First published by Portfolio / Penguin, a member of Penguin Group (USA) LLC, 2015

Courtesy Joy Warner: Insert page 1 (top, center, bottom)
Courtesy Harold Nizamian: 2 (top, bottom)
Courtesy of the author: 3 (top)
Courtesy Sondra Schlossberg: 3 (center), 5 (top, center), 6 (bottom), 7 (top, center), 8 (center)
Courtesy Patricia Smith-Roche: 3 (bottom)
Courtesy Lina Trivedi: 4 (top, center), 6 (center)
Courtesy Peggy Gallagher: 4 (bottom), 5 (bottom)
Courtesy Lauren Boldebuck: 6 (top)
© Kevin R. Johnson/Press Line Photos/Corbis: 7 (bottom)
© Andrew Nelles/AP/Corbis: 8 (top)
Nick Presniakov: 8 (bottom)

LIBRARY OF CONGRESS CATALOGING-IN-PUBLICATION DATA
Bissonnette, Zac.
The great Beanie Baby bubble : mass delusion and the dark side of cute / Zac Bissonnette.
pages cm
Includes bibliographical references and index.
ISBN 978-1-59184-602-4 (hardback)
1. Warner, Ty, 1944– 2. Ty, Inc.—History. 3. Beanie Babies (Trademark)—Collectors and
collecting—History. 4. Toy industry—United States—History. I. Title.
HD9993.T694T923 2015
338.7'688724—dc23
2014038639

Printed in the United States of America
1 3 5 7 9 10 8 6 4 2

Set in ITC New Baskerville Std
Designed by Alissa Rose Theodor

CONTENTS

THE GREAT
BEANIE
BABY
BUBBLE

INTRODUCTION

The greatest toy salesman in the world looked out at his 250 employees gathered for the Ty Inc. holiday party.

"Wow!" fifty-four-year-old Ty Warner said. "I've never been in a room with so many millionaires!"

The salespeople cheered because it wasn't an exaggeration. It was December 12, 1998, and Ty Inc. was three weeks away from closing out a year of sales that would break nearly every record in the annals of the toy industry. Andi Van Guilder was seated in the back with the relatives she'd hired to answer the phones that hadn't stopped ringing with orders for Beanie Babies in close to three years. She thought about it. In 1993, she'd made less than $30,000 lugging trunks of porcelain figurines and collector plates to stores in two states. In 1998, selling Beanie Babies to independently owned toy and gift shops in Chicago's northern suburbs had paid her more than $800,000 in commissions. She was thirty years old. Life was perfect.

The applause died down. Ty made the announcement he'd been planning for weeks: he would be giving all his employees Christmas bonuses equal to their annual salaries.

Pandemonium ensued. "Ty was their God," Faith McGowan, Ty's then girlfriend, remembers. He basked in the adulation of the workers who, in the span of three years, had helped make him the richest man in the American toy industry. His annual sales for 1998 had surpassed $1.4 billion—virtually all of it coming from the $2.50 wholesale price on beanbag animals that frenzied speculators had turned into a craze that was the twentieth-century American version of the tulip bubble in 1630s Holland.

Ty had created the toys in 1993 in the hope that they would be popular among children, but they had become so much more than that; and they had also become so much less than that because most collectors, aware of the soaring values for the rarest styles, wouldn't let their children anywhere near them. Humorist Dave Barry explained the mania in a 1998 column: "Beanie Babies were originally intended as fun playthings for children, but as the old saying goes, 'Whenever you have something intended as innocent fun for children, you can count on adults to turn it into an obsessive, grotesquely over-commercialized "hobby" with the same whimsy content as the Bataan Death March.'"

The first buyers had been children with allowances. Then their moms had started collecting. By the time of the 1998 Ty Christmas party, Van Guilder remembers, it was mostly "creepy, belligerent men" she saw lined up when she dropped in to check on retailers. The little animals with names like Seaweed the Otter and Gigi the Poodle had become, as Van Guilder puts it, "something really cute that just brought out the worst in people."

The "worst in people" was inspired by a popular belief that Beanie Babies were a long-term investment. A self-published author sold more than three million copies of a book that touted ten-year predictions for their values. The magazine *Mary Beth's Beanie World*, started by a self-described soccer mom, reached one million copies in paid monthly circulation. In it, a full-page, full-color ad for Smart Heart tag protectors led with this headline: "How Do You Protect an Investment That Increases by 8,400%?" The answer was to buy hard-shell lockets in which to encase the animals' heart-shaped paper tags that read "Safety Precaution: Please remove all swing tags before giving this item to a child." More than any other consumer good in history,

Beanie Babies were carried to the height of success by a collective dream that their values would always rise.

Warner's announcement of bonuses wasn't his only gift to his employees at the Christmas party. He also presented them with #1 Bear, a signed and numbered red Beanie Baby with the number 1 stitched onto the chest. The inside of the hangtag explained that only 253 of the bears had been produced. It also listed the company's achievements for the year: more than $3 billion in retail sales, number one in the gift category, number one in collectibles, and number one in cash register area sales.

The workers inspected the bears and cheered some more. No doubt some were moved by sentiment, but they also knew that the bear could be listed on eBay, where Beanie Babies comprised 10 percent of all sales. On eBay, Beanie Babies sold for an average of $30—six times the price they had originally retailed for. Within a few weeks, #1 Bears would be selling for $5,000 or more apiece.

Not everyone at the luncheon was so thrilled. Faith McGowan sat quietly. In late 1993, Warner had shown her and her two daughters from her previous marriage who lived with them the first prototype for Legs the Frog. Since then, the animals had been the sole focus of their time together. Even as sales exploded, Ty personally designed every piece the company put out, and that meant spending several months each year at the factories in Asia. The frantic pace of their life together was exhausting, and Ty, a throwback to an entrepreneurial archetype that no longer exists, wasn't slowing down. Today, most rags-to-mega-riches stories involve hot technology, venture capital, and high-profile initial public offerings. Ty skipped all of that, marketing his own products based on his own ideas and the feedback of everyone around him without ever hiring a marketing consultant or assembling a focus group. He'd been the business's only shareholder since he'd started it in his condo in 1983, and when the investment bankers came peddling nine- and then ten-figure deals, Warner declined the dinner invitations. "Most guys would at least have the decency to jerk you around," remembers one banker. "He wouldn't even talk to you."

McGowan worried that she was losing him. He'd told her they would get married, and he'd even shown her father the ring he'd gotten her. But that had been more than a year ago, and there was no sign of a wedding on the horizon. She was terrified about what would happen if their life together came to an end. A few weeks after the party, Ty informed her that his pretax income for the year had come in at $700 million—more than Mattel's and Hasbro's earnings combined. Over in England, Ty's ex-girlfriend Patricia Roche had become rich running the company's distribution there. Faith was apprehensive about Ty's continuing relationship with Roche. More pressingly, Faith was worried that, for all the money Ty had made, she had no assets in her own name. "If Ty changed the locks on the Oak Brook house while the girls were at school or I was at work, I had nothing," Faith remembered in an unpublished memoir. "No house. No money in the bank. No employee severance. Not even a credit card."

After the party was over, McGowan prepared for the worst. Ty had presented her with the first #1 Bear—1 of 253—and she quickly sold it to a local collectibles dealer for ten thousand dollars and a promise not to tell anyone where he'd gotten it. She used the money to seed an emergency fund in case her five-year relationship with a man who was now a billionaire imploded.

Her decision to sell was well timed. That Christmas party happened to mark the absolute height of the Beanie craze, and the beginning of its spectacularly rapid decline. The new millennium was approaching, and the bubble was about to burst.

———

I was in middle school when the Beanies hit and I remember a couple I had. But mostly I remember the Beanie Baby dealers who sprouted at Cape Cod's Dick & Ellie's flea market, which my mother and I visited every weekend. I remember the adults wearing fanny packs and visors, eagerly discussing the "secondary market" fluctuations driving up the prices of pieces they'd paid $5 for a few weeks earlier. The Beanie sellers had the busiest booths and, for a couple of years, it really did look like the dealers sticking with Shaker furniture and oil paintings were as out of touch as Warren Buffett seemed to be when he eschewed Internet stocks in favor of acquiring Dairy Queen in late 1997.

I hadn't thought about Beanie Babies at all in at least ten years until, on a wintry day in 2010, I stopped at Kimballs, an auction house down the road from the University of Massachusetts, Amherst. I was a year away from graduating into the worst job market in a generation, and the fallout from the recent speculative mania in real estate was never far from anyone's mind.

At Kimballs, I was given a reminder of the aftermath of a smaller speculative mania: three large Rubbermaid containers on a table in the back of the room holding at least five hundred Beanie Babies, all with plastic lockets protecting their hangtags. Some were preserved individually in Lucite containers. There was another large box of magazines and price guides with names like *Beanies & More, Beanie Collector, Beans! Magazine,* and *Beanie Mania.* Then there were spreadsheets and checklists—how many of each Beanie Baby the collector/speculator had, which ones she was missing, how much was paid, and estimates of current value (as of 1998 or 1999). More interesting than the Beanies themselves was the manifest conviction of whoever had assembled the collection that it would one day be of great value. Everything on display was perfectly preserved and, as we found out when the auction started at 6:00 p.m., almost worthless. The entire lot sold for less than a hundred dollars—probably well below 2 percent of its value at the height of the Beanie Babies market, which, not coincidentally, was also the height of the Internet stock bubble.

That the speculative episode in Beanie Babies took place in tandem with the Internet bubble suggests that the cultural forces that were alchemizing Internet stocks had the same effect on Beanie Babies. They rose in an era of unreality defined by magical thinking; as economist Dr. Robert Shiller writes in *Irrational Exuberance*: "Speculative market expansions have often been associated with popular perceptions that the future is brighter or less uncertain than it was in the past." They also, Shiller notes, have a way of clustering around century turns—as if the prospect of going from '99 to '00 is so fantastic as to make all things seem possible. In the new millennium, the residents of America's high culture thought, the Internet would change everything, making everyone who bought Internet stocks rich, no matter how much they paid. Those in the lower culture adapted that optimism to a belief in the investment potential of stuffed animals, and it's hard to say which view was proven more wrong.

When I got home from the auction, I Googled Beanie Babies. There were pictures of Beanie Babies and stories noting that there had once been a craze for them, but nothing of any depth. Why had anyone ever thought Beanie Babies were a good investment? How had people decided that they were no longer worth anything?

There was also almost nothing on the man behind them. Ty Warner had an education that consisted of one year studying drama at Kalamazoo College and a net worth that *Forbes* estimated at $2.6 billion, all of it the product of the three-year Beanie Babies craze. That was enough to make him the 209th richest man in America. That was about the extent of the publicly available information about him. He hadn't done an interview since 1996, before the height of the craze, and no one who had known him personally or worked for him had ever spoken about him publicly. A *Chicago* magazine profile of Warner once described his life as hidden "behind an impenetrable wall of plush."

Wondering whether there might be a story worth telling about Ty Warner and the Beanie Babies that had driven a large swath of America into a state of greed-fueled delusion, I called one of the handful of people connected to the company I found mentioned in an old news clipping: "It was an incredible ride," a man named Bill Harlow told me. "But it's a shame it ended as badly as it did for us."

But don't focus on the negative, Harlow said. If you want to understand Ty Warner and how he became who he became, which was also the story of how Beanie Babies became what they became, he said, go see him at a toy and gift industry trade show. That was where Harlow had first met Warner in the late 1980s when Harlow was in his twenties, running a quilting store with his wife. Warner was in his forties—a flamboyantly dressed, perfectly coiffed bit player in the sleepy industry of stuffed animals, fastidiously grooming his plush Himalayan cats, the first toys he'd ever created. Everyone who saw him at trade shows in those days remembers him, usually alone, plucking around the cats' eyes with tweezers to accentuate "eye contact," as he put it, and blow-drying them to enhance the thickness of their fur.

Ty stopped the Harlows when they walked by his booth, asked them about their store, and then declared that nothing could possibly sell a quilt better than a stuffed cat sitting on top of it. They were skeptical, but they ordered when Ty's then girlfriend and business partner of sorts, Patricia Roche—Patti, as Ty called her—made the decision easier: "I guarantee this order," she scribbled on the invoice, and signed it.

As it turned out, Warner was right. Cats sold quilts and quilts sold cats, and Harlow reordered quickly. That $125 order set in motion a chain of events that led to Harlow becoming the exclusive Ty

Inc. distributor for all of Canada a few years later. At his peak, Harlow's annual revenue was more than $80 million—a level of Canadian sales no other plush-toy seller had ever reached. Harlow became a multimillionaire in his thirties, and it just went to show: Ty Warner's presence at trade shows could lead to incredible things. A trade show, Harlow said: that was the place to see the king of the stuffed animals in his natural habitat.

1

The Greatest Toy Show on Earth: No Kids Allowed

American International Toy Fair, February 2012, Javits Center, New York City

No children are admitted to the exhibit halls. Absolutely no one under the age of 18 (including infants and toddlers) is permitted to attend Toy Fair. There are no childcare facilities at the Javits Center. Please save yourself and your child the stress and embarrassment of being turned away.

—FROM THE BACK OF MY ADMISSIONS TAG

"He'll be here in eight minutes," said a company vice president, looking down at his cell phone.

Instantly, the twelve or so employees manning Ty Inc.'s booth got to work. Dust was brushed from the pink pedestals displaying stuffed bears, cats, and gorillas. A pair of handlers wielding lint brushes furiously patted down the costumes on the three people who, with the help of a cockney-accented jester, were promoting the company's latest toy: Monstaz, a line of small, round, multicolored beanbags that retail for around $6.99 and spew gibberish when you squeeze them.

"Remember Beanies Babies?" the jester asked a group of five onlookers. "When everybody went c-c-c-craaazy?!" he said, twirling his finger at his temple. It wasn't the cuteness, affordability, or long-term play value of Beanie Babies that he was evoking; it wasn't even the volume of sales. It was the memory that, for a few years, Beanie Babies had driven many Americans insane.

The jester's reference to the time when everybody went "c-c-c-crazy" is about as much information as the company provides about itself. Ty Inc. is the most successful stuffed-animal brand ever, but there is no "About Us" or "Corporate" page on its Web site. There's no Ty Warner archive at a university library, no corporate-financed vanity history, and Warner has never given a public speech of any kind. A single 1996 interview with *People* magazine is the source of the biographical sketch in every news story about him, but, as I would learn, very little of what he told the reporter was true.

At Toy Fair 2012, a Ty employee told me that earlier in the day Warner had sent people to change the fabric on a curtain (a different shade of pink was needed, he'd decided) and swap out the eyes in a display model. There was still more to be done. When I asked one of the workers how much involvement Warner had in Ty's day-to-day operations, her eyes widened. "You have no idea," she said.

It is strange and noteworthy that Warner is still so focused on plush. He's at an age where most people are eyeing retirement— and, in any case, these days the stuffed-animal business is a small portion of his wealth. His annual income from Ty Inc. is well under 5 percent of what it was in the late 1990s and his real estate investments are a much bigger part of his financial life. In the early 2000s, he handed off day-to-day operations of his toy company to focus on renovating the hotels he was buying. He devoted seven years to renovating the Ty Warner Penthouse at his Four Seasons Hotel in New York City, spending $50 million on the 4,300-square-foot suite and then making it the most expensive hotel reservation in North America at $45,000 a night.

But beginning in the mid-2000s, his first love called him back.

He spends several months each year at factories in China, working on designs for new products and making sure that his standards for quality control are upheld. For all of his company's thirty-year existence, Ty Warner has been involved in the selection of every piece of fabric that goes into each of the more than five thousand distinctly designed plush animals he's sold. He recently turned down dozens of samples for the eyes in Beanie Boos, another of his new lines because, as Warner knows, the eyes are the most important part of any stuffed animal.

Wandering around the Ty booth, I told the company's vice president of global sales about the book I intended to write and my hopes for an interview with Warner.

"There's no way," he said. "He's just a very private person." Then, after a pause: "Sucks, doesn't it?"

Finally, with no fanfare, the sixty-seven-year-old billionaire who, one Ty sales rep told me, was "the Steve Jobs of plush" arrived. Ty Warner is just short of five-foot-ten—shorter than you always expect someone you've waited hours to meet to be. College classmates remember mocking him for wearing lifts in his shoes. He had on a black suit over a black turtleneck, with a wedding band that had led to speculation among the company's sales reps that he'd finally married for the first time. (He hadn't.)

The twenty-year odyssey of plastic surgery funded by the largest personal fortune in the history of stuffed animals is the first thing anyone who sees Warner will notice—although the cosmetic work began years before he was notably wealthy. A former teddy bear designer for the company told me that Ty would "get his face stretched" a few months before Toy Fair every year. More recently, he's used black sheep embryo injections to further maintain his youth. His face was tight and pale, and it had a certain porcelain-doll-like appearance. One former employee thought that the work focused around his eyes made him look Asian, and others said he was having sinus issues as a result of too-frequent procedures. Cosmetic surgeons had warned him that he had long ago reached the point of diminishing returns, but he persevered in an obsession with his own face that mirrored his meticulous micromanagement of his company's stuffed animals. His eyebrows were sculpted and his light hair was colored and carefully styled into a sort of mullet that had been his look for at least fifteen years—partly because it helped to hide any incision marks from the cosmetic procedures.

Standing away from the booth, Ty whispered a list of changes to a thirtysomething female assistant, and then he smiled. "It looks pretty good, doesn't it?" he said.

"Mr. Warner," I said as I approached him.

He walked over, stuck out his hand, and looked at me while I introduced myself.

"Nice to meet you," he said.

I told him that I was working on a book about Beanie Babies; I told him that I thought it was the most intriguing entrepreneurial success story in American history—I really thought that and I still do. I said I knew that in the past he hadn't exactly been media-friendly but that he had the most incredible story to tell and that I hoped he would tell it to me: how, starting with nothing, he had become a billionaire with beanbag animals that he'd convinced the American public were rare even while ships from China delivered them by the tens of millions as quickly as the factories could make them.

"There's a lot of people who can tell the story a lot better than I can," Warner told me in a deep but soft-spoken Midwestern voice that had a certain folksiness to it. But there was no hesitation in his delivery that suggested he'd cooperate. "It was a lot of trials and a lot of tribulations, a lot of ups and downs—and we were just trying to keep up with it. A lot of good and a lot of bad. And I would probably just tell you the good and then it wouldn't be balanced."

"Well, I would talk to other people, too," I said.

"No, I think it's better if you just talk to other people."

That, over the next two years, is what I did. I talked to current (but mostly former) Ty employees and executives and the two women who were by Warner's side during the most exciting parts of his career: the first from the beginning of the company up until the launch of Beanie Babies, and the second from the launch on through the end of the craze. I also talked with his sister, who told me the story of an early life that Ty himself described as "unhappy" in a 2013 court filing. I learned that that was a profoundly understated assessment.

Perhaps most important, I met with the collectors, dealers, and bestselling authors who transformed Ty Warner's creation from a popular toy into a collectible and, finally, a token for speculation. I talked with a retired soap opera star who, with too much time on his hands in the twilight of his career, lost his children's six-figure college funds hoarding Beanies at the peak of the market.

The story of Ty Warner and his Beanie Babies shows the dynamics that drive people into and out of speculative manias, but it's also about every other manner of human dysfunction, turmoil, and trauma. "As you have learned," Faith McGowan once told me, "this is a dark story."

But first, while I was at the Javits Center, I walked just a couple hundred feet downstairs—but a long drop in other ways—to talk to the man who gave Ty his start in the toy business.

2

The Lower Level

I can see the world without many things, but I cannot see the world without a teddy bear.

—HAROLD NIZAMIAN

The lower level of the Javits Center is filled mostly with smaller, less elaborate booths for the upstarts who can't afford prime space on the upper floor. With exhibition costs starting in the four digits, every aspiring Geppetto with some credit cards or a home equity loan has a chance to get his toys in front of every buyer worth courting. Catch the eye of the right buyer, and a fortune-making share of the global toy industry's $80 billion in annual revenue can be yours. With that bump in sales might come the means to afford a larger booth, which will make you easier for the buyers to spot and, maybe more important, announce that you've arrived.

Held annually since the turn of the century, Toy Fair tracks the history of the industry and, in many ways, the rise of consumerism in America. The U.S. market is so dominant that although major manufacturers exhibit on every continent, retailers from more than a hundred countries come to New York City to see what's hot. It was easy to get distracted as I walked away from the Ty booth and downstairs to find Harold Nizamian, who had been the CEO of Dakin Inc., a plush-industry leader, when Ty Warner worked there in the 1960s and 1970s. The Lennon Sisters of *The*

Lawrence Welk Show fame—now in their sixties and seventies—
were at Toy Fair to personally take orders for their line of Best
Pals rag dolls, inspired by their childhood in Venice, California.
Elsewhere, a fiftysomething Italian man wearing a seersucker suit
galloped by, demonstrating his product: a life-size mechanical
pony. "Why don't you already order?" he hissed at an older
woman who was watching him.

Forty years ago, Harold Nizamian would have had a booth
not all that different from the one Ty has now. Harry, as everyone at Dakin called him, would have been the star, posing for
reporters with the company's newest products, smiling and en-
thusiastically pointing out every feature on whatever teddy bear
he was pushing. Dakin's sales force came from all over the country to man the booth; they loved Harry and Harry loved them.
"It was Harry's enthusiasm and love of people that built the company," remembers one former Dakin executive.

When I met Harry, close to fifty years after he gave Warner
his first job in plush, he was back on Toy Fair's lower level, trying
to show his toys to everyone who walked by. Harry, who once ran
a $200 million toy business, watched his empire crumble just as
Warner's was ascending. He's in his early eighties now, and he
manned the booth for his company, Timeless-Toys Inc., alone.
His son had risen at dawn to help set up. Nizamian's been at Toy
Fair to sell something nearly every year since 1962, and age and
ailing finances haven't stopped him. Things had gotten so bad
recently, he confided, that he was struggling to find the $3,000
he needed to fill a retailer's order for an out-of-stock line of
hand puppets.

He showed me a set of jumbo-size pick-up sticks, rolled a
multicolored die, and then bent over wearily to pick up the
stick of corresponding color. These sticks, which he's had in inventory since 2001, help kids develop spatial skills, social skills,
integrity, and critical thinking, he said. But the thing that still

gets Harry most excited is plush. When he put down the pick-up sticks to show me a big black bear puppet named Bart, and Sasha, a Russian blue cat, decades seemed to evaporate from his face, and it was easy to see Harry as he had once been: a child of poverty raised in a string of orphanages, separated from his father, clinging to any form of sweetness that happened to enter his life.

Nizamian was born in Philadelphia in 1930. His father was an Armenian candy maker and his mother died shortly after Harry was born. When his father's financial fortunes crumbled with the Depression, Harry and his three siblings were placed in foster care on a farm run by the Edwin Gould Foundation for Children. Once a year, a bus brought them to New York, where they had medical and dental work done at Columbus Circle—about a mile and a half from the Javits Center. Nizamian is reminded of his youth every year when he makes the trip to Toy Fair. He has no memories of any stuffed toys from his childhood. It is, perhaps, that lifelong thirst for comforting objects that has kept Harry in the soft-toy business, even though it hasn't treated him well in decades.

"It's the look on a kid's face when he gets a teddy bear," Harry told me. "I love that. I love the game." He paused. "A teddy bear, to me . . . is just endless and unconditional love."

The stuffed-animal business has declined over the past couple of decades, but with a funny quirk: the people who find the most success in it seem almost without exception to come from deeply broken childhoods, and few of them ever really leave the industry. Ty Warner still goes to Toy Fair every year. Virginia Benes-Kemp, who was creative director at Dakin in the 1960s and remembers Warner's frequent drop-ins to discuss ideas for new products, is in her eighties now. Every day she goes to work at

Down to Earth Designer Gifts, her store in Pacifica, California, where she sells—for reasons that will later become clear—pretty much every major plush line except for Ty Inc. Sally Winey, who was a star designer for Ty and a celebrity of the 1990s collectibles world, ended up bankrupt after the decline of the mania and a legal battle with Warner. Still, every summer, she rents a shop in Southport, North Carolina, and tries—mostly without success—to sell her handmade bears.

Part of this is a gambler's mentality: every toy manufacturer is one break away from striking it rich, and if you've had that happen once, you spend the rest of your life fantasizing about its happening again. Yet there's more to it than money. Like the Velveteen Rabbit of Margery Williams's perennially best-selling children's book, plush makers are animated by the prospect of their creations becoming the first thing a child loves and values. The speculative bubble that emerged for Beanie Babies is probably best understood as late-1990s speculative capitalism merged with a massive collective flashback to the comfort stuffed animals provided in our early years.

Psychology textbooks tell us that a stuffed animal is the most common transitional object for American children—the thing that helps them detach from their mothers and begin life as independent beings. In his 1984 memoir, *They Cage the Animals at Night*, Jennings Michael Burch recounts the violence and neglect he faced in a childhood spent in orphanages and foster homes. One incident stood out above all others: at age eight, when he was removed from an orphanage and placed in foster care, a nun told him he couldn't take his stuffed dog with him. "Doggie was gone," he recounted. "I felt the worst pain I had ever known. It wouldn't go away."

The nurturing that stuffed animals provide doesn't exactly mesh with the reputation of the industry behind them. Several toy executives I spoke with repeated the same old joke about the plush business: "It's for people who aren't nice enough for the Garment District."

————————

Ty Warner met Harry Nizamian in the mid-1960s, when Warner was selling vacuum cleaners door to door in Northern California—a gig he worked in between pumping gas, stocking shelves at a grocery store, and auditioning for roles in movies. Warner, vacuum cleaner in hand, knocked on the door of a lavish mansion; when the homeowner opened it, Ty tossed a handful of dirt on the man's carpet, then quickly vacuumed it up. The homeowner turned out to be Harold Nizamian, and he was impressed. "Kid, you're a hell of a salesman," he said. "You ought to come work for me." Thus began Warner's entry into the world of soft toys.

Once Warner had his own company, this story was recited to every new salesman he hired. He also told it to the women he dated, and it's easy to see why: it reads as if plagiarized from a Horatio Alger novel. As a story about the wonderful things that can happen to anyone with pluck and a willingness to take some risks to close a sale, it's hard to beat. And so, naturally, it isn't true.

Actually, Ty got the job through his father, Hal, who sold Dakin's line of plush products all over Ohio. Ty had recently dropped out after a year of college to move to California to try to become an actor. That didn't work out, so he tried selling cameras door to door. Joy remembers Ty excitedly bringing home the samples and how deflated he was after his father mocked the business idea. Hal was proven right and when the camera buyers failed to materialize, Ty was left badly in need of an opportunity. But his father still had to push him to take a job with Dakin. "It's a good company," Hal told him again and again. Reluctantly, Ty agreed to start work as his dad's sub-rep.

The vacuum cleaner story wasn't true, but Warner quickly established himself as such a gifted salesman that it's easy to see why people believed it. "He was the best salesman I have ever known in my forty-four years of being a manager," says Paul Roche, who was Nizamian's head of sales and Warner's direct supervisor. As Dakin grew from a small business into a global leader in plush during the 1960s and 1970s, Ty Warner became its highest-paid employee within just a few years of entering the business—outearning Dakin's CEO, an unusual accomplishment for a commissioned sales rep with no college degree and no significant prior sales experience.

Warner had found his passion; and it was at Dakin that he began to develop the ideas—low prices and high volume, selling only to independently owned retailers, obsessive attention to every detail of product design, and a fixation on putting PVC pellets in stuffed animals—that would make him rich. As he told journalist Joni Blackman in the only extended interview of his life, "I learned marketing, impulse items—I learned this company [Ty Inc.] from Dakin. They were the best." Later, when he had his own business and new employees to train, his notes on the philosophies that he hoped to convey to them always began here.

———

On April 1, 1955, San Francisco entrepreneur Richard Dakin started a business importing shotguns from Europe. In 1957 Richard's son Roger joined him and tried to spur growth with a line of imported battery-operated trains. Along with the trains, the manufacturer sent samples of six small, sawdust-filled toys covered with a cotton velveteen fabric. At the urging of his employees, Roger took the samples down to a notions buyer at a nearby department store. They immediately ordered three hundred pieces, and Dakin was in the toy business. Roger branded the line Dakin Dream Pets, and they quickly became a steady seller in gift and toy stores. The trains and the money-losing gun business were jettisoned shortly thereafter, completing Dakin's improbable transformation from the Dakin Gun Company to a fast-growing stuffed-animal concern.

The Dream Pets look dated today, but they were quite a novelty at the time. The velveteen gave them a boldness of color that softer plush with a thicker pile lacked. They were stuffed with willow sawdust and a small amount of straw, and the look was vibrant and expressive. They were too hard to be cuddly, but they had wonderfully creative designs and characters, and at a wholesale price of sixty cents, they sold well as impulse buys. When the popular antiques guide *Warman's* published its *101 Greatest Baby Boomer Toys*, Dream Pets made the list at number sixty-six. They were probably the Beanie Babies' closest ancestor, and in the late 1990s many antiques dealers peddling Dream Pets marketed them as "the original Beanie Babies" although they had no knowledge of the Ty Warner connection: the Dream Pets were the first toys that Ty Warner ever sold.

The first stage of Dakin's growth ended on December 20, 1966, when Richard Dakin, his son Roger, both of their wives, and four of Roger's children died in a plane crash. By then Dakin was large enough to have a small board of directors, which handed control over to Nizamian, the company's executive vice president, then in his midthirties. Dakin was up to $3.5 million a year in sales, with virtually all of it coming from plush toys—mostly Dream Pets.

Under Nizamian Dakin rose to become one of the most prominent sellers of stuffed animals in the world. By the late 1970s Dakin was selling close to 70 million toys per year in 87 countries, divided among a product line of 650–700 pieces, and Ty Warner was the company's star salesman.

3

Selling the Dream Pets

No one who remembers Ty Warner in the first two decades of his life remembers him for any notable ambitions or for any interest in business. "I would swear in a court of law," says high school classmate Donald Danald of Warner's billion-dollar net worth, "that aliens kidnapped the real Ty Warner." The alchemy of Ty Warner happened almost instantaneously upon his entry into the plush business. Before Dream Pets, Warner had no particular dreams—other than a vague, adolescent aspiration for wealth and fame, but no plans for how to achieve it. All that changed when he started at Dakin. As his lawyers described his time there in a 2013 legal filing, "Ty especially enjoyed selling a product intended for children, and he developed a keen sense of what particular plush toys children enjoyed."

That knowledge brought him tremendous success at a young age: earnings of well over $100,000 per year in the late 1960s, a time when the median household income was less than $7,000. With that income came the hatred of almost everyone Warner worked with. "He was a smart-assed shithead," remembers Mike Ingram, a former Dakin sales rep. "He was arrogant and thought he was somebody that he wasn't. I would guess you're gonna be hard-pressed to find anybody who liked him."

Paul Roche, Warner's supervisor, adds that "I never liked him as a human being. I found him to be niggardly and not honest in his dealings with people. I didn't find any level of trust between him and the company or him and anybody else. At that time in his life, he was very selfish, totally into himself."

But couldn't some of that antipathy be attributed to professional jealousy?

"I don't think anybody was jealous of him because we all knew he had a lousy life. He had no close relationships; they were close insofar as they served him. There were no relationships with men, only if he could get something out of you at the moment. No real friends. None. That was part of the guy's problem. He didn't have a lot of contact. He was into work and pussy, in that order. He was a very persuasive character, a salesman. He was endearing to his customers, and ladies loved him. Once you scrape the surface away just a little bit, he was an asshole."

Former Dakin employees saw his father, Hal, as one-dimensional and excessively materialistic. He had no hobbies outside of selling, according to Roche, save for an antiques collection. When Roche asked him about it, the elder Warner quickly pointed to its investment value. Nizamian adds that "you couldn't talk to him about anything except the business."

Roche says Ty Warner was similar, but with a stronger work ethic. "He was persuasive, tenacious, wouldn't take no for an answer," he says. "He kept coming back to the sale, as most good salespeople do. I just think he practices that better than most people."

Success aside, Warner's relationship with his father was strained at best and, by most accounts, bizarre and dysfunctional. Ty and his father dated the same women on several occasions. "Dad really knew how to treat a woman," Ty's sister remembers. She says that Ty was jealous of his father's charms, and channeled that energy into seducing women his father had been with. Nizamian took a personal interest in Warner—and sought to become a mentor to the young salesman. "Ty, there's so much more to life than money," Nizamian lectured him. "Learn about the arts, learn about history."

Unlike his father, Ty seemed to have a genuine passion for the product. He was making a lot of money, but he was also using it as an extremely well-paid internship in the business of plush. Retailers Warner once sold to recall him quizzing them on which products were selling and which ones weren't; Warner sought feedback on competitors' products, too. What did they think of this idea? What about that? What if you combined this with that?

He also pitched his ideas to the executives at Dakin. Dressed in a camel hair coat, he frequently strolled into product development head Virginia Benes-Kemp's office with advice about new products. "He thought he was God's gift to women," she remembers, and she mostly ignored his suggestions. Sometimes Warner took his ideas straight to the CEO. Nizamian is quick to admit that Warner's product sense was uncanny. Ty could look at a new product and declare on the spot whether it would sell—and he turned out to be right far more often than the executives were. One idea Nizamian declined to pursue: a line of teddy bears holding World's Best Dad plaques.

Warner developed his entire arsenal of knowledge on the road in his Rolls-Royce, fur coat, and top hat; sometimes he even carried a cane. He knew what it took to get the attention of buyers, and his devotion to learning about plush gave him knowledge of the industry totally unheard of among the ranks of commissioned salespeople. Warner had been a shy high school athlete, but he transformed himself from a guy who, as one classmate put it, "went out of his way to avoid being noticed" into one of the most persuasive and eccentric personalities in an industry known for them. Other salesmen might throw their hats into a slamming door to try to get a retailer's attention, but Warner never resorted to that. He was always smooth and, with women, especially, flirtatious. Warner had carefully crafted a stage persona that was perfect for toy sales.

He remained largely inscrutable and distant from other Dakin employees, with the exception of Roger and Betty Ericson, a husband-and-wife team who represented Dakin to retailers in Indiana while Warner was selling in Ohio. The Ericsons, by all accounts, were extremely nice people—and were able to bond with Warner in a way that few others did. When they told him they planned to name their son Roger, Warner scoffed: "Nobody needs more than two letters." So R. J. Ericson it was. When Warner was in Indiana for toy shows, he stayed with them at their house; when they were in Ohio, where Warner was based, they stayed in hotels. Warner once offered to take their five-year-old daughter out for ice cream, but when he pulled up in his Rolls-Royce, he asked her if she had any money. She said no and he told her to go ask her parents because he didn't want to pay for it. They were puzzled but handed her a few dollars, and she and Warner had a nice time together. Betty found the incident bizarre, but that was Ty. She didn't hold his idiosyncrasies against him.

Warner's attitude was less endearing to the company's management: he skipped the sales conferences to play tennis—while still taking advantage of the all-expenses-paid junkets. On the court he was a fierce competitor and a bad loser; Nizamian remembers beating him once and then watching Warner storm back to his car without saying good-bye. He was also stingy—a bad tipper who was focused on the return on investment on every purchase; the strong resale value was behind his decision to buy a Rolls-Royce instead of a Mercedes. And when it came to health insurance, Warner wasn't seeing a good expected rate of return. His father approached head of sales Paul Roche with concern. Roche called Ty and told him, "Just listen to Hal," but Warner wasn't buying it. "I'm healthy, I don't need it, I'm not gonna spend the money," he said.

Warner's success and product instincts made Nizamian consider bringing him in to work on the corporate side, but Warner's relationships with other employees—he was in a constant state of war with some members of management—and his lack of formal education led Nizamian to decide against it. He worried that Warner was too "narrowly concentrated" for the vagaries of corporate life.

————————

After fifteen years as a top salesman at Dakin, Warner overstepped. Dakin had built itself first as a traditional plush business, but as brand- and licensing-driven products took over the industry, it adapted with great success. It started manufacturing products based on the cartoon cat Garfield in 1978; sales exploded with a line of plush Garfields with suction-cup paws that people stuck to the windows of their cars. As Dakin grew, it sought to expand its sales ranks and, as a consequence, shrink the territories of the existing account reps. It's a common practice—Warner later did the same thing at Ty Inc.—and with sales increasing at each account and more accounts being opened in each market, salespeople often make more money with less work. Yet it is also not uncommon for existing salespeople to be displeased with the changes. And Warner was pissed. He started pitching his own stuffed animals to the same buyers he was paid to sell Dakin products to.

Paul Roche received a few calls from customers who were surprised by Warner's behavior. Ty had been smart enough not to approach the biggest accounts that had the strongest relationships with Dakin, but he overestimated his customers' loyalty to him relative to their loyalty to Dakin. Roche and Nizamian hired a private investigator to look into it, and he reported back that it was true: Warner had rented office space for his new venture. Roche gave the greatest salesman he'd ever worked with thirty days' notice.

On Warner's last day with the company, he approached Roche

and another executive at the Chicago Gift Show. He insisted that the whole thing had been a misunderstanding. The other executive asked whether there was a way to give Warner another chance. "You can manage this whole company by yourself because it's either him or me," Roche replied.

That night, Warner showed up at a company dinner, with a date. "He had just been fired, he wasn't wanted. That's the way the man was," says Roche, speculating that Warner was mostly there for the free food. Roche also tells a bizarre story illustrating Warner's vindictive side. When Warner dropped off his final retailer orders at Roche's hotel room, Roche took the sales sheets, and Warner left without incident. Years later, Roche found out that Warner had told some of their coworkers that Roche had greeted him wearing a dress and had hit on him. This story illustrates three of Warner's defining characteristics from this period and, most say, the rest of his life: creativity, ruthlessness, and, judging from the apparent credulity of some of his former coworkers, an aptitude for persuasion.

As for the plush Warner was selling that got him fired from Dakin? Nothing ever came of that: inflation soared to 13.5 percent in 1980, and unemployment reached historically high levels as consumer spending tanked. It was a bad time to fund a small business and a worse time to try to sell impulse items. Interest rates soared, savings and loans failed, and Warner's little stuffed start-up disappeared. He sank into a depression that some of his former coworkers and industry contacts worried might end his life.

4

Plush Dreams

Hal Warner left Dakin shortly after Ty did, and the two teamed up to import a line of jewelry boxes. That business didn't go anywhere, though, and Ty's listlessness worsened. In letters to Ty's sister, Joy, from around this time, Hal expressed concern about his son and his seemingly zapped ambition.

"Ty's been here for better than three weeks eating breakfast and just about every meal available during this time," Hal wrote. "I am sure that he must sense that I am very irritated and very sick both mentally and physically because he is not working and is not looking for a job, and avoids doing anything unless it is mandatory. He is just waiting to sell one of his condominiums so he can get some cash, but so far no buyers. But in my mind this is a poor excuse for being idle, non-productive and failing to earn his daily bread. I guess this run-in with me doesn't set very well with him. I can only hope he'll see the light and take some kind of action. He's sure not like you or me."

With his relationship with his father in trouble, Warner invested some of his savings in a partnership with Pasquale Capra, an Italian American craftsman he'd hired to refinish furniture for his condo. "He didn't have no social life," remembers Capra. "When I got involved with him, he was very withdrawn. I said 'Guy! You better wake up; you're the mega-million-dollar salesman!'"

They were equal partners, with Capra working on design and manufacturing and Warner providing a few thousand dollars and his sales prowess. Their product was a line of Otagiri-style music boxes, but from the beginning, the relationship was troubled. Capra and Warner butted heads on pricing almost instantly. Capra felt that the margins were too low to make a living, even though Warner could move close to $100,000 in merchandise at a single trade show. "He had this thing that low price could make you rich," says Capra, who felt strongly that they needed to raise prices, particularly given the supply constraints that prevented them from turning it into a high-volume business. Warner was adamantly opposed to the idea of price increases; to compound the problem, he was obsessed with maximizing the quality of the product. "We were buying a fifty-cent musical movement, and he wanted to hire a pianist to tune them. That's the perfectionist that he was," says Capra.

The partnership was short-lived. "He didn't see the light at the end of the tunnel and so he picked up his briefcase and left," says Capra. Capra couldn't make a go of the business and filed for bankruptcy. He's still tinkering with music boxes but has struggled ever since, having watched in horror as Warner ascended the *Forbes* list with the very idea—low prices and obsessive attention to quality could make you rich—that had been the source of their conflict. In Ty catalogs Warner sometimes brags that his company has never raised its wholesale prices; how many of your suppliers, he asks, can say that?

After Warner ditched Capra, he continued to spend down his savings while turning over ideas in his head. He knew that his neighbor, Patricia Roche, a bold, brassy lady who looks and acts like Liza Minnelli, was taking classes at a nearby community college, so one day he approached her in the garage: Could he, he asked, use the college's library for some research?

Warner explained that he was looking into obscure patent issues. He'd been told that in the aftermath of World War II, an American company had sold a portfolio of patents to the Japanese. One of these patents was for a process for making an exceptionally soft synthetic fur. Warner had an idea for a line of plush but was concerned that the thickness of fabric he wanted was available only in Japan. By the early 1980s, the cost of manufacturing there was prohibitively high. He was seeking some sort of industrial-espionage loophole—a way to get the thickness of the pile that he sought while manufacturing it at a lower cost in Korea.

Roche was intrigued by Warner. She'd caught him on a rare good day, and his charisma and ambitious plans lured her in.

He and Roche started spending a lot of time together—hanging out in his condo after she'd finished up her day job at a convenience store. They were, as she puts it, "after-school buddies." She was married to a wheelchair-bound man, and she helped him with his car-painting business, but the marriage was disintegrating. She spent most nights at Warner's, trying to keep his spirits up, kicking around his ideas, and learning about business from him.

Roche loved Warner's condo. He kept everything immaculate, and he had beautiful Persian carpets and antiques from all over the world. There was also a baby grand piano in the living room. Warner only played it when he was badly depressed, but when he did play, he played exceptionally well. His father could play jazz by ear and his mother had been a concert pianist; she'd required Ty and his sister to practice for several hours each day when they were children. Hal Warner told Dakin coworkers that Ty might have made a career of music if he'd stayed with it.

Warner was probably playing the piano a fair amount in those days because he was still depressed. He was neglecting his personal hygiene and flailing about for some new venture that would bring in cash and restore the swagger that had once made him prosperous and something approximating happy. Two concerned friends from the gift industry were calling regularly to make sure he wasn't going to hurt himself. In his late thirties, Ty had been selling plush full time from his early twenties until the day Dakin fired him. For the first time since he'd entered the business, he was going nowhere—which was also, not coincidentally, what he'd been doing before he discovered his love of stuffed animals.

Finally, Roche told him to trim his nose hair. In Roche's telling of it, the nose hair was "down to his chin." Roche describes the nose-hair confrontation as an inflection point in Warner's psyche, the beginning of his return to superstar salesman status.

On the way out of his depression, Warner was still devoting most of his time to the music box idea (by then, without Capra), and he went to Korea to explore manufacturing possibilities. Six weeks later he came back.

"I'm going back and forth with this," he told Patricia Roche. "There's no way to mass-produce it because it takes too long for the varnish to dry."

And then he told her of a vision he'd had.

"I was in my room and I couldn't sleep. There's this flashing light going on outside my window, and I looked outside, and it was the Dakin Bear."

The Dakin Bear was the old-fashioned yellow teddy bear that had been Dakin's logo for Warner's entire tenure at the company.

"It's an omen," he continued. "Plush is what I should be doing."

Warner asked Roche what she thought about going into the stuffed-animal business.

"Wait a minute. I've gone from a convenience store to cars with my husband to music boxes to plush. I don't know anything about plush."

"I can teach you," he said.

Roche didn't know it at the time, but the idea of starting a plush company in the early 1980s was no one's idea of smart. It was a stagnant industry, fifty years past its prime, with no growth in sight. Ty Warner might have brought a level of perfectionism to it that no one else did, but it seemed unlikely that could compensate for the business's horrible economics. At one end, the rise of technological toys attracting younger fans each year was squeezing demand for plush. At the other end, vertically integrated Asian factories were crushing margins as they churned out cheap, low-quality animals that were good enough to put on the shelves of the big-box stores that were destroying the locally owned toy and gift shops. There seemed to be little demand for a better product. Yet a vision told Warner to start his own plush company, and so plush it was.

How exactly Ty Warner got the money to start his stuffed-animal business is a subject of some dispute. I went to Camano Island, Washington, to meet with his sister, Joy, and see what I could find out—and to learn a little more about his early life.

While Ty and Joy were growing up in a Frank Lloyd Wright house in the Chicago suburb of La Grange, Hal was on the road, selling toys all over Ohio and, at times, three other states. He provided well for his family in a material sense—but not in any other way. Warner's mother, Georgia, at that point not yet diagnosed as a paranoid schizophrenic, spent many of her days lying in bed with a washcloth over her face, getting up only to puke green bile into the toilet. She stood in front of the mirror and screamed at people who weren't there. Once, Joy awoke to see her mother hovering over her with a butcher's knife. When Hal was home, Georgia demanded that he hit the children with a belt; Hal hated the idea, but, not wanting to incur his unstable wife's wrath, he did it. Ty and Joy were generally on their own for the most basic needs of childhood. Georgia was rarely up to cooking, and Ty poured cereal for himself and his sister most nights.

Joy remembered how kind Ty was to her then. He always made sure to include her in baseball games with the neighborhood kids, and when they were on a boat with their grandfather going so fast that it terrified her, Ty, then around ten, held her hand and told her that everything would be okay. But their parents offered little comfort.

"There's really nothing to say," Joy told me of their child-hood. "I don't think they knew how to give us love. That's the one thing I can say, and I think Ty would agree with that."

When Hal died of a heart attack while playing tennis on May 15, 1983, Ty was living a short drive away—and he didn't tell Joy, who was then living in New Mexico, about it for five days. During that time, she says, he cleaned out their father's antiques collec-tion. "By the time I got there, Mom was talking about what a crook Ty is, and what a good crook he is."

Warner told *People* magazine that his inheritance was $50,000, but others say it was more; while he was ostensibly broke, Patricia Roche found documents for a $200,000 savings account Warner had. He told her he'd gotten the money from his father. Whatever the case, with money in hand and Patricia Roche's moral support, Warner's post-Dakin depression lifted. He was ready to return to plush stardom, with a chance to execute the ideas that Dakin's product development office had ignored during his impromptu pitch sessions.

When it was time to name the business, Ty Warner figured that with Russell Berrie's toy company being called Russ, and the Dakin family founding Dakin, his company would be called Ty. The logo he chose later made people who knew him earlier in his career snicker: a heart with just his own first name inside it. His first product idea was a line of Himalayan cats he'd de-signed based on pieces he'd seen while traveling in Italy. He went to Korea with no contacts and knocked on doors until he found a factory that agreed to make samples. Then he flew back to Chicago, drove home, called Patricia Roche, dumped the samples out on the floor of his condo, and smiled. It was 1983, and the cats were out of the bag. Ty was now a stuffed-animal brand. His first product would be a long-haired white cat he named Kashmir, after one of his favorite Led Zeppelin songs.

5

"You Can Make a Lot of Money with
a Good Cat." —Ty Warner

They were indeed good cats. Prized collectors' items that still occasionally sell for hundreds of dollars on eBay, the cats had thick
hair, a light texture, and a certain floppiness that made them
cuddlier than anything else on the market. And in a foreshad-
owing of future glory, there were beans in the buttocks and feet
to provide weight and "poseability," as Ty put it.

"No one had put the combination of under-stuffed with beans.
All the animals were stiff and hard," Warner told *People* in 1996.
He was on to something with his under-stuffing. Rigid animals
couldn't do much except sit, but softer ones with less stuffing were
moveable—more realistic, he thought, than hard stuffed animals
that lacked flexibility and had all the long-term play value of
papier-mâché. Beans made it possible for you to pose his stuffed
animal, and posing it anthropomorphized it: a stuffed cat that
was under-stuffed and had beans could, in the hands of a child,
wave, dance, and cuddle. A stuffed cat did the same thing in Ty
Warner's hands. At toy shows Warner sometimes spent as much as
ten minutes showing anyone who agreed to watch all the ways the
head on a single animal could be cocked. One man Warner was
trying to recruit to be a salesperson was seriously unnerved by Ty's
enthusiasm for the product but signed on anyway and became a
multimillionaire in his late twenties once the Beanie craze hit.

Nina Terzian, who owned a Chicago toy store called Beauty

and the Beast and had known Warner in his Dakin days, placed the company's first order for $200—Warner kept the check on display in his office for years. "They were these beautiful animals," she later told a reporter. (She declined to be interviewed for this book, citing her professional relationship with Warner.) "Everything about them was impeccable. They were cuddly and the material was the softest, and the eyes and everything about them was just right. He really paid attention to the details. I bought everything that he had, because they were done so beautifully."

Then Warner returned to the trade shows where he'd shined as a Dakin rep—this time with his own brand and a valuable sidekick in Patricia Roche. She didn't have any more formal business training than Warner did, but she made up for it with a sense of organization and office management skills. Their ability to play off each other during sales calls and trade shows quickly made them stars of the plush circuit. Their first show was in Chicago, and their space was six feet long—tiny, but money was tight and Warner had a plan to attract attention. He arrived hours before anyone else to set up his booth so that his venture's sign, with the big heart logo, towered twenty feet in the air, dominating the auditorium and ensuring that his company would be the name on everyone's lips. When groups arrived at the show, Roche remembers, the plan was obvious: "Meet me in forty-five minutes under that enormous 'Ty' sign."

And so it began: the seasoned toy salesman but first-time entrepreneur and the neophyte, barnstorming every regional trade show they could find and soliciting orders from everyone who walked by. They went to the Atlanta Gift Show, rented part of a table from another vendor, and sold $30,000 worth of cats in a single hour—the same cat in ten different colors, each with its own name. Of those early trade shows, Roche remembers: "Oh my God, that man could sell sand to an Arab." She pauses. "I don't think you can say that anymore." Within three months of the business's founding, Warner's condo association told him to get an office after neighbors complained about the UPS trucks backing up to his door.

Warner wore fur coats with ostentatious Italian scarves, and one year, when he'd designed his catalog and booth around a pink theme, he wore nothing but pink to every show: hot pink suits with pink ties and pink socks. He was as good at selling to men as he was to women, Roche says—not a small feat given that so much of Warner's sales ability came from his magnetism. When he was dealing with a husband-and-wife team of buyers, Warner knew just when to shift his attention back to the guy.

"If for two seconds that man thought he was flirting with the woman, you just lost the sale," says Roche. "So you better get the focus back on the man."

For this, Warner had a go-to move: picking up George, a baby gorilla that was among the company's most popular offerings, placing it on the man's chest, and saying, "I want you to look into his eyes and tell him you hate him."

"He would groom those animals the entire show," Roche says. "If somebody picked one up and set it back down, he would brush the hair on the cat so it would look perfect." He used tweezers to pluck around the eyes to accentuate them, and blow-dryers were brought out to fluff the fur. *Make sure the animals are set up to make eye contact with the buyers*, he explained. There was never any excuse for a cat to be looking down; it had to be posed so that it had good posture and was looking straight ahead. It was, recalls one former employee from the early shows, just part of the "values of the company." As Ty grew, Warner was equally demanding of the workers who accompanied him to the shows to help sell his expanded line of stuffed animals. "Why aren't you grooming them?" he'd ask any employee who was standing idle. "That woman just *touched* that animal! Get over there and *brush it!*"

If Warner arrived at his booth after his staff had already set it up and it wasn't to his liking, he didn't hesitate to tear everything down—even if the sales reps were in the middle of presenting the line to a possible buyer. "He'd flip over everything in the booth while you were in the middle of showing them," remembers one early employee. "He'd shout 'What is this? This looks atrocious!'" Some buyers walked away appalled, and his antics cost Ty more than a few sales.

But that didn't matter. Everything had to be perfect—far more meticulous, certainly, than any of the competitors' displays at the same events. Often those competitors found him annoying. "If he had ten feet, he'd take fifteen feet," one remembers. "He would take his tables with his pink shit all over the place and in order to get into his booth to see the product, you'd have to walk through someone else's space." Warner was also vigilant about keeping overweight women away from his cats. "He was afraid they'd sweat on [them]," Roche remembers.

His fear of competitors' stealing his designs was also present, years before anyone was paying much attention to him. When Russ Berrie—the "trolls" tycoon who had created the gift shop model by persuading sellers of greeting cards to carry other impulse items—approached the Ty booth, Warner greeted him warmly while simultaneously trying to hide his newest toys. "Hi, Russ!" he'd say, his arms spread out, pushing his plush to the back of the table.

"Ty, you look a little crazy," Roche would chide, but Warner was insistent: the toy industry was rife with copying, and he didn't want any competitors seeing his newest products. Even at the height of Beanie mania, Warner insisted on personally filling out all of his own trademark and patent forms—and sometimes he flew to Washington, DC, to file them personally. Ty Inc.'s 1989 catalog had this on the back cover: "WARNING: If anyone dare copy our creative designs or patents without written permission, ownership of your eternal soul passes to us and we have the right to negotiate the sale of said soul. Furthermore, our attorneys will see to it that life on Earth, as you know it, is not worth living."

Yet he also went into toy and gift stores almost every day in search of design inspiration. "You can't reinvent the wheel!" he always told his employees. Warner frequented a mall in Geneva, Illinois, where he bought pieces from Boyds, Russ, Gund, and Steiff. He carefully inspected the fabrics, tags, and stitching, and he dissected them in his office to learn how they were made. When he went to the factories in Asia, his carry-on bag often contained competitors' products. He showed them to the factory owners and seamstresses, and spoke in clipped English with a twangy accent to describe his ideas for ribbon colors and how much distance there should be between the eyes on his cats. Back in the United States, he often lay in bed late into the night, talking on the phone in that same twangy voice, telling the factory exactly how each animal needed to look. The animals—and the desire to make them softer, cuter, and better—consumed every part of Warner's life.

In the early days he sometimes used freelance designers, especially for the traditional jointed teddy bears that he couldn't quite figure out how to create himself. Sometimes he paid them a few hundred dollars for their drawings. As his company grew, he offered them just a credit on the hangtag in exchange for the rights to their work. The credit helped drive demand for the designers' upscale, handmade pieces—and gave Ty Inc. the cachet of being associated with "designers," thereby making the company seem a little more high-end than other lines where a bear was just a bear. Ruth Fraser, a teddy bear designer who ran a Toronto gift shop, met Warner when he came into her store and wandered around with his hands behind his back, saying nothing, carefully examining every piece she had. Then he offered her $800 for one of her patterns. She made the deal and was later annoyed to discover that

Warner had produced endless variations based on the design she'd sold him. Then Warner decided that he didn't want the designers' names on his pieces after all, and removed them peremptorily, leading to a lawsuit with one designer.

"He wanted to think he designed everything," Fraser says— but Warner's actions were never a source of conflict for her. "We're not Americans. We don't sue, we don't argue."

By the late 1980s Warner was frequently shouting at his subordinates, "I am the designer! I designed everything!" Controlling every aspect of the animals' existence was a fixation, and it stood in stunning contrast to his nearly total disregard for the feelings of the people he was closest to. He carefully excised everyone else from the story of his rise: his father hadn't gotten him his first job, he hadn't used freelance designers to create his bears, and he'd started the company all by himself.

"It was all him," says Roche of the personal myth that Warner was concocting. To his credit, though, he combined his self-absorption with an incredible work ethic.

An early high point in Warner's plush-focused compulsiveness came at the photo shoot for the cover of Ty Inc.'s 1988 catalog, the first the company ever distributed to retailers—a simple full-color foldout brochure printed on glossy paper. That cover features Angel, a white stuffed cat with a Ty tag around the collar and a pink ribbon, posed against a black background with no props of any kind. The photo shoot was a last-minute affair in the office of a local printer.

"Ty would look at it and say, 'Nah, it's not right. Take another picture. It's not right. I don't like it,'" Roche says.

"His attitude was, 'I am the designer, I know how I want it to look,'" she remembers. The single-image photo shoot took nine hours, but the result is a cover that is equal parts regal and seductive—to the extent that a stuffed cat can convey either of those things. He had taken the primary colors out of his sales

copy—they're ubiquitous in ads for Dakin and other manufacturers of that era—and displayed the cats in a way that might
capture the sensibilities of adults, not just adults looking to attract the attention of children.

The catalog also evangelized Warner's ideas about under-
stuffing: "Ty's introduction of POSEABLE PLUSH™ is featured
throughout this catalog. Ty has formulated a special weighted
lining . . . that enables you to 'pose your plush' into many different positions creating a look that is totally unique in the marketplace today." The catalog features the toys carefully posed in
positions made possible by the beans and carefully sewn stuffing. Jake the Monkey is shown holding his hands over his head—
as though he's been caught in the middle of a jumping jack.
Beanie Bear, a large teddy bear, is shown midsprint. Lovie Lamb
is lying with her front and back legs stretched out, her head an-
gled toward the camera. Some of those early animals had the
words "bean bag" on the hangtag to further promote Warner's
ideas about the play value that his stuffed-with-beans animals
provided.

For the first few years, Roche and Warner personally trimmed
and brushed every single piece that came in from the factories;
it was work too painstaking for any supplier to undertake, but
Warner didn't want any of his cats going out the door looking
anything other than their best. As sales grew, such punctilious-
ness risked becoming a liability. In fact, says Roche, the primping demands of the bigger, furrier animals were part of the
motivation for a line called Beanie Bunnies; their smaller size
and flat pile made brushing and primping unnecessary—there
was no fur to brush. Without his obsession with grooming his
long-haired, full-size stuffed animals by hand, Ty might never
have found it necessary to create Beanie Babies.

In a crowded category full of better-financed competitors,
Warner had created something that stood out. His two biggest

competitive advantages—obsessive attention to detail and trade-show charisma—outweighed his myriad disadvantages: lack of scale, no advertising budget, a small and not especially competent sales force, a limited product line, and little in the way of a track record with retailers. He was also selling only to the small stores—a market that was in decline. As Russ Berrie wrote in 1981, "Seventy percent of all stuffed animals and plush purchases used to be made in toy stores. . . . [T]he toy store's share of the market has declined to less than 50 percent." Warner wasn't interested in selling to discounters, however. He wanted his pieces to be special, and each hangtag had a note about his dedication to quality. While this sounds like typical corporate hyperbole, it really did reflect the Ty Warner ethos: "Ty represents the ultimate in soft toys. Only the world's finest fabrics are selected and meticulously tailored by dedicated craftsmen to provide maximum quality for many years of love."

The only problem was that, as Ty Inc.'s sales climbed steadily, the company had no employees with any background in business, accounting, or law—or human resources.

6

Business and Pleasure

Within about six months of Ty's founding, Warner's relationship with Patricia Roche became romantic—a "twenty-four-hour obsession," as she puts it. Or, alternatively, as she wrote in an e-mail, "Two neurotics feeding off one another's insecurities."

In the beginning Warner was endlessly romantic. If they were in a restaurant, he always made sure they sat on the same side of the table, and if they were out walking, they had to be holding hands at all times. There wasn't much money, and they often split value meals at a local diner—although Ty was always ready to splurge on clothing. She questioned his judgment when he showed her a hundred-dollar belt he'd just bought, but Ty was adamant: you had to look successful before you could be successful.

For Roche, who was coming out of a marriage that had ended badly, Warner's energy was wonderful. Even the bad times were good because Roche felt like she was in business with the man she loved. When some of the animals were declared to be choking hazards because of the tags around their necks, Warner and Roche went through four container loads—around forty-eight thousand animals in all—to remove all the tags and then photograph the dumpster they filled with them to satisfy the demands of the Consumer Product Safety Commission. It was tedious, and a run-in with regulators was never fun, but they worked together magically—almost able to read each other's minds when it came to the business, Roche remembers. Nothing stressed them out as they traveled to trade shows together, and Roche managed the office when Warner went to Korea to work on designs.

When it came to the finances of a rapidly growing business, neither of them knew anything. Within a few months of starting Ty Inc., of which Warner was the sole owner, they were running everything free of debt, using only letters of credit from Harris Bank to float inventory costs. The bank required annual budgets, which Warner and Roche had a strategy for: go to Barbados for the holidays, sit in beach chairs by the pool, and create sales projections—double every year. "We were just making it up," remembers Roche. Their banker laughed at them but continued to sign off on their accounts. The pair delivered what they'd promised, year after year.

"He can be a lot of fun," Roche says. They often sneaked onto construction sites to look at new buildings, and on Sundays when they were bored, they might go test-drive Jaguars and Mercedes-Benzes. "He always had to have something to do," she says. In California on a business trip, they drove by a lavish home with a FOR SALE sign in front; Warner insisted that they stop and knock on the door. He had nothing like the means to afford a Southern California mansion, but he told the owner that he was in town only for a day and was looking for a nice place to stay when he was on business trips. Just as Ty could sell toys to anyone, he could talk his way into anything. The homeowner took them on a tour of the house, and Roche ogled the Sub-Zero appliances and expensive modern finishes while Warner shushed her, whispering that she shouldn't act so impressed.

He was also something of a cultural polymath and a prodigious name-dropper; he read business magazines obsessively and knew who owned every major hotel in America. When he went shopping for a new car, he made sure he knew the name of the owner of the dealership—and any other biographical tidbits that might help him look connected. He was more up to date on popular culture than anyone, following the headlines closely and constantly making predictions about which songs were going to be hits. Usually, just as with his predictions about which toys would sell, he was right. There was one exception: "He was wrong about Billy Ray Cyrus," Roche says. "Ty thought he was gonna be the next Elvis. But now the daughter is . . . really something. So who knows?"

Their relationship was also defined by drama. They argued constantly. One of their first employees remembers entering the office on her second day to hear Ty and Patricia screaming at each other. When they noticed that she was there, they moved their argument to the parking lot. Their most pleasant moments, Roche says, were always punctured when Warner needled her with the things he knew she didn't want him talking about—one of which was her mother. On a romantic interlude at the St. James Hotel in San Diego, Warner opened the door to the suite; while Roche started to unpack, he stretched out in the bathtub, still wearing his suit, and called out to her, "It's a beautiful tub!"

"Yeah, it sure is!" she replied.

"I bet your mother would never fit in it!" he yelled back.

Nasty comments about overweight people were a recurring theme with Warner. In restaurants he sometimes loudly remarked on the physical fitness of patrons at other tables. If his meal was too big for his liking, he'd send it back to the kitchen to be halved—with a lecture about how such portion sizes were making America the fattest country in the world. He also made a habit of entering a restaurant, sitting down, looking at a menu, blowing his nose on the napkin, and then announcing that he wanted to go somewhere else.

He also introduced Patricia to his mother, Georgia. Ty and Patricia went over to the apartment where Georgia was staying to sew stuffing into the cats' bellies. Warner had told Patricia about his difficult childhood: how his father had once locked him in a closet as punishment for showing affection to his mother; how Hal had gotten rid of his puppy because Ty, then five years old, hadn't cleaned up after it. He also told her that he'd taken his mother to an Illinois mental hospital in the late 1970s where she was diagnosed as paranoid schizophrenic.

Roche still wasn't prepared for Mrs. Warner.

"You're an ugly whore!" Georgia screamed at her while they worked. "My son will never marry you because you're so ugly!"

"Can you leave us alone?" Patricia yelled back. "We're trying to work."

"You're in my house!" Georgia shouted.

She started telling neighbors that the stuffed animals were filled with illegal drugs. Once she was kicked out of a Piggly Wiggly for shouting racial epithets in the middle of the store. She was also tossed out of a hotel after she tried to hit people with her car.

Ty's father's letters from a few years earlier show the difficulty Ty had had trying to maintain a relationship with her. "Ty's here but mother wouldn't let him drive her car," he wrote to Joy. "She thought he'd run it into flood waters and ruin the brakes. He's breaking his back for her in every way that I can see without the slightest thanks or appreciation. At times she's not sure if he's trying to poison her, [or whether it's] the mafia. [She] has conversations with herself and other people through airwaves."

While there was stuffing to attend to, however, Warner somehow tuned out his mother's ranting.

"He did teach me about focus," Roche says. "That's the secret: focus. If this is what you want, then go for it. Nothing crosses that road, nothing gets in the way, nobody changes it.

"This man wakes up in the morning, and he's thinking about the product. He goes to bed at night, and he's thinking about the product: Should it be a blue ribbon or a red ribbon? I can't tell you what we went through to get the eyes to be absolutely what he considered perfect. Every detail on every animal was gone over fifty times. It had to be as close to perfect as you could possibly get. Or do it again: 'Do it over, I don't like this. Do it over.'" Roche remembers late-night conversations about product when she was just trying to get out of the office. "'What do you think about that? What do you think?' he'd say. And then you'd agree, because you'd get worn out. And then he'd go, 'What about if it was purple?' And you'd go, 'No! Goddamn! There he goes again! Now we've got to go through the same thing, over and over.'"

After a few days of harassing Patricia while Ty demonstrated his superhuman capacity for focus, Georgia packed up, stole her son's car, and left. Ty seemed to be the only person on the planet with any interest in her, but he couldn't figure out where she'd gone. It would be years—and half-a-billion dollars in stuffed animal sales—before Ty found her.

7

Patti's Last Stand

By late 1992, Ty Warner's deal with Patricia Roche was falling apart both personally and professionally—mostly because of the unexpectedly strong business he had built with her by his side. What had begun almost a decade earlier with selling stuffed cats out of his condo had become a bustling business with twelve employees and sales that doubled every year. Warner was in Korea for several months at a time, designing an ever-expanding and ever-changing line of plush cats, dogs, rabbits, and bears. Sales for 1992 topped $6 million. Warner had done this without building much of a brand: his charisma pushed the products on retailers at trade shows, and the charm of the stuffed animals made them top sellers in gift stores, even though few consumers went in looking for the Ty logo.

Warner understood things about toy sales that others didn't. He understood the importance not just of low pricing but also of simple pricing. Other manufacturers had dozens of wholesale price points, but Warner stuck with two. As he wrote in a 2008 letter to retailers, "In 1983, I built my company on great quality and great prices. My only retail price points were $5 and $10. I believe that these retail price points were critical to our success."

As part of keeping to a limited number of price points, Warner also kept a very tight, focused product line. Dakin, in its heyday, offered 650 to 700 products; Ty Inc.'s roster of offerings rarely topped 100, and in the early days it was well below 25 pieces. This hurt Ty's chances with retailers who needed a wide variety—and Warner never did build a particularly large share of the zoo market—but it kept his costs down by allowing larger orders of a smaller number of pieces. As one retailer told *Playthings*, the industry's leading trade magazine, in 1994—the first media mention Warner received anywhere—he had "come on very strong . . . [and] put pressure on some of the larger companies to bring down their prices."

Warner's other stroke of weirdness was to demand payment in full, up front, while his competitors were offering as much as four months to pay. This was partly out of necessity—Warner didn't want to take on a lot of debt or factor his receivables, which would have forced him to raise prices. Collecting cash quickly allowed him to float his costs without lenders or investors. "We couldn't afford to carry people," Patricia Roche remembers. "[They'd say] 'Well, everyone else gets thirty days.' And everybody thought we were crazy. We didn't want to carry people for that thirty-day crap." The payment terms also demonstrated a certain bravado that might have been enticing to retailers. *Trust me*, Warner seemed to be saying, *with my high quality, impeccable taste, and low price points, you won't need extended terms on these babies.*

It was audacious and arrogant. "He was trying to build his business out of nowhere, and yet he wasn't giving them time," says Julie Lynn, a retailer who sold Ty Inc. products long before the company was an industry leader. He was able to get away with it, she says, on the strength of his product and the fact that he passed the savings that came with his lower cost of capital on to stores in the form of reduced prices: "No one was doing plush like that with that kind of price point," she remembers.

Just as he had done at Dakin, Warner focused on a certain kind of store: mom-and-pop toy and gift shops, retailers who had little bargaining power and sold to customers who weren't going to check prices against mass merchants. "By keeping them in the mom-and-pops, you kept them really loyal to Ty," Bill Harlow of

Ty Canada remembers. Warner liked the idea of being in stores small enough that his sales would be crucial to their bottom lines. He was also focused on getting his products distributed in airport stores—partly because he thought the small toys were a perfect last-minute gift but also because he knew that putting his animals in places where they'd be flown around the country would help spread his brand. In a big-box toy store, plush was an afterthought: higher-priced, TV-advertised toys commanded the bulk of the attention, and even a category killer in plush wasn't material to a company's results.

With five-hundred-square-foot gift shops, however, Warner's sales reps could push for better space, visiting each account at least once a month, per Ty Inc.'s training manual and distributor agreements, to count inventory and ensure that his stuffed animals were well promoted. Warner once explained his focus on the mom-and-pops: "[I]t's better selling 40,000 accounts than it is 5 accounts. It's more difficult to do, but for the longevity of the company and the profit margins, it's the better of the two. . . . If we were to sell to Wal-Mart, we would not be paid in 30 days."

One company that was selling to Walmart was Dakin; like the rest of the plush industry, Dakin was in trouble. The business model for decades had been to import products from Korea, slap a logo on them, and hire a sales force to get them in stores. By the 1980s the Koreans had grown wise to the markup the U.S.-based brands were making and started hiring their own teams to sell plush direct to retailers, cutting out the middlemen. Dakin's suppliers had become its competitors in a market that was in decline.

Dakin tried desperately to lure kids away from the plastic, marketing-driven violence that was gaining market share. In 1988 it partnered with the antiwar group Alliance for Survival to give teddy bears to kids in exchange for their violent toys. In a single year Dakin spent $2 million on an ad campaign blasting violent video games, action figures, and toy weapons. It didn't accomplish much. According to the Toy Manufacturers of America, sales of traditional plush toys and dolls without an electronic component fell by 44 percent in 1988.

Facing fading prospects as an independent business, Dakin's board of directors sought out a deal to sell the company to Hallmark, the greeting-card and gift empire. Hallmark was among Dakin's biggest customers, and it was, Nizamian says now, a "match made in heaven." On January 6, 1990, the companies issued simultaneous press releases announcing the sale. Nizamian's 8 percent stake in the $120 million sale was set to let him walk away with $9.6 million.

The deal never closed. A few weeks later, Nizamian says, one of the Dakin heirs—an aunt whose nephew owned 52 percent of the company's stock—called an emergency meeting and announced that the family was backing out of the sale. She also asked Nizamian to resign and handed control of Dakin over to a team of management consultants she'd hired to evaluate the Hallmark offer. Others say that it was Hallmark that backed out of the sale over concerns about Dakin's international business.

Either way, Nizamian found himself out of a job; as the company plunged into insolvency over the next few years, his life's work—and that equity stake—evaporated. Between 1989 and 1991, Dakin sales fell from $225 million to $75 million, and in just two years the company lost $50 million. In 1991 a majority stake was sold at scrap value to a private-equity firm. The business Nizamian took over after its founders died in a plane crash was, in every meaningful way, gone. He was unable to look at a toy again for almost a decade. During that decade, Nizamian's one-time protégée made more money in stuffed animals than anyone ever had, adding his own unique spin to the business model he'd marinated in as Dakin's top salesman.

———

The seeds of the Beanie Baby mania were sown by Warner's strange approach to product development, which began with the very beginning of his company. He changed his product mix more frequently than any of his competitors. Other companies were content to keep strong sellers in their lineup for years, but Warner, a designer-artist at heart, was always tinkering and always discontinuing old products, changing existing ones, and adding new ones.

A constantly changing product line is sometimes referred to as a "rolling mix." Mattel implemented a rolling mix strategy in 1994 to revive Hot Wheels, which were rapidly losing market share to Matchbox cars. Faced with stagnant sales and low consumer excitement for the line of toy cars, Mattel changed the product introduction schedule based on research showing that increased in-store variety—and frequent changes—could drive sales. The idea of the rolling mix was to change the assortment of each seventy-two-car display every two weeks. Instead of introducing all new products once or twice a year, Mattel rotated pieces in and out in a random and unpredictable way; collectors went into stores to check the displays more frequently, and there was a "ticking clock" incentive to buy new pieces because you never knew when they'd disappear from the rolling mix. Over the next three years, Hot Wheels picked up enormous market share as sales of Matchbox cars fell. In a paper on the toy industry, Professor M. Eric Johnson, associate dean of the Tuck School of Business at Dartmouth College, calls the rolling mix "the most interesting and successful variety strategy" that toy marketers use to manage supply-chain risk. When Warner introduced Beanie Babies a couple of years later, he combined the Hot Wheels rolling mix strategy with P. T. Barnum–style showmanship.

In the beginning, this wasn't a strategy. It was a reflection of Warner's own creativity and, perhaps more important, his compulsion to create the most perfect stuffed animals possible before affixing the swing tag featuring his first name inside a heart. His name on the tag, he once told an employee, was part of the reason that he could never sell the company. It was more than a business. Ty's life, Patricia Roche explains, is "about a never-ending striving for a perfect that doesn't exist."

As the company grew, Warner began to resent the deal he'd struck with Roche when Ty Inc. became her full-time job. For the first three years, neither he nor Patricia had taken any money out of the business. Then he started paying her on a percentage of sales—and as Ty Inc. found success, her earnings far surpassed either of their expectations. In 1992 Roche's annual income soared to more than $200,000. Yet with no formal role within the company—"I didn't exist," Roche explains—she would have had little leverage if Warner decided he wanted to get rid of her.

He called her one day to suggest that she switch to a flat salary of $50,000; she bristled, and the dispute over how she should be paid was magnified by issues in their personal lives. Roche didn't want to leave the business and Ty didn't want to end their relationship.

Ultimately, Roche says, she ended it with Warner because of his possessiveness. He had been physically abusive in the past, she says, but that had stopped. The relational issues hadn't.

"I had to get away from him. His control—basically, it's the control. He mesmerizes you into thinking that you are the only person on earth that he cares about," she says. "And then, gradually, after he's brought you up and gotten you into this thing, then he starts stripping away the layers, and then he's the only one in the world who likes you, because you have walked away from friends. I have friends who didn't see me for a year and a half—I was busy. And he didn't go out with anyone! He didn't need anybody!"

The finale of their personal relationship—Warner told the

same story to others—came in February 1993. They were on the outs, but she dropped him off at the airport for his flight to Korea regardless. Two hours later, he called her; he had canceled his flight and wanted her to come get him.

"And I said, 'I can't.' And he said, 'What do you mean, you can't?' I said, 'I have a date. I can't sit here and wait anymore for you for when you're going to call so I can come get you. So I have a date.' Well, I went to dinner, and I came back. And when I came back—and he did follow me several times in my life—he came through the back parking lot and called me, and I turned around and said, 'What are you doing?' And I told my date, 'Oh, just go in. Go in the building.' And I said to Ty, 'Why are you here?' And he goes, 'I wanted to see this date. Is that your date?' And I said, 'Why do you care?' "

Warner left and Roche and her new guy went back out. Roche assured him that nothing had changed: they would still go on vacation to Cancun the next day as planned. When they got back home, Roche's passport was missing; Warner had taken it. She went and got a birth certificate the next day and the pair left for Cancun.

On their second day in Cancun, there was a knock at the door: "Room service!"

"We didn't order anything!" Roche's date shouted back, groggy from a night of partying.

"It's complimentary!"

Roche's date got out of bed to open the door.

"And all I hear is, 'Hi. I'm Ty Warner,' " Roche remembers. "I'm thinking, No no no! Son of a bitch! So we sat there for three hours and talked. About how he had wanted to marry me, how he had wanted to have children with me. And [my date] said, 'Do you want me to leave?' And I said, 'No. I don't want you going anywhere. I don't know what he'll do.' "

Warner left Cancun feeling more depressed than he'd felt in

years—and Roche's tenure with the company and with Warner was over. Ty Inc. was closing in on $10 million in annual sales at that point; Roche left with around $100,000 and started selling insurance.

Warner banned her from his office after she started showing up daily to harangue him, and he contemplated filing for a restraining order. "She was super pissed—like psychotic pissed," one employee remembers. "Everybody was really nervous because we didn't know what she was going to do." It was 1993, and the woman Warner had started the business with was out of the picture; just as he'd excised his father from the stories about how he got started in the plush industry, Warner now dropped Roche from his narrative about the early days of the company. From the day he and Roche split up, it was, in Warner's telling of it, a company he'd run entirely on his own in the beginning.

After the breakup, Warner started seeing a psychotherapist. He was reading Melody Beattie's *Codependent No More*, and, now that he had the income to finance it, beginning to experiment with plastic surgery, focusing especially on his eyes and nose.

Yet the plush show had to go on; from the time Warner had joined Dakin, it had been the one constant in his life. He was about to turn fifty, he'd never married, and he had no kids. In 1993 he reported a personal income of $1.3 million—a fortune but, he hoped, just the beginning. Within a few months of his breakup with Patricia, Ty had two new things in his life: designs for a line of $5 beanbag animals and a new girlfriend named Faith McGowan—a tall, redheaded Chicago native fourteen years his junior.

8

New Beginnings

Faith McGowan met Warner at the lighting store where she worked when he came in looking for help. Faith was recently divorced with two children in elementary school, and her first impression of Ty was that he was charming: "A little peculiar; cute. Very boyish. He was very intense—you could feel the intensity of what he was doing with the lighting." Former Ty Inc. executives recall Warner's obsession with lighting; he had memorized the serial numbers on dozens of light bulbs, and, once he was a billionaire, he would wander his hotels' corridors with complaints about lights. New hires were instantly warned: when Warner had a complaint about lights, chain of command didn't matter. Whether you were the CFO or a warehouse worker, it was your responsibility to fix the problem—immediately.

On the day he met McGowan, Warner was working on a complicated plan to install lights under a set of cabinets. McGowan explained why his plan wouldn't work, and Warner seemed impressed. He asked her to come to his home on her day off to look at the kitchen and help him with ideas, and she agreed.

When McGowan arrived at the expensive modernist house in Oak Brook, he wasn't there yet. His contractor filled her in on the work. The house had been under continuous renovation since Warner had moved in more than two years earlier. When Warner showed up, wearing alligator shoes with three-inch heels, he showed her his makeshift bedroom, which had no lighting except for the ambient light provided by a window. The room had green shag carpeting, peeling wallpaper, and magazine cutouts about lighting fixtures taped to the walls. There were other, finished rooms Ty could have lived in; his choice of the worst room in the house struck Faith as a sort of self-flagellation for his inability to finish the renovations.

Ty was oddly forthcoming about his personal life. He told her about his breakup with Patricia Roche and that his therapist had told him he was codependent, and he talked about the plastic surgery he'd had. He showed her how he had his hair cut in a bob to hide the still-healing incisions. McGowan later wrote of him in an unpublished memoir, "His sexually explicit references in talking about Patti, his cosmetic surgery, and his lifestyle warned that this man was very different. But I was struck by the drama he created and his personal flair. His unique presence and obvious intelligence started to suck me into his drama, almost as if I were auditioning for a part."

Not that Warner told her about all the drama in his life: not only was he depressed about the breakup with Roche, but he was also keeping a close eye on her. "He stalked me for two years after we broke up," Roche remembers. "Ty knew where I was morning, noon, and night." He had concealed an audio recorder in her home and once, years later, played for her the tapes he had made of her with another man.

A few days after their first meeting, McGowan went back to Warner's home to discuss lighting possibilities with the electrician. When she arrived, Warner asked her to count all the switches and receptacles in the house and help the electrician order parts, and then he retreated to his bedroom to call his lawyer. McGowan felt manipulated into working for free, and told the contractor that she was leaving. However, when she went out to her car, she saw that Ty had parked his black Mercedes behind her jalopy. She went back inside. "Excuse me," she said.

"You need to move your car. I'm leaving." Later she called him to explain that she wasn't a salesperson, she was a manager. She told him she had kids to pick up, and didn't have time to count receptacles for free while he talked to his lawyer. "I've got tickets to the White Sox game tomorrow night," he told her. "I've gotten to know you a little bit. I really want you to get to know me better. I think you'll find I'm not such a bad guy."

She accepted the invitation, and on the following night, as they sat in the bleachers together, Ty told her his life story—about his dysfunctional family and his time at Dakin and the high hopes he had for his plush company. She was hooked: they became a couple almost immediately.

The first time they went to his bedroom together, he was more interested in showing her his pillow collection than he was in taking her clothes off. He told her in detail about each of the pillows on his bed and where he'd gotten them; some he'd bought on trips to Asia, others he'd pilfered during stays at luxury hotels. He asked her to try out each one. Just as he grilled customers about plush products, he wanted to know which pillows Faith liked best.

The questions about how she could help with his business came quickly—after he helped her get fired from her job. He told her that she was underpaid at $30,000 per year and that if she didn't demand a doubling of her salary and a more prestigious title, he couldn't be with her: "You let them take advantage of you, and I don't want to be with someone like that," he said. She took a stand, lost her job as a result, and, in a panic, called Warner in Korea. He told her not to worry, but when her unemployment ran out and she started to fall behind on bills, he wasn't helpful. He advised her to cancel her cable-TV subscription. Finally, he told her to send him a tally of her monthly expenses and presented her with a check—for the exact amount, down to the penny—held in the arms of a stuffed bear, a combination of romance and exactitude that she thought was strange.

Once McGowan and her two daughters had moved in with him a few months later, keeping his white carpets clean was an all-consuming family affair, with bottles of cleaner scattered throughout the house. Living with Warner also meant developing the same devotion to the business that he had. She and her children remember dinners at Boston Market where they weren't allowed to eat until they'd settled on a name for a new stuffed rabbit or frog.

As the relationship heated up, most of the discussions concerned the development of the line he'd started thinking about right after his decade-long relationship with Patricia Roche ended: $5 beanbags that were small enough for kids to slip into their pockets and then, Warner hoped, bring to school to show their friends. "Unfortunately, as Beanie Babies came to dominate our evenings," McGowan remembered, "our lovemaking became less frequent."

9

Ty's Big Idea

In late 1993 Warner summoned Bill Harlow, the quilting store operator he'd met at a trade show who was by then the exclusive distributor for Ty products in Canada, to his office in Oak Brook, Illinois. Warner had considered a handful of people as partners for the Canadian business, many of whom had much more experience than Harlow and some who were better capitalized. Warner, however, had conditions. He wanted someone who would focus exclusively on Ty products full time; he wasn't interested in wrapping his line in with a sales organization that sold dozens of other gift products.

He also didn't want anyone who brought a lot of his own ideas and strategies to the business. "He wanted someone he could mold," Harlow remembers. "Someone he could control. I knew nothing about plush toys at all, and I learned everything about it from him. I was young, I was full of energy, and I was moldable. I knew nothing and had no preconceived notions. Ty is the closest guy I've met to someone who understood every facet of a business: the design, the manufacturing, the sales. Everything. He was my mentor."

The Ty Inc. world headquarters and distribution center that Harlow beheld consisted of a few thousand square feet and fifteen employees. The warehouse and the office were all in one building, making it a terrible place to host visitors—which was fine, because in those days no one much worth impressing went there anyway. The furniture and office supplies looked like they'd been assembled from the leavings of dozens of yard sales; nothing matched. Ty's promotional items from trade shows were stacked all over the office because they'd have gotten too dusty in the warehouse. There was a big Dry-erase board with a calendar for all the trade shows the company went to each year, and the office was filled with messy wires and arts-and-crafts decorations put up by Warner's secretary—much to the annoyance of his more corporate-minded head of sales, Karmen Kohlwes.

Harlow sat across from Warner, who reached into his immaculately organized desk filled with plush prototypes. He pulled out the first factory sample for the first Beanie Baby—Legs, a frog with little detail and, competitors soon snickered, a serious problem with under-stuffing. He placed it in Harlow's hand. Warner was always excited about his products, but he was particularly enthused about Legs because Legs didn't have much stuffing—a little in the legs, a little in the head, and a little everywhere else, but mostly what you noticed about Legs was his beans and his floppiness. Legs was the platonic ideal of what Warner had been searching for since his drop-ins at the Dakin product office in the 1960s. He'd started his own business with under-stuffed cats with beans in the feet, then moved on to beans in other stuffed animals. Now, Warner had made beans the defining characteristic of his plush; the stuffing was incidental. The result was incredibly floppy and "poseable," that word Ty had liked enough to trademark back in the 1980s.

"From now on, every penny you have goes into this," he told Harlow.

When Harlow first told me about the conversation, my reaction was *Oh, come on. He did not really say that.* It just sounded like an obvious turning-point line in a bad version of *Citizen Kane*—a cocky line from a cocky entrepreneur ready to put it all on the line for the thing he'd concocted and believed in with everything he had.

However, the conversation probably did happen exactly that way. Everyone who was in Warner's life at the time remembers how entirely absorbed he was with excitement over the creation of Legs the Frog. McGowan's daughter Jenna, then in elementary school, recalls the first time Warner showed Legs to her. He was ecstatic, she says, because of how little stuffing it had, and he kept pointing that out to her—how floppy Legs was, how you could toss him into the air and he'd land with a satisfying plop. Jenna's sister, Lauren, also remembered Ty's excitement over the new animal. He tossed Legs to her and smiled. "See!" he told her. "It's fun to play with!"

In consultation with Faith McGowan, who had no official role with the company but with whom Ty discussed everything, he changed the original dark green color to a lighter, more child-friendly shade. He was ready to introduce Legs, along with eight other Beanie Babies he had painstakingly designed to complete the collection: Brownie the Bear, Chocolate the Moose, Pinchers the Lobster, Spot the Dog, Squealer the Pig, Splash the Whale, Flash the Dolphin, and, not coincidentally, Patti the Platypus—"Patti the Puss!" Ty told Faith.

––––––

Beanie Babies were first introduced at Gatlinburg, Tennessee's Smoky Mountain Gift Show in November 1993. Always prepared to build hype, Warner had only two of the Beanies available for sale at that event: Brownie and Patti. The other seven were on display, but he told retailers they couldn't be ordered just yet. He had thought up the line, in part, to have an affordable impulse item on hand to get his foot in the door with retailers at trade shows. Sell them the cute, colorful, completely irresistible low-priced beanbags, he thought, and then he'd be able to upsell them on his full line of more traditional plush. Warner was wary of novelty items: the problem with trying to chase or create trends was that they could evaporate quickly, leaving you with a lot of worthless inventory and no steady, sustainable business. He thought that traditional animals like bears, rabbits, cats, and dogs were the way to go. The Beanie Babies were mostly a means to an end: not expensive enough to be much of a cash machine on their own but so perfect that they were destined to be a hit.

"For the first year—at least—they just didn't move," says Lina Trivedi, who worked for Ty at the company's trade shows in the early and mid-1990s. She remembers walking buyers through all of the larger animals, clipboard in hand, taking their orders for cats, dogs, rabbits, and gorillas—but when she got to the Beanie Babies, they passed. Gift shops were more interested in traditional teddy bears and animals with stuffing, not beans, and certainly not more beans than stuffing. And the thin pile and bold colors had some retailers worried that they would cheapen the look of their stores. Some told the Ty sales force that the inexpensive Beanie Babies would cannibalize sales of higher-priced products. Whatever the reason, almost no one ordered them. Warner was originally soliciting orders for Beanie Babies in twelve-packs of each style, and the company's former sales reps remember calling the head of sales seeking permission to split the twelve-packs and accept orders for six. Warner was hesitant: If he couldn't sell a store twelve beanbag animals at a wholesale price of $2.50 each, why even bother at all?

This was the opposite of what Warner was used to. In the past he'd sometimes told buyers that they could only purchase a maximum of twelve of a stuffed cat, then watch in astonishment as a buyer who was probably going to buy only eight bought twelve instead. There's some research suggesting that limiting order sizes can promote the idea of scarcity and lead to larger purchases. A 1995 study, "Framing the Deal: The Role of Restrictions in Accentuating Deal Value," found that advertising limited quantities leads consumers to associate the limited-quantity brands with higher quality.

Warner agreed to accept orders for six pieces. Ty's sales for 1994 climbed to $28 million, which was more than double the previous year, but that was driven by his traditional plush lines and a new brand he named Attic Treasures. The Attic Treasures were modeled after antique stuffed animals—some were designed by artists, all had textured fur, and many of them were jointed. They were selling well in gift shops to adult collectors, and seemed like they might be the future of the company.

Still, Warner wasn't ready to give up on the Beanies. In June 1994, more than six months after their inauspicious launch, he introduced a bunch more: Ally the Alligator, Blackie the Bear, Bones the Dog, Chilly the Bear, Daisy the Cow, Digger the Crab, Goldie the Goldfish, Happy the Hippo, Humphrey the Camel, Inky the Octopus, Lucky the Ladybug, Mystic the Unicorn, Peking the Panda, Quackers the Duck, Seamore the Seal, Slither the Snake, Speedy the Turtle, Trap the Mouse, and Web the Spider, along with a teddy Beanie that was available in brown, cranberry, jade, magenta, teal, and violet.

On January 7, 1995, he released Nip the Cat, Tank the Armadillo, Tusk the Walrus, Zip the Cat, and Valentino, a Valentine's Day–themed white bear. He also added wings to Quackers and changed the design on the colored teddy bears, making the faces less flat and, incidentally at the time, creating the first discontinued Beanie Babies that anyone looking to build a complete set would have a hard time finding. Soon "New Face Teddy" and "Old Face Teddy" would be household names among collectors, and a pair of Old Face Teddies would be worth enough to pay for a semester of college. For the time being, though, Beanie Babies were selling poorly enough that most traditionally minded businesspeople would have considered scrapping the whole line.

The future of the company changed with a lamb named Lovie.

10

A Lamb Named Lovie

One of Ty's more popular traditional stuffed animals was Lovie, a lamb that sold especially well in hospitals. However, at the Atlanta Gift Show of 1995, there was a problem: Lovie had been discontinued because of supplier issues in China—something to do with the fabric—and the buyers were none too pleased to hear it. Companies have always discontinued poorly performing products; usually, no one cares because the pieces they stop selling are the ones consumers aren't buying.

Lovie, though, was different: no one was eager to see her go, and the buyers complained endlessly to the salespeople. The tension over a stuffed lamb was complicating the sale of the rest of the Ty collection.

The King brothers (Bryan, Chris, and Kevin) were a trio of siblings who sold Ty products in the southern United States through their company, RBT Enterprises (Rich Before Thirty—a goal they accomplished with the help of the conversation they had on this day). They were working at the Ty booth at the Atlanta Gift Show, listening to angry buyers lament the unavailability of Lovie. When they broke for lunch they sat in the food court, eating sandwiches and talking about Lovie. And then one of the brothers recalled a microphenomenon he had seen at their parents' gift shop in Clearwater, Florida, where they sold a line of figurines called Tom Clark gnomes.

Tom Clark gnomes were designed by Dr. Tom Clark, a

professor of religion at Davidson College. Each of Clark's gnomes, with names like Coastie and Hogan, was manufactured in a large quantity. Without warning, though, Clark would break the mold for one of the figurines and inform retailers that the piece had been "retired." When the King brothers' parents heard about a newly retired piece, they moved it to a special shelf and charged double for it. It wasn't a craze, but a few collectors were willing to pay the premium prices.

"Let's just tell people Lovie's been retired," one of the King brothers suggested, and that's what they did after lunch. It worked: customers who were upset by the idea of a discontinued Lovie were intrigued by the prospect of a retired Lovie. Retailers who were pissed off if you told them you were discontinuing a piece they wanted out of necessity were delighted if you told them you were doing it on purpose. A few buyers asked the King brothers whether other pieces were going to be retired. The brothers said they weren't sure—but suggested that it might not be a bad idea to stock up just in case.

They told Warner about it later that day, and he was intrigued. He'd tried selling an Annual Collectible Bears line a few years back, but that hadn't really gone anywhere. His use of artist-designed bears, with the names of the designers printed on the tags, showed that he was definitely interested in the possibility of moving his product from popular gift into object of desire.

Warner started thinking and talking about how to use "retirements" to create demand for the $5 beanbags he had thought would become his breakout product but that were, to date, mostly a flop. He had reservations: Ty Inc. was producing as many of each piece as it hoped to sell, which seemed to undermine the idea of promoting them as scarce. Yet in other ways Beanie Babies were ideally suited to the retirement gimmick: they had sold too poorly to have many of the early, already "retired" (i.e., discontinued) pieces in circulation, so it wouldn't take much of a cult following to start to create a market for them.

"Most importantly, we would plant the seed in consumers' minds that the Beanies they could buy on the primary market for $5 would be retired and immediately take on a higher value on the secondary market," Faith McGowan remembered in her unpublished memoir. This assessment, however, overstates the depth of planning that went into the retirement idea; for the time being, retiring Beanie Babies was a random marketing stunt that came with no costs and few expectations.

"He was open to listening to the guys in the field. A lot of CEOs didn't do that," says Bryan King. While Warner is almost universally described as a micromanager obsessed with controlling every aspect of the market for his toys, he was also constantly on the prowl for new ideas and new insights, wherever they might come from. At home with Faith McGowan's daughters, plush was never far from anyone's lips. "Constantly, all the time. The prototypes were all over the place. What would make this one or that one better was always a topic of conversation," is how Faith's daughter Jenna Boldebuck describes it. Ty generally interacted little with his company's fans, but when he did, he always asked children the same question: What's one animal we haven't done that you'd like to see? In February 1999, a child at a trade show told him she'd like to see a snail Beanie; Ty introduced Swirly the Snail four months later.

At a family dinner at a local restaurant in early 1995, Ty mused on his desire to create a ghost Beanie—but said he couldn't figure out how to do it because ghosts don't have legs and he hadn't done one without legs before. Jenna, then in elementary school, drew her idea for a ghost on the paper tablecloth, and Warner was impressed. He tore it off and put it in his wallet. Within a few months Spook the Ghost was ready to ship—with "Designed by Jenna Boldebuck" on the hangtag. Two months later, Warner changed his mind and removed her name from the tag and changed Spook to Spooky. Jenna was hurt by it, and Faith was puzzled: Was Ty's self-esteem really so fragile that giving a designer credit to his girlfriend's school-age daughter was a problem? But it worked in everyone's favor: once Beanie Babies got hot, a Spook with Jenna's name on the hangtag was instantly one of the most highly sought variations, and collectors paid as much as $1,000 for mint-condition examples.

A couple of years later, Faith McGowan suggested creating a Princess Diana bear to raise money for her memorial fund, and Ty dismissed it outright—only to announce it later that night as his own idea.

"I sat there stunned but not surprised," McGowan remembered. "At that point, all good ideas were Ty's, regardless of who first suggested them. The idea for Beanie birthdays, Beanie poems, the Beanie Web site, and even the retirement of Beanies, had all originated with other people. One thing you can say for Ty: when he recognized a good idea, he got it done. But he also took ownership of it."

The release of a purple Princess Diana bear on October 29, 1997, generated more headlines promoting the craze. Warner announced that stores were only allowed to order twelve Princess bears; and while that was just an initial-order size limit, many speculators assumed that Princess would be a limited-edition bear. The price soared into the hundreds of dollars, and Princess remains one of the best-remembered Beanie Babies, sparking memories of minor fortunes paid for this bear. Yet Ty was more generous in filling reorders, and as the supply increased, prices tanked. The Princess bear raised more than $20 million for the memorial fund; fifteen years later, McGowan was still irked by Warner's unwillingness to give her any credit for it. But all that would come later.

In late 1995, at the suggestion of the King brothers, Warner had begun subtly marketing his products as collectibles. There was no sophisticated packaging and no complex strategy involved. But by directing its sales force to tell retailers that certain pieces had been "retired," the company was now moving its plush animals into the category that was, at the time, a major driver of sales at the same gift shops where Beanie Babies were being sold as a toy. Still, the strategy had no immediate impact. A few weeks before Christmas 1995, McGowan set up a kiosk at the Yorktown Shopping Center, not far from Ty Inc. headquarters. She hoped to push Beanie Babies as stocking stuffers but didn't end up making enough to cover the rent. She closed the booth on Christmas Eve and went on vacation; retirements or no, Beanie Babies still weren't hot.

In 2005, in a rare e-mail exchange with a reporter from the *Santa Barbara News-Press* (offered as part of an effort to drum up support for Warner's plans to renovate the Miramar Hotel, which preservationists were opposing), Warner offered this as his best piece of business advice: "If you know in your heart it is a good idea, don't give up or compromise it. Before I started the Beanie Baby line, the industry rule was that a $5 collectable item could not work. Enough said?"

That was true. Before Warner, no one had had the gall to try to market such low-priced items as heirlooms to be put in display cases and held for investment. However, the business model had its roots in the 1960s, when another entrepreneur, Joseph Segel, had a similar idea: manufacture something of little intrinsic value and then, through hype, marketing, and sometimes outright misrepresentation, persuade people to believe that the trinket is actually a precious heirloom. At the very least, you convince the public your heirs will be honored to receive it when you pass, and perhaps (and more likely) you'll sell it at some point for a handsome profit.

When I asked one former top-level executive at Ty about Warner's greatest strength, he was succinct: "He was a master of selling useless shit to people and making it seem really important." That business of mass-produced collectibles began with Segel, a 1951 University of Pennsylvania graduate who became the youngest faculty member in the history of the university's Wharton School when he began teaching Marketing 101 and 102 there at age twenty. He was also running several of his own businesses on the side. Little more than a decade later, he had the idea that made him spectacularly rich—and provided the capital for his next big idea, which turned out to be the cable shopping channel QVC.

"In June of 1964, I saw an article in *Time* magazine about the last U.S. silver dollars being sold by the government," Segel remembered years ago. "A picture showed people [lined up] around the block waiting to buy silver dollars from the United States Treasury Department in Washington. That gave me a brainstorm. My idea was to issue a series of solid sterling-silver medals, a little larger than a silver dollar, of the highest quality . . . and the edition would be extremely limited. Only one hundred specimen[s] of each medal would be available, at a fixed price, to each member of a society formed to issue the medals. Membership in the society would be open for a short period of time. . . . I called it the National Commemorative Society." The National Commemorative Society was a direct-marketing invention and was not a society of any kind. It launched without an office or members.

The ad first ran in June 1964 and used a ticking clock to drive sales: if the "membership application" (i.e., order form) was postmarked within the first two weeks, the price was $10. It rose to as much as $40 the longer you waited. Segel gained 5,250 members on the strength of that ad—and more important, the medal appreciated in value because the price of silver was soaring. It was perfectly timed and incredibly lucky. Segel's medals had increased in value because of commodities prices, not some sort of alchemy on his part. Nevertheless, the auspicious timing launched a perfect feedback loop, and the word spread. Segel's commemoratives went up in value, and the actual reason—the price of silver—was obscured because who really cared? "Buy the National Commemorative Society's medallions and get rich" was a better story.

Segel quickly expanded the National Commemorative Society and renamed it the Franklin Mint—another fabricated title with no connection to anyone named Franklin. I asked Mr. Segel in an e-mail about the marketing strategy: Had he really set out with the idea of creating something out of nothing—and selling it as an investment? "Initially, I thought it was important," he wrote back. "But, very soon thereafter, I changed my thinking based on the realization that the more a collectible is promoted as an investment, the less likely it will turn out to be a good investment . . . because promoting collectibles as an investment tends to cause too many people to buy the product primarily for that reason, eventually resulting in too many people trying to sell at a profit and too few people interested in buying."

Yet once Segel made his venture a public company aiming for the annual revenue and income growth that would boost the stock price, the probable long-term failure of the Franklin Mint's products to generate returns for consumers wasn't much of a concern. All that mattered was the perception and the quarterly sales growth that perception could drive. In 1972, with his company's sales at more than $50 million, Segel told UPI that "new as they are, collections of our medals have already appreciated in value since issued, some fairly significantly."

Segel (and especially the copycats who followed him) began introducing pieces of less intrinsic value than the medals, promoting them both for their aesthetic merit and their chance at appreciation. The company's 1971 annual report noted that "Norman Rockwell's 1971 Christmas plate sold out even faster than his trend-setting 1970 plate. Meanwhile, resale price of the 1970 limited edition soared in the collector market. A major market in silver plates appears to have formed, posting bright prospects for 1972." In 1974 sales soared 48 percent to more than $166 million.

The *Wall Street Journal* juxtaposed the performance of collector plates with the bear market in stocks: "While You Were Going Under, Grannie Got In at $100, Out at $450" was the headline for a page one story on December 21, 1971. "Over the past few years," it began, "you, being a clever, with-it affluent fellow, have played the stock market like a plane, buying, selling and swapping up and down the Dow Jones average. Meanwhile, your sweet old Grannie in Grundy Center, who doesn't know a short sale from shortbread, has been using her savings to buy those corny Christmas plates that come out each year adorned with engravings of Norman Rockwell paintings or bas relief angels or other such sentimentalities. . . . We have some news for you. While you've been taking a bath in the market, Grannie has been getting rich."

A 1973 advertisement in the *Boston Globe* led with the headline, "How to Double Your Money in Collector's Plates: Guaranteed Return with No Risk." The free booklet promised readers an opportunity to learn how to "guarantee a return of at least 30% per year on your investment with no risk what-so-ever." And lest the appeal seem avaricious, readers were also assured that they could "own and enjoy the beauty of true works of art."

Eventually, the watchdog media barked. On November 12, 1978, *60 Minutes*'s Morley Safer took Segel and his Franklin Mint to task in a devastating exposé. Noting that precious metals had been a powerful inflation hedge of late, Safer explained, "There is one area of collecting in which you almost certainly would have lost your shirt and that's in the material sold and advertised by the Franklin Mint." More than 75 percent of Franklin Mint pieces, Safer estimated, were worth substantially less than their issue price. Yet the growth continued.

The Bradford Exchange—a knockoff of Segel's business—created a murky secondary market for its collector plates, complete with advertisements featuring its "brokers" hovering over computers, tracking plate prices. To underscore the idea of these mass-produced tchotchkes as upmarket, sophisticated investments, the company deployed some of its most aggressive ads (which later led to lawsuits) in magazines like *Kiplinger's Personal Finance* and *Architectural Digest.* A 1986 sales pitch offered "The Sound of Music," the first plate in a new series from the Edwin M. Knowles China Company, at a price of $19.50. Yet the ad copy didn't emphasize the plate itself. Rather, bold type introduced two so-called facts: "Fact: 'Scarlett,' the 1976 first issue in Edwin M. Knowles' landmark series of collector's plates inspired by the classic film *Gone With the Wind,* cost $21.60 when it was issued. It recently traded at $245.00—an increase of 1,040% in just seven years." And "Fact: 'The Sound of Music,' the first issue in Knowles' The Sound of Music series, inspired by the classic film of the same name, is now available for $19.50." Later the ad advised that "it's likely to increase in value." Currently, those plates can be had on eBay for less than $5 each.

In 1993 U.S. direct mail sales of collectibles totaled $1.7 billion; in 1994 the Franklin Mint spent $121 million on advertising, enough to make it the twenty-seventh most advertised brand in the United States and the number one advertiser in Sunday magazines. The close to one hundred Franklin Mint employees on the advertising side made it the largest in-house ad agency in America, according to *Advertising Age.*

Segel left the industry in 1973 and calls the hard-sell tactics that predominated in the following years despicable. "I was sickened by aggressive pitching of those products as investments, but there was nothing I could do about it. It's a shame. A lot of people got burned," he says. Segel had invented an industry that used marketing to circumvent a process that the market, over centuries, had taken to organically determine what was valuable. The collectibles business preyed on all the behavioral fallacies that cost investors money: our overreliance on past performance as a predictor of future results, our tendency to have an inflated concept of the value of things we own (known as the endowment effect), and our tendency toward movement in herds.

It worked. By the mid-1990s, selling less-than-limited limited editions was a bigger business than ever. Brands like Department 56 and Boyds Bears were growing quickly and drawing the interest of investment bankers looking for hot IPO candidates. Warner followed the gift industry obsessively, reading every article in every trade magazine, carefully monitoring all his competitors' moves, and now he was entering the red-hot collectibles business.

It was the smartest decision he'd made yet, and he was to make more money in collectibles than anyone ever had. First, though, he needed a few collectors to get the sentimental little scheme going.

11

The First Collectors

"When I look back, the one thing I remember so much about Beanie Babies was how they made people feel so warm and fuzzy inside," Mary Beth Sobolewski explained from her home in Naperville, Illinois. She'd been one of the first collectors in the Chicago suburbs—chasing Beanie Babies with her kids and trading with other mothers in the area to get the harder-to-find ones. "It was so much fun."

She paused as her mood darkened. "Then it just became people who saw dollar signs—that was by far the majority of it at the height of it."

By early 1996, following close to two years of weak sales, Beanie Babies were a popular toy for children, just as Warner had hoped and predicted. Demand was strongest in the Midwest, where Ty Inc.'s suburban Chicago headquarters gave it an in with local stores, and the low-priced toys sold well on impulse. Kids who grew up in Naperville remember trading them in the first half of 1995, close to a year before the rest of the country had heard of them, and a few teachers had banned Beanies from their classrooms because they'd become a distraction.

One sales rep remembers that when the product was first building a following on Chicago's North Shore, the company was shipping more than half of all Beanie Babies to stores in Illinois. Merchants had disagreed with Warner at first about the potential of Beanie Babies, but as he once wrote in a Steve Jobs–like note to an employee, "Most retailers don't know what they're doing. When retailers are angry with you, it means you have a good product." Warner thought that the play value of a stuffed animal with mostly beans and a little stuffing would appeal to kids, and he also thought that a stuffed animal that could be slipped into a back-pack would spread through word of mouth far more quickly than one that required at-home play dates. He was right on both counts.

On December 9, 1995, nearly two years after the Beanies' launch, J.T. Puffin's in Madison, Wisconsin, placed one of the first newspaper ads for them: "Beanie Babies: At Puffins, on Dec. 6, we had 27 different styles of Beanie Babies. At only $5 they disappear quickly. Puffins, trying hard to be your Beanie Baby Boutique." On December 7, Crescent Bear & Bath Boutique advertised "Beanie Babies Bean Bag Animals. Only $3.99." On February 27, 1996, the *Wisconsin State Journal* reported on their popularity: J.T. Puffin's had sold out of forty-eight Bongo the Monkeys instantly and was ordering more as quickly as Ty could ship them. A nine-year-old told the newspaper, "One of the things I like is they're really soft. You can like toss them up. I just find it kind of fun to watch them when they're coming down."

A local newspaper story in April 1996 noted that a few had been retired, but no collectibles craze was mentioned. In June 1996, *Playthings* gave Beanies their first bit of industry trade press, mentioning that two gift shops had singled them out as a fast mover in a recent survey. Other papers in the Midwest began reporting on the popularity of Beanies in April 1996, tracing their rise to the 1995 Christmas season. "I had a few in October [1995]," one retailer told a reporter. "They weren't selling. Then in mid-January [1996] they took off like crazy."

No one was talking about an emerging secondary market, and there were no references to rare pieces. Occasionally, a reporter noted that retailers had explained that certain Beanie Babies were being "retired," but with no further discussion of any impact on values. A couple of midyear stories mentioned that some parents were willing to pay $10 to $20 each for Beanies they were having trouble finding—but that wasn't out of the ordinary for an in-demand toy whose supply hadn't yet caught up with demand.

The beginning of the Beanie Baby's transition from children's toy to adult obsession was a product of the 1990s relationship between mothers and children—a connection that was often centered on shopping. The term "soccer mom" entered the lexicon in 1995, a year before the Beanie craze began. In her 2010 paper, "Public Choices, Private Control," Boston University professor D. Lynn O'Brien Hallstein writes that America's soccer moms are part of an ethos that "encourage[s] consumerism as the solution to the work/life struggle." Quickly, though, at least in suburban Chicago, the mother-daughter toy collecting hobby was taken over by the mothers.

———————

Becky Phillips of Naperville, Illinois, started collecting Beanies with her daughter in early 1996, just as they were catching on with other kids in the neighborhood.

Becky's daughter lost interest quickly—but Becky was just getting going. Already a devoted collector of Disney memorabilia, she was also a Type A elementary school teacher who was intensely focused on organization. When I met with Becky at the Coldwell Banker office in Naperville, where she now sells real estate, she was prepared with two boxes full of carefully filed, pristine documents from her days first as a Beanie collector, then as a Beanie maven.

In mid-1996, Becky started noticing which ones were harder to find and which ones had been discontinued. The first Beanie Baby to be retired, with no announcement or reaction, was Humphrey the Camel in mid-1995. With four long legs, he was difficult to pose, and his tan color wasn't particularly appealing; kids didn't buy him, so Ty stopped making him. Slither the Snake, Web the Spider, Peking the Panda, and Trap the Mouse were retired later that year for similar reasons. Other Beanie Babies were redesigned because Warner was constantly looking for ways to make them cuter. Becky was trying to sort through it all. She devoted days to tracking down the differences between Old Face Teddy and New Face Teddy—and she was the one who first noted the distinction for the benefit of other enthusiasts.

For a compulsive collector with a desire to create order and organization, there was a lot to do. Becky Phillips roped in her friend Becky Estenssoro, and they started collecting together, acquiring multiples of some pieces that they then used to trade for hard-to-find ones with the handful of other collectors they met at gift shops. It was "two Tabascos for one Kiwi," as Estenssoro later remembered. Still, it was mostly just trading, and if parents occasionally paid more than $5 for a hard-to-find Beanie Baby, it was probably because they were trying to please their kids. No one was cataloging values, and certainly no one could see that the collecting had the makings of a speculative episode.

Not far from Becky and Becky, local children introduced Glenview, Illinois, collectibles dealer Richard Gernady to Beanie Babies. His store was named the Cat's Meow, and he became one of the first retailers to place large orders. He also saw the collectability potential that came with the so-called retirements the Ty salespeople were telling him about. He displayed Beanie Babies alongside the more traditional limited-edition lines like Precious Moments, the Franklin Mint, and the Bradford Exchange.

Before there was an established market for Beanies, Gernady started highlighting the retired pieces for his customers and pricing them at a premium, just as the King brothers' parents had done with Tom Clark gnomes. This would never have worked at Toys "R" Us or even most independent toy stores, but Richard had the advantage of a built-in customer base used to paying high prices for rare Hummel figurines. At first the reaction was slow, but Gernady was an enthusiastic evangelist, and he offered his customers a chance to get in on the ground floor of an affordable collectible. Sharon Altier, Ty Inc.'s general manger before, during, and after the craze, says that more than anything, it was retailers who made the product a hit. Selling to the mom-and-pops meant that Ty's account executives could explain the idea of the retired pieces to the store owners—who were also, as often as not, the people who were interacting with the shoppers. As the Ty reps started to get stores on board with Beanie Babies, word of the retirements spread. When early collectors called the company's office in search of information about Beanie Babies, Warner's secretary usually referred them to Richard Gernady.

I called Gernady, who was excited to tell his story and meet with me in person. He said he could show me tapes of his TV appearances commenting on the toy craze. He also mentioned that he'd spoken with Warner occasionally and that in their initial conversations, when Beanie Babies were starting to pick up locally, Warner was nonplussed. As good as the sales were, he wasn't sure he'd ever be able to monetize such a low-priced item in a big way. Gernady said he assured Warner that there was room to run with Beanie Babies; Gernady, it seems, believed in the collectability potential of Beanies more than Warner did.

The next time I was in Chicago, I called Gernady. This time, he was less friendly. He'd thought about it and decided that he didn't want to talk—he was afraid of Warner's penchant for litigation and didn't want any trouble. "He's cuckoo," Gernady told me before hanging up.

Gernady's contribution to the rise of the Beanie Baby bubble was significant. He was the first retailer to produce a checklist of all the Beanies he knew of, current and retired. Gernady had seen the power of checklists to induce collecting, and he was hoping to make that happen for Beanie Babies—at a lower entry point. Give a person who is genetically hardwired for collecting a checklist and he'll attempt to buy everything on it, Gernady knew.

Richard and his wife brought Beanie Babies to collectibles shows, where he wore a homemade hat with Beanies dangling off the rim. They told everyone that Beanies were the next big thing. In the week before Valentine's Day 1996, Gernady sold five thousand of them, and he made this prediction in an interview with one of the first reporters to write about Beanie Babies: they might become "the biggest thing ever in retailing—Elvis, Sinatra and the Beatles combined."

As for the kiosk that McGowan had set up and then quickly closed at the Yorktown Shopping Center: when she and Warner got back from a post-Christmas vacation in St. Bart's, her mother phoned her with news. The leasing manager had been trying to get in touch because the mall had been overwhelmed with chatter about Beanie Babies. He wanted to know if McGowan would be interested in reopening the booth. At Toy Fair in February 1996, a stranger approached Warner and offered him $2 million for the Beanie Baby line. Warner replied that he'd consider $100 million—which at the time was just a gibe. But it would soon represent less than one month's sales. The biggest toy craze of all time had begun.

———————

It's tempting to view the market that was developing for Beanie Babies as something entirely apart from the product itself: a greed-fueled lust for objects that might have been anything. However, like few other things, the stuffed animal is completely entrenched in the childhood experience of the Western world, and its place in our lives often lingers into adulthood. According to one British survey, 25 percent of men bring a stuffed animal along when they travel—and the deep, strange, and seldom-discussed connection between people and plush toys is a not insignificant part of the answer to the question "Why Beanie Babies?" Stuffed toys' popularity has risen and fallen over the years, and the business model has certainly changed. Yet almost from the day they came into existence, they've captured our imaginations and driven us to do things we wouldn't ordinarily do.

In 1880 a German polio survivor named Apollonia Margarete Steiff used the proceeds from teaching zither lessons to buy a sewing machine. She started making elephant-shaped pincushions as gifts for her friends and relatives. They were probably always intended as toys or ornaments, but calling them pincushions assuaged the nineteenth-century guilt that came with making something frivolous. Steiff had grown up in a well-to-do but dour and toy-less family and later recalled her gratitude at being allowed once to play with a pile of lentils, which she poured between cups. Whatever her initial intent, Steiff had created the first stuffed animal. On December 29, 1880, she went into business selling her elephants, and in 1886 she sold 5,170 of them; a line of dogs, lions, camels, and monkeys followed in quick succession.

It was a struggle. Steiff's grandniece writes of the challenges that a polio survivor faced in starting her own business: "School was easy and fun for her, but learning to sew was not. . . . When she realized that she should learn to use a sewing machine—a new thing then—it again seemed to pose a special problem: the wheel that gave the machine its impetus was on the right, and her weak right hand simply could not turn it. . . . But then she had a great idea: she would turn the machine around and learn to sew everything backwards!" In the beginning Steiff employed almost exclusively the physically disabled—people who were then considered unemployable—based on her belief that gratitude for the opportunity would inspire them to overcome their obstacles.

Margarete Steiff's introduction of stuffed animals revolutionized the world of toys. Up until then, toys had been hard; there were dolls, but their heads were generally made of porcelain, and the bodies might have been stuffed, but the fabric was coarse. The sales side also left room for improvement. Before Steiff, dolls were grouped by material type (primarily bisque, wood, and rubber); creepily, the body parts were often sold separately. This was possible because when parents made purchasing decisions without the input of children, sentimentality could (it was thought) be stripped from the sale.

The rise of teddy bears paralleled the rise of industrialization and the rise of the child as a person seen as worthy of pampering. Between 1880 and 1910, the percentage of the American labor force that worked in farming fell from 49 percent to 31 percent, and as the population moved away from the realities of life with animals, it romanticized them in its children's toys. Steiff's company was growing rapidly; then she got lucky.

On November 14, 1902, President Teddy Roosevelt was in the South to mediate a dispute over the Louisiana-Mississippi border and took a few days off to go hunting. He hadn't shot anything in four days; his hosts, feeling sorry for him, found a bear—an elderly female according to some accounts, a bear cub according to others—and tied it up so that Roosevelt would have something to kill. Roosevelt was offended and refused to shoot—although the fact that a member of his party subsequently slit the bear's throat with a hunting knife has been dropped from the popular recollection.

The story—or, rather, a romanticized version of it—was immortalized by *Washington Post* cartoonist Clifford K. Berryman, whose cartoon "Drawing the Line in the Mississippi" depicted Roosevelt standing indignantly, refusing even to face the leashed bear being offered by an eager local. By the end of the month, the phrase "teddy's bear" had entered the lexicon (although the phrase didn't appear in the cartoon), and toy sellers had begun peddling teddy bears.

Many later retellings of this incident—especially the dozens of children's books about it—neglect to mention that the bear had been tied up, which changes the connotation significantly, substituting a pleasant myth for a darker reality. The popular version says that Roosevelt refused to shoot the bear out of pity; actually, Roosevelt refused to be patronized. For an industry that was to become as cutthroat and tinged with tragedy as the cuddly business of stuffed animals, it's perfect that the teddy bear's genesis—and the birth of the stuffed animal as a popular toy that was linked, from the beginning, with President Roosevelt—was an act of pride misconstrued as an act of mercy. Yet while Roosevelt might have been the spark that ignited the teddy bear boom, the popularity was really driven by the uniqueness of the product: its softness was unheard of in toys up to that time.

Margarete Steiff introduced her first stuffed bears in 1902, and sales skyrocketed. Steiff was also among the first toy companies to build a brand and sell its products as something other than an easily substituted commodity. The *Knopf im Ohr* (Button in Ear) was Steiff's signature bit of branding, and the company fought hard against knockoffs and counterfeiters. By 1906 teddy bears were a full-blown phenomenon that approached, without the speculative element, the mania that enveloped Beanie Babies ninety years later. An ad in *Ladies' World* magazine that year advised that a teddy-less child "now-a-days is quite out of fashion." Even then, it wasn't just children. A story in *Playthings* from the same year advised that "the Teddy Bear fad has not confined itself to children. . . . If the German toymaker who invented these new playthings had been told, when he [Steiff avoided publicity, and it was generally assumed that a man was behind the company] put them on the market, that grown women would be making a fad of them, toting them around, he probably would have remarked 'Ach, himmel! Nein!'—'Oh, heavens! No!' " The story added that teddy bears were especially popular among New York's wealthy and cited a Newport, Rhode Island, socialite who always kept one with her in her carriage.

Playthings predicted that "any toy in the shape of an animal will have a good sale in 1908," but that didn't happen. Contrary to its bullishness of a year earlier, *Playthings* reported in 1908 that "the so-called craze for them has entirely subsided, that is, as far as women carrying them around is concerned." Steiff remains the most prestigious stuffed-animal maker in the world, but it never again shipped more bears than the 975,000 it sold in 1907. The real decline in the relevance of teddy bears—and all traditional toys—came forty-five years later.

Hasbro launched the first seasonal television toy commercials in 1952, and Mattel followed with the first year-round commercials in 1955. They were the first two toy companies to take their marketing directly to children. Those first ads were wildly successful and reshuffled the ranks of toy companies in America: Hasbro and Mattel, once also-rans, became the two biggest toy brands.

The business of toy selling became corporatized; the big companies that failed to jump into TV saw their sales dwindle, and the start-up toymakers who lacked the resources to advertise found themselves shut out of an industry that had once had few barriers to entry. As Michael Lewis wrote in *Next: The Future Just Happened*, "Without the television, there never would have been Tide or Rice Krispies or Alpo, but fifty smaller versions of Tide and Rice Krispies and Alpo."

Close to half a century later, the market for consumer goods was still driven by television—and toys were more dependent on TV than any other industry. That Ty Warner's Beanie Babies were able, without the benefit of a single ad, to outpace the combined annual profits of the largest toymakers in the world for even a few years was an astounding and unprecedented achievement. That he did it in spite of the interpersonal drama that reentered his life right as the toys were taking off is perhaps equally impressive.

12

The Return

In January 1996 Faith McGowan walked into Ty Warner's office, looked down at his desk, and screamed.

McGowan had been with Warner for close to three years by then—living with him, raising her children with him, "doing the business with him," as she puts it, and ceding to his demand that she reinvent herself in his image. He'd hired a personal trainer for her, and he'd begun picking out her clothes—spending hours at a mall with her in search of a winter coat, only to leave empty-handed after proclaiming there wasn't a single one that he liked. At his insistence she'd had jaw surgery to correct a slightly open bite, even as she tried to tell him that his own obsession with cosmetic surgery had gone too far. She'd gone to Dallas to visit him while he recuperated from a touch-up he'd had because he was concerned that his eyes didn't match.

His appearance shocked her: he'd opted to have both eyes redone, and he'd gotten another face-lift, too. His rapidly changing visage scared Faith and her daughters, but they loved him. They loved the time they'd been spending with him and had no reason to question his devotion. They traveled all over the world with him, played tennis almost every day, and enjoyed his slapstick comedic sensibility. When he played with Faith's dog he pretended to be a dog. The Beanie Babies business had taken off after the 1995 Christmas season, at least regionally, and things couldn't have been going better—personally or professionally.

Yet there it was, sitting on his desk, peeking out of an envelope: a one-way plane ticket to London for the woman Warner had insisted was completely out of his life. Patricia Roche was back.

There was a perfectly innocent explanation, Warner told Faith. A few weeks earlier, he had called Roche to express concern about his company's flagging sales in England. He'd contracted with a few Jehovah's Witnesses to run distribution there—and they'd recruited more Jehovah's Witnesses while Warner was busy focusing on the booming U.S. business. The Jehovah's Witnesses' experience with rejected soliciting probably prepared them well for selling plush, but the territory wasn't making money.

"How would you like to go to England?" Warner had asked Roche at a meeting he'd set up under the guise of giving her some stuffed animals that her mother could use for a charity fund-raiser.

"How the hell far away do you want me?" she'd replied.

Going back to work with Warner would be awkward, but in the three or so years since he'd booted her out of the company they'd started together, she'd barely been able to make a living. And she'd never wanted to leave the business in the first place. For Warner, the appeal was obvious: he knew she would never steal from him, and she'd been the one who'd run his office in the early days. They'd worked well together once, and she knew the business and Warner's unique approach to it better than anyone. And so, three years after their dramatic confrontation in a Cancun hotel room, Patricia Roche went to England.

While she ran Ty UK, buying product from him at below wholesale and then selling it to stores at a markup, Roche made a point of giving Warner every possible reason to regret their new partnership. As his Oak Brook office started to pick up MBAs and industry veterans to serve as executives, Ty insisted that people call him Mr. Warner. He even went through a phase where he asked to be addressed as Owner. He started to call meetings even though the social requirements bored him. He often read magazines while his executives discussed ideas, and sometimes interrupted to share a fun fact he'd come across. "Like a child," Roche says. During conference calls, if he droned on pompously, she called him out—and not tactfully.

"Oh, shove it up your ass, Ty!" she once shouted.

"Patricia, you know I hate it when you swear, and a little decorum would be nice. You're on speakerphone," he replied.

"Good, I'll talk louder, you dumb shit," she said. No one at Ty talked to Warner like Patricia did. She also believed that she was above talking to anyone at the company other than Warner himself. She screamed at Sharon Altier, the general manager who had been her replacement after the episode in Cancun, whenever she called to discuss inventory. After a few months, Altier started answering the phone with "Hello, Patricia. If you swear at me, I'm going to hang up."

In time, Sharon and Patricia developed a certain rapport. When Ty's behavior struck Sharon as odd—like when she discovered that he had bugged her office—she would call Patricia for advice. "No one understands Ty better than her," Sharon remembers, and there was one tip Roche gave her that she never forgot: everything, Patricia told her, was a manipulation. "He doesn't fart without planning it weeks in advance," Roche explained.

———

With Faith and her daughters, Warner, now in his fifties, had a basically conventional personal life for the first time, which surprised those who'd known him as a perennial playboy. At Toy Fair, an old acquaintance of Warner's approached him and McGowan and exclaimed, "I want to meet the woman who would live in a house with this man and her children!" There were still eccentricities, some of them fun: a resolute individualist, Ty instructed the girls to pay no attention to peer pressure about fashion. Create your own style, he told them. He also, as every-one who's ever driven with him recalls, indoctrinated people in his philosophy of never paying tolls. "Just throw pennies and keep driving! It's an illegal tax!" he'd shout.

Other eccentricities were more off-putting. When Faith's daughters were preteens, he insisted that everyone join him to watch his favorite movie: a 1945 adaptation of Oscar Wilde's novel *The Picture of Dorian Gray*, the dark story of a wealthy and immoral young man who never ages. He took them on lavish vacations and paid for everything, but they generally experienced him as stingy. When the girls were older, he never bought them cars or contributed to college funds. Ty was a master of appealing to sentimentality about family life when it came to his products, but family life opened a Pandora's box for Warner. He once stayed home with McGowan's daughters while she went to a Christmas party. He was distraught when she returned. "I don't know what I'm doing. I'm out of here," he told her, and left immediately. When she didn't hear from him for two days, McGowan drove over to his house—they were living at her house while his was under construction—and found him sitting in a dark closet upstairs. "He said that while babysitting for Lauren and Jenna, he felt responsible for them," she remembers. "This triggered bad memories of when his parents failed to provide the care and nurturing that he needed during his childhood. Because his parents had emotionally abandoned him, he said he couldn't do the family thing."

"I need to be taken care of like a five-year-old boy," he told her.

While Ty Inc.'s sales grew tenfold in the span of a few months, Warner received word that his mother, who had fallen out of communication with both of her children, was living in the Palm Beach area. Warner was eager to see her, so he and McGowan got on the next flight, then drove to the hotel where she was staying. "The manager called the room, but she refused to see us,"

McGowan recalls. "We went back to our convertible and drove through the parking lot, where Ty spotted his old brown Mercedes, which was now in bad condition. When we looked back at the hotel, we saw a woman with long black hair peeking out from behind the drapes. So we went back into the hotel and Ty knocked on her door. No response. Ty then told her in a loud, firm voice that he was there and he loved her." Georgia told them to leave.

A few months later, Ty received a call from a hospital in Palm Beach: Georgia had recently been there for treatment. She had no money, no insurance, no home, and had told the hospital that she was living out of her car.

Ty wasn't known for his empathy or his willingness to accommodate other people—but he would do anything for his mother. He rented a hotel suite for her and arranged for the hospital to move her there under some false pretense he'd concocted with the staff. Next he flew to Palm Beach and hid in the bushes at the hotel while Faith, dressed as a nurse, went to the desk, asked for Georgia's room number, and knocked on the door. They sat talking in the living room for half an hour. Georgia said, "My son would like you. He'd charm you." She told Faith that Ty was a criminal who imported drugs in stuffed animals from Asia. Faith replied that she doubted that and that Ty sounded like a successful businessman. Yet Faith's protest came off a bit too eager, and Georgia caught on to the ruse. She spit at Faith and ordered her out. Faith walked out the front door and found Ty, who was still waiting in the bushes. They flew home in tears.

Back in the Chicago suburbs, not far from the home he was returning to, a few women Warner had never even heard of were doing the groundwork that was to make him richer than even he, the supremely cocky salesman, ever could have dreamed of becoming.

Beanie Babies creator Ty Warner and his sister, Joy, circa 1949.

Warner's mother, Georgia, seen here in 1937, struggled with paranoid schizophrenia. Once, Ty's sister awoke to see Georgia hovering over her with a butcher's knife.

Ty Warner at age sixteen.

Ty's father, Hal, was a top salesman at Dakin, a leading plush company in the 1960s and 1970s. Hal got Ty his first job in the toy business, but their relationship was bizarre and dysfunctional. They often dated the same women.

Within a few years of dropping out of Kalamazoo College and then signing on as his father's sub-rep, Warner became the most successful salesman Dakin had ever seen, outearning the company's CEO in the process.

After he was fired from Dakin at the end of the 1970s, Warner sunk into a depression that industry friends worried might end his life. It was the bear in Dakin's logo (lower right) who came to him in a dream, and told him: start your own plush company, and you can be a star once again.

With this Spring, 1980 catalog, R. Dakin & Company celebrates its 25th year in business. That's a silver anniversary. We hope you will pardon our pride and the bits of 1955 nostalgia scattered through this publication.

Twenty-five years of service. That's Dakin's slogan for 1980. It's as important now with worldwide sales to many thousands of customers as in 1955. We cherish each of you; you have the right to expect excellent treatment from Dakin -- as well as excellent merchandise.

We are pleased, in this connection, to announce that our Mid-western customers will be serviced from warehouse facilities near Chicago beginning in late Spring, 1980. This will reduce shipping time tremendously.

What's ahead for 1980? We're optimistic, and hope you are too. We look for record sales, with the finest lines we have ever assembled, presented at fair prices and backed by service. We know it will do a great job for you.

Inflation at all levels has forced us to establish modest price increases in many categories. We will never sacrifice quality; Dakin is still the best value on the market.

Join us in celebrating Dakin's 25th year in business. Our present to you is the truly outstanding merchandise you see illustrated in this beautiful catalog.

R. Dakin & Company

CATALOG © R. DAKIN & COMPANY 1979

R. DAKIN AND COMPANY
DAKIN
OUR 25th ANNIVERSARY

Warner started his own business in 1983 with a few impeccably designed plush cats that he stuffed himself and groomed obsessively during trade shows. "You can make a lot of money with a good cat," he once said.

Warner and his girlfriend Patricia Roche ran the business by themselves for the first few years. When this photo was taken in 1990, the company was up to a few million dollars per year in sales. Two years later, their relationship imploded spectacularly. Shortly after they broke up, he named one of the first Beanie Babies, Patti the Platypus, after her. He wrote this poem for its hangtag: "Ran into Patti one day while walking/Believe me, she wouldn't stop talking/Listened and listened to her speak/That would explain her extra-large beak."

Lina Trivedi was a sociology major at DePaul University when she became Ty Inc.'s twelfth employee in 1992. Here she is at the Atlanta Gift Show in 1995. A year later, Lina came up with the idea that changed how the company marketed Beanie Babies and helped make them the weirdest speculative mania of all time.

The King brothers were distributors for Ty Inc. products in several southern states. After they pitched Warner the idea of announcing "retirements" for Beanie Babies, a global craze ensued. The brothers became multimillionaires in their twenties.

Before anyone had heard of Beanie Babies, an eccentric collectibles dealer named Richard Gernady, owner of the Cat's Meow, a gift shop in Glenview, Illinois, was telling anyone who would listen that they'd be the next big thing. He pushed his customers to pay higher prices for retired pieces.

Warner, a perfectionist who one employee called "the Steve Jobs of plush," was constantly tinkering with his products to try to create the perfect stuffed animal. When he changed the face design on his Teddy Beanie Baby in early 1995, he inadvertently created the first rare Beanie Baby, who soon became known as Old Face Teddy. Within a couple of years, the early Chicago collectors who'd picked up dozens of old-faced teddies at $5 each were sitting on six-figure fortunes.

At its 1998 peak, *Mary Beth's Beanie World*, a monthly magazine edited by a self-described soccer mom from suburban Chicago, had a paid monthly circulation of more than one million copies. The highlight of the magazine was the price guide that tracked the Beanies' rapidly fluctuating values.

Former commodities trader Peggy Gallagher and her sister, Dr. Paula Abrinko, both of suburban Chicago, were two of the first serious, systematic Beanie collectors. When they had trouble finding some pieces locally, they ran up four-digit phone bills calling all over the country in search of Beanie Babies and spread the craze in the process. Perched on Dr. Abrinko's left hand is Peanut the Royal Blue Elephant, the rarest of all Beanie Babies, worth more than $5,000 at the height of the market.

Warner and his girlfriend Faith McGowan at the company's employee appreciation party on Lake Michigan, September 13, 1997. Ty Inc.'s sales were growing at a rate of more than 1,000 percent per year as sales of Beanie Babies like Congo the Gorilla (center) soared.

A worker at Ty's warehouse stands amid the boxes that carried fifteen thousand orders of Beanie Babies per day to retailers all over America. A few months after this picture was taken, complaints about collectors stalking UPS trucks and boxes of Beanie Babies disappearing during shipping forced Warner to remove the company's logo from its boxes. "If you were shipping diamonds, would you put a diamond on the box?" said one former executive.

Released in August 1999, The End bear announced the end of the millennium and, Warner hoped, the end of Beanie Babies.

Warner's original plan for the new millennium was to replace Beanie Babies with Beanie Kids. "Ty, they're ugly," the head of Ty UK told him. "They'll buy it," he replied. "I could put the Ty heart on manure and they'd buy it!" The Beanie Kids were the biggest flop of Warner's career.

The living room of Leon and Sondra Schlossberg, a father-daughter team of collectors. Their tens of thousands of Ty products have taken over their home and, Sondra says, they haven't been able to use their living room since 2012.

As the owner of Wallos.com, the biggest of the Beanie Baby dealers, Brian Wallos made millions in his twenties. When the mania ended, he used his winnings to start a line of trading cards featuring porn stars.

On January 14, 2014, sixty-nine-year-old Ty Warner arrived in court for sentencing in the largest bust of the government's crackdown on Swiss bank account tax evasion.

Even after he became a billionaire, Warner never stopped experimenting in his quest to make the most beautiful stuffed animals in the world, poring over every detail of every piece his company ever released.

The day after Warner's sentencing of probation for tax evasion, a local photographer took this shot of workers painting the wrought iron gates to his $150 million Montecito, California, home gold.

13

Force Multipliers

It had been a half century since a major toy craze had started locally; even the Hula Hoop fad, which is generally thought to have begun with product giveaways on the playgrounds of Southern California, really only began with a demonstration on *The Dinah Shore Show*.

The rise of Beanie Babies, by contrast, really was an incremental, peer-to-peer phenomenon that began in the Chicago suburbs. The localized variations in knowledge about rare Beanie Babies created a natural way for the craze to spread. As local collectors geographically expanded their search for early and rare Beanies, awareness of a Beanie craze expanded. Had demand started out strong, there would have been no early Beanie Babies produced in small quantities for collectors to hunt for—and, more important, spread stories about.

While Richard Gernady was promoting Beanies in his store and at local collectibles shows, two pairs of intelligent, well-educated Chicago women—Becky Phillips and Becky Estenssoro, along with a doctor and her sister—were working to assemble complete collections, egged on by the checklists they obtained from Gernady. "My downfall was the checklists," one early collector told me. "Once you have a checklist, you don't look at what you have. You look at what you don't have."

Dr. Paula Benchik-Abrinko first got hooked by a pile of Beanie Babies she saw in the gift shop at the hospital where she worked.

She bought several dozen and brought them along when she met her sister Peggy Gallagher for lunch a few days later. "She said, 'Look at these little stuffed animals,'" remembers Gallagher. "She said, 'Peggy, you figure this out for me—how many of them there are and who makes them.'" Benchik-Abrinko wanted to collect them all for her daughter, and while Peggy didn't have any children, she decided she'd start a collection, too. Then she decided she wanted Beanie Baby collections for her older sister's two daughters as well. "I started showing them to people, and they'd say, 'Well, when you get them, get me one,'" she remembers.

Gallagher and Benchik-Abrinko, along with the two Beckys, were the first serious, systematic Beanie Baby collectors. Demand was already high among children in the Chicago suburbs, so they needed to cast a wider net to find the rarest pieces. Once you got out of the Midwest, piles of Beanie Babies—even the early retired pieces—could still be found in Hallmark stores, toy stores, zoos, and hospital gift shops. This set the stage for a classic arbitrage trade: buying something in a market where it's not in demand and then selling it where it is in demand.

That was when the phone calls started.

Dr. Benchik-Abrinko was working as an internist on a study about women who were undergoing dialysis while pregnant. She was calling hospitals all over the country in search of patient records. At the end of each call, she'd ask to be transferred to the hospital gift shop. Credit card in hand, she asked puzzled clerks who'd only vaguely heard of Beanie Babies to describe the ones they had in inventory. Benchik-Abrinko ordered the ones she didn't have, along with the ones that were hard to find in Chicago. When she found stores with duplicates of hard-to-find Beanies, she ordered as many as she could to build a stockpile for trading.

"It was trading in the beginning," remembers her sister Peggy. "But then Richard Gernady started telling us what he was selling them for. He'd say, 'These are retired so they cost more.' So we'd pay. Then we'd tell other people that we paid more, and so they would need to pay more. That was how the higher prices started happening."

At this point, none of it was especially insane. Higher prices were being paid, but only by parents and collectors. No one thought of them as an investment. There were many things for which people with discretionary income overpaid—so why not tick off another box on the Beanie Baby checklist? In March 1996 a local newspaper reported that "people are so desperate to collect the Beanie Babies, they're now offering to pay $10 to $25, plus shipping and handling charges, for animals that are still on sale in stores for just $5." Once people could buy them for $5 and flip them for two to five times that much, the speed of the fad's spread multiplied—because humans have an insatiable need to brag. The idea of making money reselling stuffed animals was so bizarre—so fantastic—that everyone who did it told everyone they knew about it. Even with relatively tiny volume, stories about profits on Beanies spread word virally of an otherwise unremarkable product.

Gallagher and Benchik-Abrinko compiled lists of retailers all over the country and racked up $1,000-per-month long-distance charges. Peggy tried to hide the phone bills and all other evidence of her new hobby from her husband, who was a lawyer. "At first I had them hiding in my office because I said, 'If my husband sees me buying these little animals, he's going to say, "What the hell is wrong with her?"'"

A year later, Peggy was telling collectors who lined up at her lectures and book signings about the treasures she'd scored in the first days of Beanie collecting: In early 1996 the Camelback Mountain Resort in Pennsylvania sold her twelve Humphrey the Camels for $5 each. Back in Chicago she traded some of those for Beanies she hadn't been able to find. She was fortunate to hold on to a few: by late 1997 Humphrey was selling reliably on-line for more than $2,000. On February 12, 1996, Gallagher scored the biggest hit of her Beanie collecting career: through a little sleuthing, she found the contact information for the Ty distributor in Nuremberg, Germany, and phoned to see what they had. Beanies hadn't yet caught on there, and Gallagher placed her first order, paying retail prices for 198 Beanie Babies that were already impossible to find in Chicago—and once the collecting craze turned speculative, they would be worth a fortune.

Among her finds: 30 Chilly the Polar Bears purchased for the equivalent of $7 each; within a year and a half, those sold for more than $1,800 each. Her 36 Peking the Pandas were worth around $2,000 each; the 84 Old Face Teddies were worth $1,800 each; the 36 Trap the Mouse Beanies, $1,200 each; and 12 Patti the Platypuses, $800 each. Unfortunately, her requests for the royal blue Peanut the Elephant and Spot the Dog, along with a few other Beanies, went unfilled.

Still, a few months later that $2,000 order, which included shipping fees from Germany, was worth more than $300,000—far higher than the annual sales of Ty Germany at the time. Peggy Gallagher knew far more about which pieces were sought after than the company did.

While Benchik-Abrinko and her sister were building their collections and asking their mother for help with the phone bills, just across town, the two Beckys were doing the same thing. Sometimes a store manager explained that a day earlier a mysterious lady from suburban Chicago had called and bought out his entire inventory. As the Chicago women called around the country, asking retailers about Beanie Babies and purchasing everything stores had—even if that was only thirty or forty pieces per store—they served as the force multipliers of the local interest.

Fads and trends are often seen as spreading virally through word of mouth—as a steady process of regular people telling one another about something until everyone has heard about it. However, journalist and best-selling author Malcolm Gladwell says that, in reality, fads are often spread "by the efforts of a handful of exceptional people." In this case it was the exceptional dedication of a few Chicago women that spread Beanie Baby collecting nationally. When they called friends in different time zones to ask them to be on the lookout for rare pieces that could fetch five times their retail price in the suburban Chicago market, they created new collectors who were equipped with stories they couldn't resist telling. As Seth Godin notes in his book *Unleashing the Ideavirus*, the investments they were making in their own collections gave them a powerful incentive to build the broader market for Beanie Babies: "If other people start collecting, your collection increases in value." While consumer goods have always gained popularity through word of mouth, word of a profitable investment always spreads more quickly. The actual universe of collectors for these early pieces was tiny—but their existence drove Beanie Babies to become something much bigger.

In late 1996, Richard Gernady introduced Peggy Gallagher to his friend Rosie Wells, a collectibles impresario and the publisher of *Rosie's Collectors' Bulletin,* a popular magazine among collectors. Wells and Gernady knew each other from the world of Precious Moments collecting, and Gernady hoped to get her on the Beanie bandwagon. At first Wells was cool to the idea of Beanie Babies as a collectible, but as she saw the momentum gathering in Illinois, she jumped on board and gave Gallagher the assignment for the first magazine piece on the emerging craze.

In that magazine Gallagher also placed an ad: send her a self-addressed stamped envelope, she wrote, and she'd send you a price list of all the Beanie Babies. Admittedly, her research left something to be desired; as Gallagher explained it to me, she was essentially making up prices based on the pieces that seemed to be the hardest to find. She tried to cull values based on what Gernady was charging and what the collectors in America Online's collectibles chat room were saying, but there was no transparent market yet. In the beginning she simply decreed that most retired Beanie Babies were worth $10 or $20 each, and then watched in amazement as the market went there. Gallagher, with her own collection, naturally had a strong incentive to be optimistic about her estimates. Among the small group of Chicago suburbs collectors, the price lists that Gallagher—and then the two Beckys—put out *became* the market.

"All the people who were driving this lived within ten miles of each other," remembers Mary Beth Sobolewski. Anyone who was collecting Beanie Babies in early 1996 was either in the Chicago suburbs or connected with someone in the Chicago suburbs who told them about the booming trade in collectible plush. As I researched the earliest Beanie mavens and collectors, one apparent outlier was Sara Nelson, who created BeanieMom .com, one of the first and by far the most popular of the fan sites. She was living in Virginia at the time of the craze; how could she have been one of the early Beanie collectors?

One of Nelson's best friends moved to suburban Chicago in early 1996. When the friend returned to Virginia to visit, she told Nelson about Beanie Babies, and Nelson started her own collection, ostensibly for her daughters. She went online and found a woman named Becky Phillips who had a fine-mane Mystic—a rare variation of Mystic the Unicorn, then worth about $100. When Phillips gave her the address to send the check, Nelson was shocked: Phillips lived across the street from the friend who had introduced Nelson to Beanie Babies. Being Becky Phillips's neighbor made it nearly impossible to avoid becoming a Beanie collector. Also on that same block lived Joni Blackman—the *People* magazine reporter who did the first national story on Beanie

Babies after Phillips told her about them. The world of early collectors hoarding the rarest pieces was indeed a tiny one, and all
of the major collectors can be traced back to the cul-de-sac where
Becky Phillips lived, not far from Mary Beth, Peggy, and Paula.

As I talked to the early collectors, their lack of insight into
what became their obsession was fascinating. Beanie Babies, almost from the beginning, seemed to have people doing things
they didn't even really want to do—and more than fifteen years
later, they struggled to explain their thinking. It was fun; they
wanted complete sets, so they acquired duplicates when they
could in order to trade for ones they couldn't find. The trouble,
as with so many things, came later—once the money involved
escalated.

14

Peanut the Royal Blue Elephant

The early collectors' excitement preceded the broader public's. In mid-1996 Becky Phillips and Becky Estenssoro began placing ads in toy and collector magazines to try to sell some of their earliest Beanie Babies—but they didn't get much response. In October they set up a booth at the Kane County Flea Market in Saint Charles, Illinois, but that didn't work either. Few people were interested in paying $20 or $25 for a retired Beanie Baby. The two Beckys were only able to recoup the $125 they'd paid for the table by buying out the stock of a dealer who had Beanies for $5 and marking them up to $6.50. Still, they persisted.

As the collectors chased Beanies and compiled lists, they realized there were a few oddities that were nearly impossible to find. The hunt for oddball specimens has always fueled collectors: philatelists made the rare Inverted Jenny one of the most valuable stamps of the twentieth century. Baseball card collectors obsessed over the 1909 Honus Wagner card that was pulled from production after Wagner threatened legal action. News accounts of the card's soaring value helped to spur a speculative market for mass-produced contemporary cards in the 1980s and early 1990s. In the tulip mania of the 1630s, the Semper Augustus bulb was the rarest and most coveted—and helped to spread the burgeoning market for tulips to its sad and inevitable conclusion: naive latecomers paid too much for tulips that weren't even a little bit rare. Just as the legitimate business model of eBay drove demand for shares of hundreds of Internet stocks without business models, it was the discovery of hard-to-find oddities that started to turn harmless toy collecting into something truly insane.

Peanut the Elephant originally shipped in mid-1995 with royal blue fabric; after a few thousand Peanuts had already been sold, Warner decided that the color was too dark to appeal to children. He stopped production and switched the fabric color to baby blue—and those original royal blue Peanuts became the most coveted of all Beanie Babies, worth more than $5,000 each. By 1997 there were few people who hadn't heard of the royal blue version of Peanut the Elephant. The toy and its incredible value became such a ubiquitous cultural meme that columnist Dave Barry could mock it in a 1998 column without bothering to provide much context: "So now Beanie Babies are big business, with grown men and women fighting over them and paying thousands of dollars for certain rare models, such as Peanut the Royal Blue Elephant (not to be confused with Peanut the LIGHT Blue Elephant, which only a total loser would pay thousands of dollars for)."

Spot the Dog originally shipped without a spot, and Quackers the Duck originally shipped without wings. "The reason people are willing to pay so much for a Beanie when it's first released," Myrtle Cecil, one of the first Beanie collectors and later an official Beanie expert for eBay, told *Good Housekeeping,* "is that Ty is famous for changing an animal after the first production run. That makes the earlier version much more valuable." Warner changed the design of Tank the Armadillo after a biologist phoned to inform him that it wasn't anatomically correct; when his redesign wasn't quite right, he changed it again, and each new variation made the older versions highly sought after by collectors seeking complete sets.

Collectors and reporters gave Ty Warner credit for brilliant marketing when it came to the variations, but that wasn't the case. In the beginning, the variations weren't driven by a desire to create buzz. Rather, Warner was just tinkering with already-released products out of his obsessive desire to create a perfect toy—the goal that had been the sole driver of his life since he'd started his own business.

The variations were dutifully cataloged by the collectors. There was Derby the Horse, introduced in mid-1995—but then there was Derby with a star on his head, and Derby without a star on his head, and both of those variations came with "fine manes" and "coarse manes," with values ranging from $5 to $4,000 by 1998. Inky the Octopus was originally tan and didn't have a mouth; then he was tan with a mouth; then he was pink with a mouth. His value, depending on which edition you had, ranged from roughly $30 up to around $1,000 by 1998. The number of spots on Lucky the Ladybug also varied; Nip the Cat's paws and face went through several changes during his production, and Patti the Platypus went from maroon to magenta. When Sly the Fox's belly was changed from white to brown, the original Beanie's value soared to close to $200.

The self-styled market experts stoked the idea that in the new Beanies there was the possibility of finding examples that would experience the same appreciation patterns the earlier ones had. The reasoning was of course flawed: by the time Beanie Babies had caught on, the Chinese factories were pumping them out in huge quantities—although the diffused distribution masked just how many Ty was selling. No one ever walked into a store and saw a pile of five hundred Beanie Babies; Ty's sales went through large numbers of small stores rather than small numbers of large stores. Every day, Ty generated eight thousand to ten thousand packing slips, and during the holiday season the company shipped fifteen thousand orders per day to retailers across America. Warner knew that keeping small numbers of Beanies in many stores was the key to the craze, telling a reporter in 1996, "This thing could grow and be around for many years just as long as I don't take the easy road and sell it to a mass merchant who's going to put it in bins."

"People didn't understand that the ones people were making $800 on were really rare," says Paula Benchik-Abrinko. "By the time they had heard that people were making money, the really hot ones were all gone"—mostly into the hands of that small group of Chicago women. In July 1996 Mary Beth Sobolewski had paid $25 each for five New Face teddy bears of various colors. "Naysayers were quick to say I was throwing money away on a fad that would be tomorrow's disaster," she later remembered. "As history played out, my investment in Teddy New Face Magenta, Cranberry, Violet, Jade, and Teal would realize an eighty-eight hundred percent increase over the next couple of years." By mid-1998 the bears were selling for at least $2,000 each, and all of the earliest Chicago collectors were sitting on six-figure fortunes. As new collectors started backtracking to acquire the earliest pieces, Benchik-Abrinko quietly sold a few of her rarest Beanies and used the proceeds to adopt her first child.

Had the initial sales of Beanie Babies been stronger, it's unlikely that a craze ever could have developed. There would have been no early oddities and limited-production rarities for collectors to hunt for—and for which to pay the high prices that would spread word of an investment opportunity. As the *Chicago Tribune* reported, "Start talking Beanies, and just about everybody knows somebody who financed a wedding, a vacation, a new van or what have you with the proceeds of Beanie sales." In his 1978 book, *Manias, Panics, and Crashes: A History of Financial Crises*, the economist Charles Kindleberger explained the self-perpetuating feeding frenzy that develops when speculators start making money: "There is nothing so disturbing to one's well-being and judgment as to see a friend get rich."

The money and the stories were flowing. Vicki Chalmers of

Cockeysville, Maryland, left her sales job at AT&T to become a full-time Beanie trader. Jennifer Sykes, a forty-one-year-old mother from Northridge, California, bragged to a reporter about the Slither the Snake Beanie Baby she'd paid $600 for in a store— and then flipped online for more than $1,000. "Now that was pretty addicting," she said.

The idea of people making money with Beanie Babies was too good for fact-checking. As Dr. Robert Shiller notes in *Irrational Exuberance*, it is perhaps no coincidence that "the history of speculative bubbles begins roughly with the advent of newspapers. Although the news media—newspapers, magazines, and broadcast media, along with their new outlets on the Internet— present themselves as detached observers of market events, they are themselves an integral part of these events." The *Wall Street Journal* ran a feature story on Michael Podraza, a thirteen-year-old who, it said, had grossed more than $1 million with the Beanie-trading Web site BeanieX.com, which he'd started with his father. In 1998, the *Chicago Tribune* reported that "the corporation earned $2.3 million in gross sales; this year, Podraza expects sales to top $3 million." Other collectors doubt the veracity of that sales figure—BeanieX.com was a site most collectors had never heard of—and today Podraza works as a stylist at a Hair Cuttery in suburban Illinois.

"The media actively shape public attention and categories of thought, and they create the environment within which the speculative market events we see are played out," writes Dr. Shiller. The microphenomenon in the Chicago suburbs was transformed by the power of the press.

The ability of stories to shape values and valuations is at the heart of every speculative event. Shiller tells the story of how Leonardo da Vinci's *Mona Lisa* became the most famous and most valuable painting in the world. It started with Giorgio Vasari's profile of Leonardo in his 1550 book, *Lives of the Most*

Excellent Painters, Sculptors, and Architects. Vasari is considered to have been the first art historian, and the book and its stories circulated widely—especially its story about the model's famous smile: Vasari reported that Leonardo had difficulty capturing it and that he'd tried a number of entertainers who, he hoped, would get the model to assume the correct facial expression. In the end, Vasari writes, the result was "a thing more divine than human, and it was held to be a marvel." That story, apocryphal at the time and believed to be entirely untrue by many modern art historians, spread the idea of the painting as something more than just a painting—and poets and songwriters responded with tributes to it. Sigmund Freud published a widely circulated essay psychoanalyzing *Mona Lisa* in 1910; when the masterpiece was stolen from the Louvre in 1911, media reports fixated on the smile. In 1950 Nat "King" Cole's recording of the song "Mona Lisa" was the number one record in the country for eight weeks. While it's interesting that the stories that made *Mona Lisa* the most famous painting in the world probably aren't even true, no one really cares.

And so it was with Beanie Babies: incredible stories about vast riches being made, predictions about rising prices, then books and magazines extolling their investment merits circulated. Preteens were making millions with Beanie-trading Web sites; soccer moms were accumulating collections that would cover the cost of college. The stories might not have started out as accurate ones, but the momentum they created sometimes helped them become true.

———

In early 1997 Peggy Gallagher released the first book on Beanie Babies—a thin, self-published volume featuring photos of every Beanie she'd been able to accumulate so far. Between the book and her wheeling and dealing over the phone, in a few months she netted $200,000. She celebrated with a new Mercedes and a vanity license plate: BBABIES. She was also appearing once a month for two hours on WGN Radio, the most popular talk station in the Chicago market with a strong signal that often made it audible all over America. When Gallagher entered each caller into a drawing to win a basket of Beanie Babies, the phone lines jammed. During one summer show, a caller asked, "Do you think there is a seasonal cycle for Beanie Babies?"

"It's not different than any other kind of investment—the stock market or the commodities market," was Gallagher's reply. Then she explained that she used to be a trader on the Chicago Mercantile Exchange. "There are peaks and valleys. It's an investment for people. There's nobody as big as the market. The Hunt [brothers] tried to do it with the silver market. There is nobody bigger than the market. The prices have stabilized a bit right now, but now they're starting to get more active. So it's just like any other type of investment."

As the women of suburban Chicago built their collections, Beanie Babies also found their way into the classroom. On January 3, 1997, the *Daily Herald* reported that two kindergarten teachers were working to incorporate Beanies into their lesson plans. Pep Tobin brought her collection into the classroom to educate the students about Beanies: "Besides showing the students 91 of her Beanie Babies, Tobin talked to them about sorting the toys and about how she finds out more about her hobby from the World Wide Web. . . . Beanie Babies sell for about $5, but Tobin told children that rare versions and ones that no longer are manufactured may fetch hundreds of dollars." One Minnesota mother told a skeptical reporter that the toys had educational value: "They read the little poems that come with the Beanies, so it helps their reading. They've learned the concept of retiring." Why it would be valuable for children to learn the concept of retiring was a question left unasked.

It was a reasonably normal-size mania, but still a mania. Ty's sales for 1996 rose to $280 million—up tenfold in a year but only a slightly larger business than that of Department 56, a seller of similarly collectible Christmas cottages. Ty was becoming a major player in the world of toys and collectibles, but not on a scale that transcended the industry. A few suburban Chicago collectors trading, then spending cash to fill holes in their collections had combined with demand from children bringing the pocket-size toys to school to ignite a bull market in Beanies. Now collector-speculators were lining up to acquire the newest pieces because who knew? Might Bruno the Bull Terrier be the next royal blue Peanut the Elephant? At $5 it certainly seemed worth a try, and they were cute enough as toys to overcome skepticism: even if they didn't go up in value, they still made great gifts.

———————

As for Ty Warner, he was watching the developing rage surrounding his line with a mixture of astonished joy—the collectors were driving his sales—and contempt. Because Ty wasn't providing any information, Becky Phillips and Becky Estenssoro had taken the lead as Beanie Baby historians, sorting through thousands of Beanies and photographing the hangtags to try to trace the history of the line. They categorized the tags into different "generations" based on when Ty had used which designs. Their efforts helped turn the hangtags into cult objects: the key to determining how early a piece was and, once the counterfeiting started, whether it was authentic. They tried to drop off a copy of their book, *Beanie Mania*, one of the first guides to collecting, at Ty Inc., but Warner's secretary wouldn't let them into the office. Warner thought the women were "totally nuts," as one former employee puts it.

He also wasn't helping with the media coverage, telling his employees that he was only interested in interviews if it was Oprah

Winfrey or *People* magazine. Robin Smith Kollman, a reporter for suburban Chicago's *Daily Herald*, wrote several of the first stories about Beanie Babies, but without any input from the company. "I recall the frustration in trying numerous times to reach him before some secretary took pity on me and flat-out told me he would not return my phone calls because he did not do interviews at the time," she told me.

He wasn't even interested in meeting with the industry analysts and investment bankers who, at a moment's notice, could have put together a billion-dollar IPO or sale of the company. "I tried calling Ty," remembers Sean McGowan (no relation to Faith McGowan), then a top-ranked toy industry analyst at the investment bank Gerard Klauer Mattison. "You got a recorded message saying send us a fax [and] if we deem you worthy maybe we'll call you back." Warner didn't call him back.

Part of this was that Ty was busy and stressed: he reported a pretax income of around $90 million in 1996, and he wasn't delegating much even as sales continued to soar.

He was spending several months each year at the factories in China, and wherever he was, he visited a few toy and gift shops almost every day, partly to make sure that retailers were displaying his toys to his specifications. His handbook for his salespeople required them to hand-count inventory in every store each month; the handbook advised that if the store owner said he would count the inventory himself, the sales rep should insist otherwise. He also required them to provide at least one piece of merchandising advice during every meeting with a store owner. But his rules weren't always followed. When a visit to a Harrods in London turned up Beanie Babies with price stickers covering the Ty logo on the tag, he called Patricia Roche and demanded that she immediately stop selling to all three hundred Harrods locations. "They put a sticker over my name!" he "shrieked," as Roche put it. (She told him to shut up, and he eventually let it go.)

As the toys became an investment, Warner's in-store visits picked up a more specific purpose: figuring out which Beanies to announce were up for retirement. If he saw that an animal was stacking up unsold, he'd announce its retirement to clear out inventory and keep the dream of ever-rising prices alive. He later hit on another strategy: by retiring pieces that were already hard to find, you could drive collectors really nuts, and get them thinking that no Beanie was safe and that all Beanies must be accumulated as quickly as possible as soon as they were available.

When Warner announced that a Beanie was retired, that meant that he immediately stopped shipping it to retailers: all outstanding orders were canceled, even on pieces he had in the warehouse that had secondary-market values of ten or twenty times their retail prices. Ty's whimsical, anecdote-based retirement decisions came with a cost: at the height of Beanie Baby mania, even as he couldn't manufacture product fast enough to keep up with demand, he filled a 370,000-square-foot warehouse with retired Beanie Babies—more than $100 million worth of product he could no longer sell only because he had announced that he wouldn't.

He sometimes shipped products to the United Kingdom only to tell Patricia Roche, while they were en route, that she couldn't sell them because they'd been retired. She'd respond, "Well, if you're charging me for them, they're not retired in England, Ty," but he wouldn't budge. Such tactics made Roche furious, and she did call him at his office every now and then to hurl obscenities at him.

Nickel-and-diming aside, however, the Ty UK distributorship was making her richer than she ever could have imagined becoming. So she reluctantly spent more than $10,000 on a machine that could rip apart the toys customers would have lined up to buy, discard the fabric, and collect the PVC pellets—which were then sold back to the factories in Asia.

For the time being, Warner had control of Patricia Roche—and now he wanted more control of everything. "Control the fad" was a phrase he used frequently around the office, but there was a problem that was starting to annoy him: his biggest fans. The collectors cataloging and profiting from his creatures weren't entirely to his liking, even if it was clear that they were making him rich. Claudia Dunne, one of the early collectors and experts, remembers the Beanie moms' limited interactions with Warner: "He hated us. He hated us. He absolutely hated us. And I never understood why. I don't know what the deal was and why it made him so angry."

"Who better to control it than him?" is how Faith McGowan summarizes Warner's deep distrust of the experts, Webmasters, promoters, and publishers who were proselytizing the idea of his under-stuffed animals as an investment. To harness the cult following that was building around Beanie Babies, Warner needed something to connect directly with his customers, and connect them with each other. The technology was there, but Warner knew nothing about computers. Like many parents and small-business owners in 1996, he found the expertise he needed from a younger generation when a twentysomething part-time employee told him about this "new thing called the Internet."

15

The $12-per-Hour Sociology Major Who
Made Ty Warner a Billionaire

Most of the negative stories about Ty Warner come from his former high-level employees. "You get beat with a stick and there is
no carrot," one of them said of his management style. "And if
you still want the carrot, you get beat again. Then he'll tell you
that maybe there is a carrot after all, and then he'll go to Europe
and fire you while he's out of the country."

With hourly workers, though, it was entirely different. When
Warner was running things with Patricia, he made sure everyone
knew that Ty was basically a family business; he was the dad and
Patricia was the mom, and everyone was valued and loved. When
he hired his first warehouse worker from a job-board posting at a
for-profit college across the street, he offered the young man the
use of his home—Warner was living in a condo while the house
was under renovation—to help him save for college.

He allowed a local police officer to use space in his warehouse
to start a dog training business, and when one of his early employees was diagnosed with cancer, Warner arrived at work the
next day with research he'd done on top specialists. He knew all
the workers in the warehouse by name and regularly asked them
about their families; he especially enjoyed talking with a four-
foot-tall employee. And years before there was media attention to
the problem, he was obsessed with the living and working conditions of the workers at the Chinese factories that manufactured

Ty's products. He always made sure they were paid above-market wages—and he was especially concerned with making sure they had enough light.

If you didn't have power that threatened Warner and he wasn't paying you too much money, he could be extremely kind. Lina Trivedi was the nineteen-year-old daughter of Indian im-migrants when she answered a classified ad for a telemarketer in 1992. She became the company's twelfth employee, making a little over minimum wage while studying sociology at DePaul University in Chicago. Trivedi, former top employees at Ty told me, was the key to understanding how Beanie Babies became a speculative phenomenon—although most had trouble remem-bering her name and its spelling. "An Indian law school student," one remembered. "See if you can find her."

Trivedi spent her first year at Ty working the phones, calling retailers who had placed orders in the past but weren't within a territory where the company's limited sales force could make regular calls.

"From the very beginning Ty was the type who would always ask people's opinions. Always, always," she says. The *People* mag-azine reporter who in 1996 scored Warner's last interview, be-fore the craze had reached its zenith, later described her visit to his office this way, and it was an experience that matched the memories of most of the people who knew him: "At the begin-ning of our meeting, I wondered whether I was interviewing him or vice versa. He frenetically jumped around the room, grabbing Beanies off the floor and out of drawers and showing them to me: new ones, old ones, prototypes. He wanted my opinion on everything and listened as if it were the most important opinion in the world. What did I think of the new poems? What should we name this one? Which color do you like better for this one?"

Most of Ty's hourly employees lacked any industry experi-ence and, unsure of how to respond to their plush-expert boss and his queries, provided effusive praise. Yet Trivedi, who was planning on law school in a couple years anyway, felt she had nothing to lose.

"I'd be the first person to say, 'I think the eyes suck!' " she recalls. "For a while I was one of the only people that would tell him what I really thought." Lina's constant and honest feedback on new products delighted Warner, and her responsibilities increased. She went to the company's trade shows, setting up the pink pedestals that are still its signature. Most employees were, at some point, on the receiving end of his tantrums over imperfect aesthetics, but Trivedi always managed to satisfy him. When she came to him with an idea, he listened: she told him she thought the insides of the tags were boring and generic—with the spaces for To and From—and suggested adding birthdates and poems for each Beanie. She did a mock-up on the computer for Stripes the Tiger: "Stripes was never fierce nor strong/So with tigers, he didn't get along/Jungle life was hard getting by/ So he came to his friends at Ty!" Then she gave him a birthday: the month and day of her own birth, June 11, and 1995, the year he was introduced.

Warner looked at it over his glasses; he liked it. The poems could give the Beanie Babies "charisma," he said—just a little outline of a possible personality, nothing that would prevent kids from projecting their own ideas into the characters. He figured that the birthdates might also make them good gifts for people who shared the same day. It was Monday, he was leaving for Asia that afternoon, and they had a new shipment ready for tagging at the warehouse. Could she create a poem for every Beanie in the collection by Wednesday? Charged with writing eighty-six poems in three days, she bounced back and forth between her desk and the warehouse, pulling five Beanies at a time in order of serial number, staring into their eyes, asking them what they did, seeking inspiration. Warner wrote one of the

poems himself. Patti the Platypus, whom he had named for Patricia Roche, was paired with this: "Ran into Patti one day while
walking/Believe me, she wouldn't stop talking/Listened and listened to her speak/That would explain her extra-large beak."

However, Trivedi's really big idea—the one that was to change
the future of Ty and raise Warner to an echelon of wealth he
otherwise wouldn't have reached—came in late 1995 when she
approached him with a suggestion: create a Web site.

In 1995 about 10 percent of Americans were online, according
to the Pew Research Center's Internet & American Life Project,
and growth was strong without yet being in the triple digits. In
October of that year, Pew Internet reported, "Our findings indi-
cate that currently 18 million homes have modem-equipped
computers, compared to 1994 when 11 million households had
such machines." Warner's wasn't one of them, and neither was
the Ty office. The Internet was the province mainly of nerds and
academics; fortunately for the future of Ty Inc., Trivedi was both.
She had been introduced to the Web by a DePaul professor, and
the school provided every student with an Internet account and
a 14.4 Kb dial-up modem.

She brought her modem into the Ty office to introduce Warner to the idea that people used the Internet to connect with
others with similar interests. She showed him the Beanie Baby
message boards and chat rooms that were starting to pop up.
Warner immediately had WebTV installed in his home and office so he could follow the action. He stayed up late into the
night browsing Internet message boards to learn what people
were saying, and he called McGowan over to show her posts that
described him as a marketing genius. When Lina suggested that
she could create a Web site for the company, he told her to go
for it.

But first, as always, drama: the domain name Ty.com had already been registered by Philip Giacalone, a Californian with a

son named Ty; he used the site to promote his tech consulting business. Trivedi contacted him to offer a small sum for the site; when he declined to sell, Warner filed a claim to have the domain name suspended on the grounds that he owned the trademark for "Ty." Giacalone responded by suing Ty Inc. and won an injunction. Warner capitulated and paid him $150,000, plus legal fees, to acquire the domain name. That Warner, who was generally stingy, paid what was at the time an exceptionally high price for a domain suggests that he had some inkling of how valuable it might be for his business.

As Lina prepared to create the Ty Web site, the first research step was obvious: scope out the competition and find out what Mattel and Hasbro were doing with Web sites for Barbie and G.I. Joe.

Just one problem: they weren't doing much.

Mattel hadn't created a Web site until mid-1995 and the site, such as it was, was extremely corporate: addresses, contact information, lists of product lines—nothing even remotely consumer facing and certainly nothing that would spur repeat visits from children or collectors. Mattel didn't even register an official site for Barbie until mid-1996, and Hasbro didn't launch a site for its Matchbox line until 1998. The inspiration Trivedi had hoped to find was absent; she would have to make it up as she went along.

From the beginning, Trivedi and her brother and part-time assistant, Nikhil, focused on making Ty.com more than a source of information and marketing. In order to really work Lina knew that it needed to become a resource that people logged on to multiple times per day. Her experience and resources were limited, but so were the expectations of consumers. She used the Ty Web site to experiment with every possible gimmick to stoke interest in Beanie Babies and speculation about what was coming next. "The whole idea behind it was to centralize the information and have a voice to provide official information, and we wanted to do it in a fun way because Ty is a little bit elusive," she says.

By mid-1996 the site was up and running; on the Ty hang-tags, right below the poems Trivedi had written, was the call to

```
Visit our web page!!!
http://www.ty.com.
```

Ty was one of the first toy companies to promote its Web site on its products and definitely the first to aggressively—three exclamation points!—drive its customers to the Internet. With the Beanie Baby trend already low-tech viral—Beanie moms and small Beanie conventions—featuring the company's Web page prominently on the tag offered a chance to centralize it, to reach out to the mob and bring the collectors together under the Ty umbrella, where they could communicate with one another and be informed about new products. "Seeing the response and the marketing potential of bringing collectors together was amazing," Trivedi says.

One of Trivdei's first creations was the Info Beanie; every month, Ty.com users voted for which Beanie Baby they wanted to be their source of information. Trivedi would then upload a post every few hours with updates written in the voice of that animal: vague gossip about what was going on at Ty, allusions to new product lines, and hints about when retirements might be coming and which Beanie Babies might be affected. On May 3, 1997, for instance, Nanook the Husky wrote of the difficulty he was having finding one of the other Beanies in the nursery: "The only thing that I have noticed—I don't know if this means anything or not—but I have not seen Stripes anywhere in the last few WEEKS! Where is Stripes? . . . He was not even at my birthday party! I was sad about that because everyone was there. I have been trying to find Garcia to tell him, but he is so hard to track down because when he is not running around trying to find this or that Beanie Baby, he is under cover. He hides in different places and just waits to see if anything happens. You know what is going to happen?" Eight days later, under legal pressure from the Jerry Garcia estate, the tie-dyed bear was renamed Peace—and Garcia's value rose dramatically, immediately enriching speculators who bought based on the Info Beanie's hints rather than waiting for the official announcement.

Messages like that caused prices on Internet auctions to shoot up as collectors speculated about retirements. Flea market dealers called their spouses at home to get the latest updates from the Info Beanies—and changed their prices accordingly. The highest-trafficked part of the Web site was the guest book: fifteen to twenty messages per minute flying back and forth with requests to buy, sell, and trade current and retired Beanies, along with rumors and speculation. "Let's talk about how you can get rich investing in Beanie Babies," Dave Barry wrote in 1998. "I have here an Associated Press story stating that in Andover, Mass., police caught somebody trying to sell a stolen Happy the Hippo for $900. The story also states that a couple in Nashua, N.H., allegedly bought Beanie Babies with forged checks, then sold them and used the proceeds to buy heroin. Fortunately, not all of the people involved in this craze are criminal heroin addicts. Many of them are merely insane. If you don't believe me, you should read their discussions on the Internet."

One collector wrote, "I have **Teddy97 and Snowball** I need **Maple** so . . . if you have Maple and don't have Teddy97 and Snowball..e-mail me and we can trade. Remember..after all the back-orders are out..these 2 beanies are history!"

Another collector wrote:

Hello! I need mint or nonmint: Spook (not Spooky), Coral, Grunt, Kiwi, Lefty, Libearty, Manny, Radar, Righty, Sting,

Tabasco, Tusk, Bongo (brown tail), Happy (grey), Inch (felt an-
tennae), Inky (tan), Lucky (retired versions), Bumble, Magic (dif-
ferent thread), Mystic (fine main), Nip (old versions), Patti
(Magenta), Pride, Sly (brown belly), Stripes (dark), Tank (old ver-
sions), and Zip (old versions). Im also interested in buying old re-
tires. These beanies can be mint or nonmint, I will pay $$ (have
lots to spend, but will only pay reasonable prices). I have Princess
*to trade for May or Jan retires (might sell). Email me! *THANX*
& GODBLESS.*

The Ty guest book was mostly a place for buying, selling, and
trading Beanie Babies—but other sites were alive with rumors
concerning new releases and upcoming retirements. On a home
shopping show, host Don West hawked a $2,000 collection of
ninety-four Beanie Babies by explaining that many of the pieces
in the collection would be retired soon: "A retirement is coming
up either September first or October first. We've been hearing
rumors." If the still hard-to-find Princess bear was retired as part
of the announcement, he said, its value would rise by enough to
cover the cost of the entire collection he was selling. "If you can
afford it, buy it!" he shouted.

On Peggy Gallagher's WGN radio show, a caller wondered
about rumors: "What about a Ty retirement in October?" she
asked breathlessly.

"There's warnings," Gallagher replied. "If you start watching
Ty's Web site, the Beanies will start talking in the nursery like
two or three weeks ahead of time. The Beanies start giving clues.
There's warnings that something's going to happen. There's like
a new rumor every week."

"We were able to use that voice to kind of manipulate the
market, so to speak," Trivedi says. A single cryptic message from
the Info Beanie could spark a buying frenzy. She and her brother
were still full-time students—he was in high school and she was

still studying sociology at DePaul—and updating the site often meant racing to the library between classes.

"I was having fun and just going by intuition and just trying to entertain people," she says. The *Cincinnati Post* described the site: "Updated constantly (some sections daily), the folks at Ty have created a kid/collector friendly site that weaves products in so smoothly you might forget that '.com' is short for commercial."

In contrast to his obsessive management of the product, Warner was largely disengaged from the Ty Web site. His advice to Trivedi mainly consisted of "Keep doing what you're doing" and "From now on, devote all your time to the Web site. If anyone asks you to do anything else, tell them to come talk to me."

On January 1, 1997, Trivedi posted an announcement listing nine pieces that were to be retired. Trivedi had decided that it would be fun to announce the retirement with a forty-minute-long Shockwave animation featuring Kiwi the Toucan, one of the retiring Beanies, performing a magic show, with the voices provided by Lina and her brother. The millions of users trying to load the animation rendered the site unavailable for most of the day, and many collectors, confused and frustrated, had their first brush with the addictive power of the Internet.

Sara Nelson, who ran BeanieMom.com, had invited friends over for dinner that night. "I spent all of New Year's Day hitting 'Reload' as did countless other collectors," she later remembered. "My guests arrived for dinner, and I was barely civil—constantly hitting 'Reload'—almost certain I'd miss the magical moment when the announcement was made. Finally, sometime after 9:00 P.M., long after my guests had left, the announcement finally appeared." However, most people had to download Shockwave in order to view it, and that could take an hour on a dial-up modem. Nelson, who already had Shockwave and a high-speed connection, was one of the first to get it to load. When she posted the list of retirees on her BeanieMom site, traffic hit a record high. Peggy Gallagher called her in the middle of the night and asked her to hold her computer's speakers up to the phone (for forty minutes!) so that she could hear Kiwi the Toucan make the announcement.

The retirement announcement was a massive success. Traffic to the site soared 3,500 percent in one day, and for the first time, prices rose instantly as the information was assimilated into the marketplace.

Mary Beth's Beanie World magazine reported, "Seeing a potentially profitable opportunity, many savvy collectors hit the streets and begin purchasing all Beanies that were retired 24 hours earlier. The market value of Chops jumps 500 percent (from $5 to $25 overnight)." As *Beanie Mania* reported of that date, "The prices started to escalate out of control. Many of the collectors pulled their Beanie Baby postings off the internet, waiting for a settling of the market. The settling just didn't happen and the prices continued to rise."

As Mary Beth Sobolewski remembered it later: "What originally began as just changes to the annual retailer catalogs [became] international events, prompting millions of Beanie fans to stay glued to their computers to wait for anticipated Ty announcements."

On March 19, riding high on the momentum of the retirement announcement, Karmen Kohlwes, a Ty vice president, appeared on *The Today Show* to announce that a new Beanie Baby was being released—but told viewers that they'd have to log on to Ty.com to find out what it was. Today, that sort of tease would be seen as tacky and intolerable by TV producers; in 1997, however, it was innovative. On May 11, Mother's Day, Trivedi posted another announcement: eight Beanies were to be retired, and fourteen new ones were to be introduced.

The Ty site also brought the company real-time feedback from its customers; when an Info Beanie diary entry implied that one of the Beanie Babies thought that Canada was part of the United States, hundreds of e-mails arrived from perturbed Canadians. The characters of the Info Beanies provided Ty—who wasn't comfortable with the idea of being the public face of a company—with an outlet to communicate with consumers. It was unorthodox but it worked. When people wrote to Ty Inc. to ask why Beanies weren't available in big-box stores, it was a Beanie Baby that responded that he was afraid of being in a building with high ceilings. It was also a Beanie Baby that took to the Web site to defend his "friends" on the Ty legal team, whose aggressive litigiousness had resulted in disillusioned message board chatter. Sometimes retailers wrote to the site to complain about slow shipping and incomplete order fulfillment—and they too would receive an unhelpful response from a Beanie Baby.

The Web site was most valuable, however, as a means of driving collectors to stores in search of soon-to-be-rare pieces. *Beanie Digest* described the frenzy that Trivedi's announcements caused:

> *The recent Ty retirement announcement has turned previously normal, level-headed individuals into crazed Beanie hoarding fanatics. How many times did we hear that people had formed Beanie teams—one at the computer waiting for the big announcement, the other team member wearing comfortable walking shoes, cell phone in hand at the mall waiting to receive the purchase orders and jockeying for position in the various stores that carry Beanies? . . . [W]ithin days after the announcement, store shelves had cleared and prices began rising for these recently retired gems. . . . Experienced collectors were . . . buying these retired items in bulk to store for the future.*

"It's exactly like the stock market," explained Mary Beth Sobolewski. "A rumor that one of them is about to be retired makes the prices go up on the secondary market. There's a lot of greed out there. If they don't retire it, you have a bunch of them worth five dollars each."

The retirement announcements were a closely guarded secret: at flea markets and shows, and in online auctions, sellers often manipulated the market into paying higher prices by floating rumors of upcoming retirements. Yet the more advanced collectors understood that only Warner knew which Beanies were up for retirement.

"There are few announcements that grab a Beanie collector's attention as intensely as rapid, strategic retirements," Mary Beth explained. "An unexpected, carefully timed retirement causes a ripple effect of Beanie gossip, Beanie purchases . . . and an almost sure-fire increase in internet auction prices."

Beanie Power magazine, to its credit more level-headed than most of the cheerleaders, warned collectors about buying into the hype that came with retirement announcements:

> With *Ty* having ritualized Beanie-retirement dates, the well-publicized retirement that occurred on May 1, 1998 is on everyone's mind. Each of the 28 Beanies that have just been taken out of circulation has already shown some increase. . . . However, speculators should be warned that each successive Beanie Baby generation has a little less growth potential on the secondary market than the previous one. Unfortunately, too many collectors are buying lots of them, dreaming they'll buy a common Beanie for $6 and be able to watch it increase in value over time until it reaches the dizzying, four-digit prices of the original retired Beanies.

No one, though, was paying much attention to the naysayers. For now Beanie Baby prices were soaring, the early collectors were rich, and the dealers and promoters who'd been pumping up the market looked like geniuses. John Tumpack, a suburban Chicago father and construction contractor, started going to Beanie shows every weekend after he realized there was money to be made.

"The first [rare] one I was able to get ahold of was in rural Illinois," he remembers. "I paid a hundred and fifty dollars and sent it to my uncle in California, and he sold it for five hundred dollars. It just snowballed." By late 1997 the arbitrage trade had inverted: the early Beanie Babies the suburban Chicago collectors had hoarded were no longer in other states' stores. In those states, new collectors were entering the market, looking to backtrack to buy the Beanie Babies that had been retired before they'd even heard of them. The early Chicago collectors could earn triple-digit profits selling Beanies back into the states where they'd been buying them by mail for $5 each plus shipping less than a year earlier.

"There were people you'd meet at the shows who were now personally coming to my office to stock their shelves," Tumpack says. "I'd become my own little store. I had thousands of them. I'm running out and buying them for five dollars and selling them for ten dollars. And they're taking them and selling for twenty dollars."

Tumpack was spending, as he recalls, at least thirty hours per week on the hunt—often slipping away from construction sites to hit Hallmark stores when he got a call from a source about an upcoming shipment. The Beanies were providing him with a decent income—probably at least $15,000 per year, he remembers—and as the money poured in, he gained the confidence to spend more time and more money building his own collection for long-term value.

As Bob Swarup writes in *Money Mania: Booms, Panics, and Busts from Ancient Rome to the Great Meltdown*, "Each increase in value rubber-stamps and diffuses the innate superiority of our chosen gurus until by the end we are all self-affirming experts and inevitably oblivious to the increasingly shaky ground underneath." Beanie Babies had increased substantially in value since the first collectors started paying premium prices for them and spending their days calling out-of-state retailers; now those suburban Chicago women looked like geniuses. Their husbands, and anyone else who'd doubted them, looked like idiots as their collections were all of a sudden worth hundreds of thousands of dollars. At first Peggy Gallagher had been hiding her collection, and especially her phone bills, from her husband. However, once those little animals started to increase in value and the media started calling on her for prognostications, she told him all about it. He became her biggest fan—and had the first magazine story she wrote on the craze framed for display in his law office. In a larger sense Peggy's husband's capitulation was mirrored by the rest of America. Rosie Wells, Richard Gernady's friend and the collectibles publisher who had initially been skeptical of Beanie Babies, launched her own Beanies-only magazine in late 1997 and a heart-shaped Beanie Babies book in 1998. Ty Warner responded to her change of heart with a copyright infringement lawsuit.

In the end Tumpack gave back most of his profits as the inventory he kept accumulating depreciated during the waning period of the craze. When I spoke with him by phone, he said that he still had several thousand Beanie Babies—along with at least a thousand more Disney beanbag animals that came out in the wake of Beanie Babies. As the Beanie craze escalated, Tumpack thought the new Disney line offered a chance to get in on the ground floor—just as the soaring price of eBay stock lured investors in to start-ups with weaker prospects.

"It happened so fast," he says—and, like most of the people whose lives were overtaken by Beanie collecting, he offers little insight into his own behavior.

The next leg up in the Beanie market came when the collectors congregating online concentrated their activity on another Web site, the idea for which had been hatched right as the King brothers were introducing Ty Warner to the idea of retiring Beanie Babies to create a sense of scarcity.

16

The Efficient Market

The story of eBay's genesis was such a media sensation that anyone who followed business news in the late 1990s can recite it from memory. In the summer of 1995 twenty-eight-year-old French-born Iranian American Web developer Pierre Omidyar had dinner with his fiancée. She complained of her difficulty in finding trading partners for the Pez dispensers she collected. In response Omidyar created AuctionWeb, a site for her to trade the dispensers, and launched it on September 3 of that year. That site became eBay, and Omidyar became a billionaire. As an inspiring story about a guy who just wants to make life better for someone he loves and ends up spectacularly rich as a result, it's hard to beat.

And just as with the story of Ty Warner and the vacuum cleaner, it isn't true. In 1997 Mary Lou Song, eBay's twenty-seven-year-old public relations manager, was given the task of bringing mainstream media attention to a site that was mostly used by geeks buying antiques or trading computer parts. Omidyar was an idealist and had been trying to explain to reporters that he'd created the site as part of a utopian vision for more efficient, friction-free markets, but the media didn't care. "Nobody wants to hear about a thirty-year-old genius who wanted to create a perfect market," Song explained in Adam Cohen's book *The Perfect Store.* "They want to hear that he did it for his fiancée." So she made up the story about Pez dispensers, and started pitching it to reporters.

The creation myth generated enormous amounts of publicity. Coincidentally, it led to some of eBay's most explosive early growth among toy collectors who had heard the Pez dispenser story. With Beanie Babies as the leader in the toy category—and the most difficult brand to find at retail—it wasn't long before they emerged as the dominant product on eBay. Seeing the momentum, eBay ramped up its efforts to court Beanie collectors. Jill Finlayson, one of the company's first three category managers, was in charge of toys, games, and dolls. She spent much of her time at collectors' conventions, "evangelizing" the benefits of eBay and cutting deals with some of the first suburban Chicago Beanie Baby collectors—who by then were Internet celebrities among the later adopters—to promote eBay as a trading hub.

eBay's decision to target collectors aggressively came with ambivalence. In the days of the Internet bubble, a sexy story was often more important than a viable business model. When eBay was looking to raise venture capital money—and later on preparing for its IPO—its dependence on collectors led to eye-rolling among investors and analysts. How could a Web site that was mostly used to help people buy and sell vintage lunch boxes and Beanie Babies possibly be worth $1 billion? As the stock price rose, investors asked whether a company could really sustain a $5 billion valuation with 10 percent of its sales tied to collectors swapping Beanie Babies? Did that mean the market was valuing eBay's business selling Beanie Babies at $500 million? Was that sane? Many analysts urged the company to move away from collectors and toward something more respectable: computers, cars, anything other than rare beanbag animals. That the media linked eBay and Beanie Babies constantly was something of a sore spot. A 1998 *New York Times* profile of Pierre Omidyar quips, "[S]ince its public offering in September, the stock has become a more treasured addition to Internet stock portfolios than the Princess Diana bear is to Beanie Baby fans." Yet in regulatory filings, eBay admitted it needed Beanie Babies. The risk-factors section of the company's 1998 annual report filed with the U.S. Securities and Exchange Commission notes eBay's dependence on the continued strength of the market: "For example, during the three months ended December 31, 1998, we had, at times, approximately 7% of our listings involved in 'Beanie Babies.'"

Inside eBay, some wondered whether the company could achieve better results—or similar or only slightly worse financial results with more respect from Wall Street—by building its business on, for instance, anything that wasn't Beanie Babies.

Meg Whitman, whom Omidyar had installed as CEO, thought about it. In her memoir Whitman notes, "[D]uring my first few years as eBay's CEO, I realized that to be successful, what we as a company needed to collect was collectors. We needed to build a core community interested in collectibles; from there, I was confident, we would be able to expand almost infinitely." Obsessive types, Whitman knew, could drive growth like no one else. Finlayson recalls that "eBay grew because people would come for a specific item, and then they'd happen upon other things." As Meg Whitman later put it in an interview with Charlie Rose on *60 Minutes*, it took eBay four years to go from Beanie Babies to BMWs. Without Beanies, however, it's doubtful whether eBay ever would have gotten to BMWs.

As fast as the Internet was growing, it's often forgotten that in its early years the growth of e-commerce was lagging expectations. In a piece on holiday shopping in November 1997, the *Pittsburgh Post-Gazette* reported that "online shopping holds more promise than profit." Only one in five households had Internet access, but that alone wasn't the problem—because those one in five households tended to be the ones with the most discretionary income. According to the report, "[O]f those shoppers in the technological know, some are scared off by lingering security fears." Others were put off by the limited selection on most sites and, above all else, the lack of any pressing reason to buy most things online. Shipping was expensive, and online retailers hadn't yet achieved the economies of scale that eventually let them undercut retail stores on price. In order to lure people out of their comfort zone and into the idea of e-commerce— and, even scarier, peer-to-peer e-commerce—eBay needed to offer consumers something that was easy to ship, couldn't be found anywhere else, and elicited passion among the people who were looking for it.

Adam Cohen describes the impact of Beanies on the company's rise in *The Perfect Store*:

> *It would be an exaggeration to say that eBay was built on Beanie Babies, but not by much. . . . It turned out that Beanie Babies, which were gaining popularity just as [eBay] was, were the ideal product to sell through an online auction. Auction theory teaches that auctions are not, in fact, an efficient way of selling most goods. They are too labor intensive and time consuming for items that are likely to sell at a price the parties could have anticipated in advance. But auctions excel when they are called on to set prices for items whose value is inherently indeterminate. . . . Beanie Babies, whose value rose and fell daily based on popular whim, could take full advantage of the dynamic pricing mechanism that auctions provided.*

As Faith McGowan writes in her unpublished memoir, "The final link in creating an easily-accessible, worldwide, 24-hour a day market for Beanie Babies was the Internet. More than anything, it was the coincidental and simultaneous emergence of e-trading on the worldwide Web that took the market for Beanie Babies to the stratosphere."

The role of auction fever in the rise of Beanie Babies can't be ignored. Business school professors have been writing for decades about the tendency of people to overpay at auctions, and the effect is thought to be most profound in novices. eBay brought millions of people into the world of auctions for the first time—and the combination of the newness of the Internet and the newness of bidding probably contributed to irrationality. In the late 1990s Kimberly Young, a clinical postdoc at the University of Rochester's Strong Memorial Hospital, became one of the first researchers to study the field of Internet addiction. She found that online auction addicts made up about 15 percent of all Internet addicts.

Predictably, Ty Warner wasn't entirely comfortable with this new secondary market for his products. Finlayson says that eBay had no contact with Ty Inc., save for a single awkward trip to the company's headquarters to pitch the idea of an eBay co-branded Beanie Baby. The online auction house was shot down immediately; Ty was Warner's company, and he wasn't interested in partnering with anyone on anything. Ty threatened legal action against eBay for using its trademarked name, Beanies, as a category on its site. The perplexed auction house changed the name to "Beanbag Plush" and Ty backed off.

As the Internet gained mass adoption, few people acquired computers with any real idea what they were going to do with them. Beanie Babies gave people a ready-made hobby to indulge online. The collecting of Beanies was made so much more novel and exciting when speculators could watch the market's gyrations and keep track of their wins and losses in real time in the same way that the rise of day trading was facilitated by the rise of online stock brokerages.

Beanie Babies were more likely to attract bidders than any of eBay's other categories. In May 1997 the site sold $500,000 worth of the animals at an average price of $30 each. The volume, while it seems high, wasn't in relation to Ty's sales: $500,000 in Beanie Babies sold on the site represented about $83,000 in retail purchases—or $41,500 at wholesale. Ty's wholesale shipments at the time were closing in on $100 million per month. That is to say, the monthly sales of Beanie Babies on eBay constituted about 0.04 percent of the Beanie Babies Ty was shipping each month. But the prices they were fetching on eBay helped drive sales volume by a huge multiplier. People who had collections could go online and see that they were in the money, which made stocking up on more retail-priced Beanies an easy decision. The media was full of stories about people flipping Beanie Babies for a profit—but most people were not flipping them for a profit. Most people were hoarding them for long-term investment.

Just as relatively minor discoveries of gold had fueled the gold rush of 1849, it only took $500,000 per month in eBay sales to help drive, at Beanie Babies' height, $200 million per month in retail sales. In his book *Contagious: Why Things Catch On*, Wharton School professor Jonah Berger explains, "People don't think in terms of information. They think in terms of narratives." The stories of people buying $5 Beanie Babies and then selling them to pay for cars spread the word of Beanie Babies more efficiently than any deliberate marketing strategy could have. As antiques expert Harry Rinker told me, "In the antiques business we sell stories and dreams. With Beanie Babies the dream was one of the most spectacular dreams ever sold."

17

The Beanie Chase

At the heart of the market for Beanie Babies was what was known almost universally as the Beanie Chase, which was enabled by the eccentricities of Warner's distribution. In March 1997 he'd started limiting retailers to ordering thirty-six of each Beanie per month at a time when most stores were trying to buy them by the gross. The decision to constrict supply originated with the supply issues Warner was having, but it also reflected his desire to control the fad. As soon as the supply caught up to the demand, he knew, it would be over. Warner had been in the toy industry long enough to know just how quickly a fad could end. He was devoted to doing whatever he could to make Beanie Babies last.

Even within those severely restricted limits on order sizes, there was no guarantee stores would get the merchandise they wanted. Ann Kanaby, former head of customer service at Ty, left the company relatively early into the Beanie craze but lasted long enough to be puzzled by its prescribed response to retailers' questions about shipping. A Ty vice president had instructed her to inform them that products would be shipped within five days, when in reality they wouldn't be ready for at least a month and a half. When she got to work each day, she had literally hours of voice mail from angry customers to listen to.

"It's ridiculous," she complained at the time. "We don't have the product. We're just going to get another call in six days if we tell them it's shipping in five days. Why don't we just tell the truth?" She was rebuffed—told that the word had come down from the top: tell the retailers that you'll be shipping the Beanie Babies immediately even when you know that isn't possible.

Predictability, Ty thought, could only hurt the market for Beanie Babies. "Expect the unexpected," was his motto around the office and that extended to his approach to customer service. Sure, it would piss off retailers when their orders didn't come—but they'd come eventually and with demand as hot as it was, what were the stores going to do about it anyway? A Ty marketing manager told a reporter that the hunt was part of the fun and that having the product easily locatable was not among the company's goals. As Warner himself said, "As long as kids keep fighting over the products and retailers are angry at us because they cannot get enough, I think those are good signs."

Even Ty's biggest accounts had to grovel. Noodle Kidoodle was a chain of specialty toy stores; with around fifty locations, it was the second-biggest Beanie seller in the United States. It was deriving more than 20 percent of its revenue from Beanie Babies, according to Stanley Greenman, its founder. Even as CEO of a publicly traded company, Greenman valued the sales enough that he took procurement into his own hands.

"I would fly to Chicago and just sit in Ty's lobby all day trying to get his attention," Greenman remembers. "We took all his people out to dinner. You could sell every Beanie Baby you could get, so we spent a lot of our time begging."

Yet no amount of begging guaranteed results when it came to dealing with Ty Inc. "They'd ship you everything but the most popular one," remembers Phil Wrzesinski of Toy House, located in Jackson, Michigan. "Then they'd cancel the back order on you. You never really knew what you were going to get until it showed up."

Many stores passed Ty's promises about shipping on to customers; the result was that the Beanie Baby hunters called the stores daily and sometimes lined up outside to look for the boxes with Ty's heart logo.

"The UPS truck would show up at our back door," remembers Wrzesinski. "Somebody at UPS was tipping people on when we were getting shipments. I would be at the back door unloading the UPS truck, and there would be people at the front door saying, 'We heard you got Beanie Babies today.' The frontline staff didn't know that; the customers knew it.

"We'd set up big tables in the middle of our store. We'd open the bag and dump them on the table. The word got out real fast, and the people came in and they went. The people that bought Beanie Babies didn't really buy anything else. It was just collectors looking for Beanie Babies; they found out we had them, they bought them, and then they left. It looked like the county fair the day after."

In 1998, concerned about customers stalking UPS trucks and merchandise disappearing from warehouses, Ty removed its heart logo from the shipping boxes. Shrinkage shrunk dramatically. "If you were shipping diamonds, would you put a picture of a diamond on the box?" says one former executive. "That's what it was."

There wasn't a single store in America that could get as many Beanie Babies as it wanted. It was not uncommon for accounts to have $10,000 in back orders outstanding with no communication on when—or even whether—they might expect delivery. One customer-service worker at Ty headquarters quit, citing religious convictions that told her it wasn't right to lie to the customers. One retailer told *Playthings* that, as popular as Beanie Babies were, she had stopped carrying them as a matter of principle: "We had shipping issues, there was a lack of communication, we couldn't get questions answered about invoices and we were totally ignored. They are solid marketers, but they have treated their customers—both resellers and end-customers—poorly. I don't believe it will serve them well in the end."

To his sales force, Warner seemed more interested in the products themselves than in the fulfillment issues. Andi Van Guilder, who was a sales rep beginning in 1995, sometimes worried that there wasn't much direction at the company. "As a sales team we were worried about who was in charge," she says. "We were like, 'He's creative but where's the sales manager?' I think he was passionate about product, so driven about product that the business part of it was not his passion."

Van Guilder remembers walking into Ty's office one day with a complaint: she was carrying a stack of orders an inch and a half thick that had gone unfilled for months—several million dollars in product. She wanted to know what was going to be done about it, what she could tell her accounts, and, as a commissioned salesperson who wasn't paid until goods were delivered, what was going to happen with her pay. Her complaint reflected the concerns of most of the salespeople: the call center took one hundred thousand requests from retailers per day, and many of those were irate follow-ups about unfilled orders.

When Van Guilder entered Warner's office, he was, as always, surrounded by bolts of fabric. "He was wearing this velour sweat suit and I was like, 'Wow, you are wearing a strange outfit, and you are a billionaire,'" she remembers. He listened to her complaint and then announced, "I'm looking for a felt color for my Pillow Pal," a line of plush animals for babies that Ty Inc. marketed from 1995 until 1999. He next asked her for her opinion on the colors for the Pillow Pals' eyes, and she never did get an answer about those unfilled orders.

Once, Ty was sitting in his office alone, inspecting a factory sample for a new bear he was planning. He wanted it to be a pearl color, but it didn't look quite right to him. He picked up the phone and summoned an employee he knew wore pearl earrings. She walked in and was confused when he instructed her to take off her earrings and hand them over. He held them up to the bear and then looked at both under a light. "It is not pearl!" he proclaimed, handing back the earrings. She never would have noticed it but she could see that he was right: the bear's fur wasn't quite the same shade as the pearl earrings. Why this was important remains a mystery to her, but it was; the prototype went back to China with instructions that the color needed to be more pearl-like.

Another executive remembered Ty wandering the office carrying artists' renderings of new animals he was contemplating. Ty stopped him in the hall one day to ask, "Do you think the ass on this one is too big?"

"Ty, I'm an accountant," the executive replied.

———————

Talk with collectors of anything for more than about a minute, and you're almost guaranteed to hear the phrase "the thrill of the hunt." Sigmund Freud, a noted collector himself, saw the root of collecting, not surprisingly, in sex and toilet training. He wrote in 1908, "The core of paranoia is the detachment of the libido from objects. A reverse course is taken by the collector who directs his surplus libido into an inanimate object: a love of things." Psychologists believe that the ownership of objects—often teddy bears and blankets—gives young children a sense of power and control in a world where they are otherwise vulnerable, and enables them to develop a sense of self independent from their parents.

Collecting is generally seen as a harmless and possibly positive influence on people's lives, but at its most extreme it seems to reflect a regression to the soothing and comfort provided by objects during childhood. Ty's retirements and scarcity allowed the acquisition of $5 beanbags to activate the same endorphins that people chasing rare books and fine art thrive on—but at an initially negligible cost and without any immediate need for specialized knowledge.

In 1998 Paula Benchik-Abrinko wrote about her sister Peggy Gallagher's quest to find every Beanie—a task she'd completed in mid-1996 and then kept up to date with new releases. At the time her collection was worth enough to cover the cost of four years at Harvard:

> *The calm experienced with owning the collection comes only after the storm of the hunt. . . . How did she do it? Thousands of dollars to Ma Bell looking for them; hours on the computer trying to find people who could trade for what she needed; harassing poor Ty reps; following overnight couriers thinking they had her beanies. . . . Why this happens or how this happens is beyond me. . . . Peggy has had many sleepless nights thinking of places she hasn't searched and nightmares of calling a store as the targeted piece leaves the store to a lucky buyer. . . . It is just about that time when hopelessness overcomes you that you then happen upon the animal that has eluded you for so long.*

Or, as Saint Augustine put it, "What is sought with difficulty is discovered with more pleasure."

In 1998 Ellie Kiehls was on maternity leave from her legal-assistant job at the Ford Motor Company in Dearborn, Michigan. She was a crazed Beanie Baby collector, and more than fifteen years later Kiehls describes those days with a mixture of nostalgia and remorse—the former for the excitement of finding a Beanie she didn't yet have and the latter for the time she smashed her two-year-old's head into a door while rushing a gift shop with a mob who'd learned of a new delivery. The idea for a board game called The Beanie Chase came to her in a dream during her maternity leave. A few months later, she put her family's life savings of $100,000 on the line. The Beanie Chase, designed for between two and nine players, featured nine profile cards, each adorned with a poem representing each of the collector types Kiehls had encountered: her crazy mother-in-law, her brother-in-law who bought for resale, and the rest of the collectors who fought their way from store to store each day.

There's Retired Ben, whose poem reads: "Retired Ben works no more/Hangs around all day at the Beanie store/Carries his phone so he can call/All of his friends from mall to mall." Best Friend Melody is a housewife with an incurable urge to collect: "Best Friend Melody, she's so funny/Hops around town like the Easter Bunny/Takes more money for the grocery store/But it's Beanies, she's out to score." There is a card for the hard-core reseller: "Dealer Dave, he's a dog/Buys those Beanies like a hog/Buys them up, not to keep/It's a profit he's out to reap." Almost as an afterthought, one of the collectors in the game is a child who actually likes Beanie Babies: "Sweet Young Gretchen, pure as snow/What they're worth, she doesn't know/Been collecting Beanies since they were born/All of hers are loved and worn."

Buoyed by an endorsement from the influential Beanie guru Janie Daniels of MsJanie.com, Kiehls ordered ten thousand copies of the game from the printer. Before they were even ready to ship, she had two thousand preorders at $24.95 each. The gamble was looking like it would pay off; dreams of a larger second printing and perhaps a deal with a publisher that could provide better distribution and marketing didn't seem so far-fetched. However, shortly before the game was set to ship, a cease-and-desist letter from Ty arrived; it was the day after Ellie had started back at work following her maternity leave. Bypassing hiring lawyers for fear of running up expenses she couldn't afford, Ellie phoned the company's law firm herself to make her case. They were just a family, she'd invested her life savings, and could she please just sell the ones she'd already had made? Ellie couldn't get an answer and, thinking it had blown over, started shipping the ones she'd sold. Then Ty sued her in the U.S. District Court in Chicago.

Her husband had an idea: tell the media. The reporters who had helped bring the message of Beanie mania to the public were now going to take the company down a peg. Regardless of the merits of the lawsuit, few people were going to be impressed with Warner's attack on a young family's first business venture. Local stories quickly emerged, and on August 15, 1998, the Associated Press picked it up; other outlets piled on behind the young suburban mother who was being sued by the most powerful toymaker in the world.

In addition to generating interest in the board game, the press also pushed Warner into a position he rarely found himself in and liked even less: on the ropes facing a barrage of criticism and pressured to yield to a weaker foe. In an uncharacteristic act of mercy that was probably motivated almost entirely by the fear of this kind of publicity, Ty settled, allowing Kiehls two months to sell all the copies she'd already printed. She'd have to report her sales weekly and, at the end of two months, turn whatever games were left over to Ty to be destroyed. Borrowing a line from the Ty playbook, she marketed the board game as a collectible; Beanie fans, knowing that there would never be another printing, bought them on the premise that they would have investment potential of their own.

After expenses, Ellie had more than doubled her $100,000 life savings. The legal drama was nerve-racking, but she counts herself among the lucky ones who came out okay after a legal battle with Warner, who was suing more than thirty companies per year on top of the hundred-plus cease-and-desist letters his lawyers were sending each month to competitors manufacturing anything that resembled a Beanie Baby.

Judge Richard Posner—a renowned jurist and prolific author—presided over many of the Beanie Babies lawsuits in the Seventh Circuit Court of Appeals.

"They were litigating very aggressively, and they brought a

large number of lawsuits," he told me by phone. "I can understand their aggressive strategy because this is a simple product to make, so it's very difficult to fend off competition. . . . Their basic strategy seemed to be to try to obtain exclusive rights over the term 'Beanie.' "

Was there any legitimacy to the idea that Ty owned the word?

"We didn't think so," said Judge Posner, chuckling. Internal memos introduced as evidence found Warner himself referring to other companies' products by this name: "We want to emphasize our Beanies are not just any Beanies—But special. Set us apart from our competitors' Beanies," he'd written. Other memos from trade shows, written by Ty employees, included references to competitors' products as "beanies": "They had beanies' [sic] that were similar in look, but fabric was inexpensive and it looked like a cheap knockoff of [our] product."

How, Posner asked in a ruling, could Ty Inc. really claim that the term wasn't generic when its own documents revealed that Warner himself was using it generically?

"Those were really fun cases; I was sad they went away," Posner said. In one lawsuit involving allegations of copyright infringement in the design of a stuffed pig, Posner attached a photograph of a real pig to refute the defendant's claim that it had designed its pig based on nature. Toy industry executives talk about the "10 percent rule"; there's no law about it, but in general it's thought that changing a competitor's product by 10 percent is enough to minimize litigation risk. What that even means is confusing: Who's to say what 10 percent of a stuffed pig's design is? All of this makes for extremely complicated and expensive litigation. That's yet another advantage for big companies.

There are few industry types who take seriously the idea that competition from other brands was a threat to the sales of Beanie Babies. In 1997, when Warner sued Imperial Toys over its line of beanbag toys, Friendly Pebble Pets, the defense recruited a seventh-grader named Katy Clune to testify about her collection of 108 Beanie Babies. "You shouldn't be so worried about them taking the business," she told a reporter she planned to tell Warner in her testimony. "You are better. Everyone knows that Beanie Babies are cuter." In any case, it was collector-investors who were driving the success of Beanie Babies; the toys' cuteness and quality was mostly a back story that had enabled the materialistic craze to ensue. No one was interested in beanbag plush that didn't have a Ty heart tag attached to it. None of the lines that launched to capitalize on the success of Beanies would have stuck around for long even if Ty hadn't sued them.

Collectors cared about the brand, and while counterfeits designed to mislead consumers were a serious problem—one that nobody faulted Warner for pursuing—the devotion of significant resources to bringing lawsuits against start-ups' selling beanbag animals was probably a mistake. For Warner, though, it wasn't about money.

"I think he really wanted to be the only one who was doing beanbag toys. Maybe it was like an ego thing. I think he sort of felt like he invented it," says Jenna Boldebuck. She and her mother, Faith McGowan, often accompanied Ty on his frequent mall trips where he rounded up what he thought were knockoffs to bring to his lawyers—much to the chagrin of McGowan, who felt that he was ruining family outings.

HolyBears, which sold beanbag teddy bears with biblical references on the hangtags as fund-raising items, found itself on the receiving end of a lawsuit from Ty over, among other things, the design of the bears' feet.

"I think they used litigation as a marketing tool, and you tie up all these small businesses that can't even afford an attorney," the company's founder and CEO, Robert LeClair, told me. LeClair decided that he too could use litigation as a marketing tool. He responded to Ty's lawsuit with a press release. "Using teddy bears to help spread the Word of God apparently does not sit well with the maker of Beanie Babies products. Ty, Inc. has filed a lawsuit against HolyBears, Inc. asking for all HolyBears teddy bears to be 'impounded for destruction,'" began the press release.

"We will fight to protect them from destruction even as we pray for their aggressors," LeClair blustered. "With all the potential good deeds that Ty, Inc. could pursue with their vast resources, they chose instead to ask the courts to impound and destroy all HolyBears teddy bears. When materialism challenges religion, there is often an interesting result—and I believe HolyBears has been put in this position for a reason.

"I'm asking everyone who understands and respects the mission of HolyBears to pray for our teddy bears—and to add a prayer on behalf of Ty, Inc.," LeClair wrote.

Finally LeClair took a shot at Ty's gimmick-laden marketing and distribution: "Unlike Ty, Inc. and other manufacturers, HolyBears neither 'retires' its teddy bears nor limits their production—thereby preventing speculators from inflating prices in the secondary market that caters to collectors."

To raise money for legal expenses, HolyBears released a "David" bear holding a slingshot to symbolize the battle with Ty. That bear included 1 Samuel 17:37 on the hangtag: "David said moreover, the Lord that delivered me out of the paw of the lion, and out of the paw of the bear, He will deliver me out of the hand of this Philistine . . ."

As Ty's litigiousness began to make headlines, collectors filled message boards and the in-boxes of Beanie authorities with complaints about what they saw as bullying tactics. One commenter noted, "He hurt himself tremendously by suing HolyBears. Many people found this to show how money hungry Ty really is." Another added, "Too many law suits. No one wants to support, or be associated with a company that goes around an[d] sues everyone. It just isn't right. . . . The bottom line is he is a control freak, and he is out of control." Added another, "His endless lawsuits, scare tactics, and silliness boggle the mind. Does this man believe he is the first one to create a bean filled teddy bear or stuffed animal? Has he ever heard of the Boyd's Co.? How about Dakin? I have a stuffed bean dog called Drooper from the late seventies. He is an exact likeness to Bones. Who do you think came first? I also have a pure white seal made from that co., a dead ringer for Seamore! Mr. Warner needs a reality check." Summarized another poster, "And the more I learn about TY, the less I like it. The Holybears thing is disgusting."

Another of Ty's tactics was causing discontent: releasing new pieces in small quantities, then following up with larger shipments the next month. When Erin, a St. Patrick's Day–themed bear, was released on January 31, 1998, retailers were limited to just twelve pieces—and secondary-market values soared to $250 immediately. In March Ty informed stores that they'd be able to place an order for thirty-five, and the price fell to between $150 and $200. "Continued supply should bring this figure down," *Mary Beth's Beanie World* told readers. Ann Atkins of Chandler, Arizona, wrote in to *Mary Beth's* to complain about the difficulty in finding Glory—another rare $100-plus bear, this one patriot-themed: "I'm very, very disappointed in Ty Warner keeping Glory from the general public, especially since this Beanie represents our nation. How very uncouth that they would put [money] ahead of customers in this respect. . . . There is no way I can afford the prices being put on this bear, nor can the children that Ty Warner says he has made these toys for." A parent wrote in to excoriate the very idea of adult Beanie collectors: "You should be encouraging people to let the children have their toys and find their own items to collect."

Perhaps to counterbalance the materialism that was taking

over what was supposed to be a toy, the collecting magazines started to heavy-handedly emphasize the more altruistic, prosocial elements of the hobby. The September 1998 issue of *Mary Beth's Beanie World*—shortly before the name was changed in response to litigation from Ty—told the story of Tim Holmes, a twelve-year-old with cerebral palsy who'd acquired a Princess bear from a retailer for $6.50 by entering his name into the store's lottery system. Not long after his purchase, Tim saw on the news that three paramedics and a child had died in a helicopter crash while en route to Children's Hospital Los Angeles, where Tim had received brain surgery months earlier. He paired up with a local store to raffle off his Princess bear, and raised $3,400 for the hospital. Holmes became a poster child for Beanie collecting. This story also circulated among collectors: on April 15, 1998, the Kankakee City Police Department just outside Chicago melted down forty guns that locals had traded in at an exchange rate of one retired Beanie Baby per gun.

There were two popular books, *Heartfelt Stories About Beanie Babies and Those Who Collect Them* and *Beanie Baby Stories*, that collected the cloying tales of the impact Beanies had on people's lives. In *Heartfelt Stories*, a twenty-three-year-old writes about how Beanie Babies saved her marriage after a move that had left the couple feeling depressed and unconnected: "When we returned to Tucson, we realized the Beanie craze hadn't hit there yet. Chris and I began to spend our free time together hunting for Beanies, learning each time we went out more information about what to look for, which ones are hard to find, etc. We began to have fun together again. . . . We have something in common that we can talk about and laugh about. . . . I know it sounds weird to say Beanie Babies have saved my marriage. . . . One day we hope the excitement we have felt about the hunt for our treasures will help our son to enjoy his own dreams, whether it helps to pay for his college or as a cherished memory to pass on to his own children."

Sentimentality combined with a quest for riches makes many of the stories unsettling: "My daughter who is ten thinks I am addicted. . . . Yes, we are behind on our house payment, and I beg my husband to buy me 'oh, just one' . . . My fifteen year old son has cerebral palsy. I tell myself that he can use the proceeds from these Beanies to help himself maintain a decent lifestyle after I am gone."

In the afterword to *Heartfelt Stories*, Angela M. S. Nelson, a Bowling Green State University professor in the Department of Popular Culture, writes, "When a mother says that her daughter's self-esteem has improved, when a mother's grief over her daughter's suicide has been relieved . . . the impact of Beanie Babies is apparent as well as the various ways people are united because of them. . . . I'm sure that people of the Christian faith will agree that the message of Jesus Christ is present in the actions of these Beanie collectors, even though Jesus is not."

Never mind all that, however: there were a few people who became millionaires in less than two years by spreading the idea that never, under any circumstances, ever, should anyone let a child touch a Beanie Baby. Beanies, they said, were destined for greater things.

18

Shovel Dealers in the Gold Rush

Henry Blodget was a thirty-two-year-old Wall Street analyst in December 1998 when he predicted that Amazon.com's shares, already flying high at $240, would rise to $400. Within weeks the prediction came true—and it made Blodget a star. He was young and good-looking, and when Blodget talked on CNBC, people listened. After the Nasdaq bubble burst, he was pilloried as the traders who rode his advice up to riches rode it back down to poverty. New York attorney general Eliot Spitzer pursued him over e-mails showing that he was trashing some dicey Internet start-ups privately while promoting them publicly for the benefit of his firm's investment banking business. Blodget was banned for life from working in the securities industry.

Blodget has been philosophical about the affair. In an interview with journalist Maggie Mahar for her book *Bull!: A History of the Boom and Bust, 1982–2004*, he talks about his recent research that helped him understand his place in the world of speculative episodes. "Have you ever read John Kenneth Galbraith's book about the history of bubbles?" he asks her, referring to 1990's *A Short History of Financial Euphoria*. "Well I hadn't—until recently. I just finished it. It's amazing how Galbraith spells it all out—what happens in every bubble, every time. He's almost yawning as he lays it out. First some new thing comes along and captures the public's imagination. Then everyone starts making money. After that, some person of average intelligence is held up as a genius. Hi, that was me."

All speculative manias rely on self-proclaimed and media-anointed soothsayers for amplification, and Beanie Babies were no different. The craze never could have inflated as much as it did without the implied credibility that came from the books, magazines, and charismatic prognosticators extolling the toys' investment value. Internet stocks had Henry Blodget, and Beanie Babies had scores of would-be experts promoting the line as a retirement strategy. The relationship between price guides and values is reflexive, antiques experts tell me. Each drives the other in a market-making cycle. Between 1997 and 1999, books about Beanie Babies were more popular than books about Y2K. A very abbreviated list: *The Beanie Encyclopedia: A Complete Unofficial Guide to Collecting Beanie Babies*; *Beanie Mania*; *Beanie Mania II*; *For the Love of Beanies*; *Encyclo-Beanie-A*; *The Complete Idiot's Guide to Beanie Babies*; *Beanie Mania Guidebook*; *The Unauthorized Beanie Baby Guide*; *Beanie Babies Collectors Guide*; *Rosie's Price Guide for Ty's Beanie Babies*; *Pocket Idiot's Guide to Beanie Babies*; *The Official Beanie Basher Handbook*; *Ty Beanie Values Guide*; *The Beanie Invasion*; and *The Unofficial Beanie Baby Coloring Book #4*.

The presence of price guides, self-published and from major publishers, in bookstores—and especially in gift shops, stacked amid the Beanies themselves—reinforced the notion of Beanie Babies as a vehicle for speculation. Indeed, the earliest secondary-market price lists actually predated the rise of a speculative market.

The bubble in baseball cards came a decade before the Beanie craze. In the book *Mint Condition*, journalist Dave Jamieson, himself a former collector, explains the impact of the price guides put out by Beckett Publications, a publisher of popular baseball card price guides founded by statistics professor James Beckett. "What none of us understood at the time, however," he writes, "was that Beckett's guides were probably creating prices just as much as they were reporting them." In a copyright infringement lawsuit Beckett filed against a competitor, a judge noted that "it is entirely possible that the prices in [his] publication not only reflect market prices, but in fact can determine market prices." The Beanie price guides and the prices they were reporting contributed to an upward-spiraling feedback loop that benefited publishers, dealers, and most of all, the manufacturer.

According to Faith McGowan, though, "Ty didn't see it that way." Warner saw the experts as overhyping his product beyond the benefits that it could reasonably be expected to produce—especially when the price guides exaggerated current market prices, as they often did. Warner was focused on the long term, and the rise of a speculative market was at odds with the longevity he sought. He once said that he wanted the Ty brand to be the Coca-Cola of collectibles, and even as the fad was making him rich, its ephemeral nature grated on him.

Others say Warner was mostly just irked by the notion that anyone else was making money from his creatures. Whatever his issue, he sued the price guide publishers relentlessly. If Warner was concerned that the publishers were getting rich off him, the financials he found during discovery proved him right. When Ty Inc. won on summary judgment in a case against one obscure publisher, it was awarded all the profits—an astonishing $1.36 million plus more than $200,000 in interest on a few low-budget, poorly researched exploitation books that were not even close to being among the most popular of the Beanie guides. It is often said of the gold rush that the people who got rich were the shovel dealers who profited from the greed of the forty-niners. With Beanie Babies, most of the lasting personal fortunes came from selling books and tag protectors, not from speculating in plush. Late in the craze Ty began collecting licensing fees from some publishers in exchange for the right to produce Beanie Baby price guides. The existence of these licensing deals was used by

Ty in litigation as a justification for the lawsuits. Judge Richard Posner pointed to a different motive behind the price guide lawsuits: a fear that independent commentators on the market would make note of declining Beanie Baby values and hurt demand on the primary market.

Warner probably didn't need to worry about that: the mavens and publishers, even if they weren't themselves Beanie dealers, had powerful incentives to keep prices high. As collectibles expert and author Harry Rinker says, "A price guide is only valuable as long as you can raise prices. The premise of selling second-, third-, and fourth-edition price guides is to show people how much more valuable their stuff has become." Just as business news viewership tanks after a market crash, no one is interested in buying a price guide that tells them their stuff is worth less than it was last year. Robert L. Miller, who published price guides for the collectible Hummel figurines for decades, solved that problem by simply raising his value estimates by 10 percent every year.

Everyone wanted to be a Beanie expert. Les Fox, a New Jersey coin dealer and aspiring novelist, ran a coin business with his wife and spent decades trying to carve out a publishing career. Les and Sue Fox were married in September 1968, began publishing their own coin guides in the 1970s, and made their first attempt at cracking the best-seller lists with 1995's self-published *Return to Sender*, a fictional account of the life of Elvis Presley's secret son. They printed 5,000 copies, sold 200, and lost $60,000. When they threw an Elvis birthday party and book signing at a Borders in Fort Lauderdale, hundreds of Elvis fans showed up for the free cake and Elvis impersonator they'd hired. The Foxes failed to sell a single book. They followed it up with *The Pizza and Ice Cream Diet*, which Les Fox said sold eleven copies.

In early 1997, following three weeks of research, writing, and photographing, the Foxes self-published *The Beanie Baby Handbook*—using their daughter's $100,000 college fund as capital.

If that seemed reckless given their track record of publishing failures, the quality of the book made it even crazier. Its 128 pages included poems, quizzes, and a "Match Game" of suggested names for future Beanie Babies. It's a wonderful combination of bad writing, uninformed speculation, and wild optimism. Every current Beanie Baby available at retail for $5 was projected to be worth at least $40 by 2007. Fox bought virtually all the Beanie Babies he used for the photos from Peggy Gallagher, paying her, by her own admission, inflated prices and then using those prices as the basis for his valuations. "It was obscene what I was charging him," she remembers. "He didn't really care about the actual true pricing. He cared more about selling a gazillion books."

"It's our own personal 'theory of scarcity' that at least 90% of almost everything gets lost, stolen, or destroyed within 10 years," the Foxes explain in the book. "Why should Beanies defy the laws of human nature? . . . The point is, only a tiny percentage of Beanies will be sealed in Zip-Loc bags and treated with TLC until the year 2007, no matter how well-intentioned their owners. . . . Whoever is lucky (and smart) enough to hang on to some top grade Beanie Babies for the long haul will be the future supplier for tomorrow's collectors.

"If this hobby continues to grow, as we believe it will, 10 years from now even today's 'shocking' high prices may seem low," they add. "After all, people were shocked when Picasso's paintings surpassed the million-dollar mark. Recently one sold for $25 million."

The Foxes also provided "estimates" of how many of each Beanie Baby had been produced, but those guesses turned out to be woefully low—as evidenced by the size of the fortune Warner had accumulated by the time the market crashed. However, the estimates did provide consumers with enough misinformation to make the idea of long-term Beanie scarcity seem plausible.

Les and Sue Fox were confident that this was the work that

would make their mark in publishing. At first they found no buyers. Distributors turned it down, and Barnes & Noble, thinking that Beanie Babies were a two-season fad, declined to place an order. Out of traditional options, the Foxes started mailing the book and a brochure to gift and toy shops all over America. After decades of publishing failures, Les and Sue had their hit. Fifteen thousand stores placed orders, apparently sensing the synergy of selling a book that predicted the $5 stuffed animals next to it were going to be worth thousands.

The Beanie Baby Handbook sold more than one million copies in its first year and was a mainstay on the *New York Times* best-seller list—an über-rarity for a self-published book, especially back then. It also appeared on the harder-to-crack *USA Today* best-seller list, spending fifty-five weeks there and peaking at number three—an astonishing accomplishment for a collector's guide on a list that included all books of every genre, including perennials. It hit number one on the *Publishers Weekly* list and was selling twenty thousand copies per week at Barnes & Noble. It was the fastest-selling collectibles book ever, and one of the best-selling self-published books of all time.

When Warner sued the Foxes for copyright infringement, Les told a magazine that he felt like he'd been betrayed by an old friend after all he had done to promote Beanie mania. The Foxes agreed to a cease-and-desist order and, reportedly, a cash settlement that still left them with millions in profits. Today, Les Fox remains all too happy to reminisce about the failure of his Elvis novel; it's the success of his nonfictional work on Beanie Babies that he wishes people would forget. More accurately, he wishes they'd remember the success but forget the topic. Les has refashioned himself as an expert on the fine arts. He and his wife have another self-published book, *The Art Hunters Handbook: How to Buy Art for $5 and Sell It for $1,000,000*, although he freely admits he's never done anything the title suggests. The cover includes the boast "N.Y. Times Bestselling Authors," but neither the book nor any of the Foxes' Web sites include a single reference to Beanie Babies.

In the YouTube video introducing this 2012 book, Les Fox is wearing an Abercrombie & Fitch sweatshirt over a green T-shirt with some kind of logo on it. He stands in front of an impressionist landscape and a primitive portrait, talking in a thick New Jersey accent.

He is, as always, enthusiastic about what he's selling.

"You're gonna love this book," he says, after introducing himself as a *New York Times* best-selling author. "This book actually teaches you even if you're not an art expert. In fact the book is not written for art experts. It's probably the only really serious art book that's ever been written that is not written for art collectors. It's written for the average person, people that play the lottery, people that go to garage sales and flea markets hoping to find something exciting. You will, you can; this book will help you do it. . . . Please buy a copy of our book. It will be the best fourteen ninety-five investment you ever make."

When I asked him about Beanie Babies, he replied via e-mail, "After thinking about our current business strategies, we have decided not to do an interview for your book. . . . If you are interested in our art or rare coin activities, please let me know as I will be happy to talk about that. But I think we are done with Beanie Babies." Today he lives in New Jersey in a multimillion-dollar home financed by the Beanie bubble, and his neighbor is Fox News anchor Steve Doocy. Fox pitches his projects to Doocy routinely in the hope of getting on TV, so far without luck. The topics he's tried to sell himself as an expert on over the past decade include online shopping, electing Arnold Schwarzenegger president, selling on eBay, publishing, and the stock market. Perhaps sensing the publicity it once brought Henry Blodget, Fox predicted in 2005 that shares of Amazon would triple by 2009—a call that worked out a lot better than his Beanie prognostications.

The Foxes and their best-selling price guides did a lot to take Beanie Babies out of the hands of children. With their best-selling book came a popular recognition that the toys were mostly for investment. None of the original Beanie collectors have anything nice to say about Les and Sue Fox. They say that they lifted material from their books, did essentially no research of their own, and made up prices and projections that were irresponsibly optimistic and, in the long run, hurt the market by giving buyers false hope and luring in too many quick-buck artists. Still, Becky Estenssoro readily admits, "It helped us," at least as far as their business selling Beanies at shows and online was concerned. After the craze had ended, a reporter asked Les Fox about the predictions, and his response was dismissive: "We had a lot of fun making predictions. We've been involved with collecting for thirty years, and we're pretty good at guessing. However, these were just guesses."

During the craze, however, the two Beckys had complete collections that were worth $100,000. John Orozco, a toy dealer who'd taken a beating in the stock market, watched the inflating Beanie market and then plowed his portfolio into early retired pieces. He claimed in an interview with the *Wall Street Journal* to have made back all his losses in less than a month and a half as prices continued to inflate.

The final step that moved Ty Warner's creations fully into the realm of financial assets, however, started with a well-meaning psychotherapist who just wanted to help frightened children find the comfort stuffed into these endearing, soft, and "poseable" little animals.

19

The Point of No Return

In mid-1996, psychotherapist Nancee Biank was running an eight-week therapy group for children between ages six and twelve who had a family member, often a parent, battling cancer. "We were talking about heavy stuff: their parents being sick and what that felt like," she says. "They knew their parents could die."

To help ease elementary school students into a comfort zone, Biank used Beanie Babies as a "transitional object," she says. The children in her group loved them instantly. "They were soft and they were cushy," she remembers. "It wasn't obtrusive. They weren't throwing them at each other. They could just hold it and touch it. The Beanie Baby was there to comfort them."

Biank's program was held at the Wellness House in Hinsdale, Illinois—about ten minutes from Ty headquarters as well as McDonald's headquarters; those two companies were located only about five minutes from each other. McDonald's was a major sponsor of the Wellness House, and one day Jane Hulbert, who worked in corporate communications at the fast-food chain, stopped by to sit in on Biank's program. Some say that it was Hulbert's story about how well the kids at Wellness House responded to the toys that led McDonald's to explore the idea of a Beanie Babies promotion, but Hulbert doubts that. "I really believe that it was a high-level marketing initiative when they saw the craze for Beanie Babies," she says. Whatever the impetus, McDonald's executives approached Ty in mid-1996 with an idea for a Happy Meal promotion that would include Beanie Babies.

Warner's fixation on control of the line and control of the market had helped make Beanie Babies an incredible cult phenomenon yet threatened their ability to catch on in a larger way. His sales were on track to surpass the $500 million mark, but that was all in gift shops—mostly in upper-middle-class areas, with a heavy concentration in the suburbs. Warner had opportunities to do things with Beanie Babies he never could have imagined, and he'd hired Kristin Edstrom as his vice president of licensing to explore the possibilities. Her initial assignment was to set up a deal for a Beanie Babies TV show. That was the kind of product-based programming that was responsible for billions per year in sales and could turn toys no one wanted into hits through sheer exposure. Lines such as He-Man, My Little Pony, and the ThunderCats had all become hundred-million-dollar brands with the help of the product-based TV shows that accompanied their launches.

Warner wanted in; at least he thought he did. Edstrom met with five top television studios and returned, delighted, with an offer from each one. Then Warner pulled the plug on the whole idea. He'd grown concerned that fleshing out the Beanie Babies into fully developed characters with personalities and voices would hurt the ability of children to interact creatively with them. He also worried that it would alienate the independent toy retailers who frowned on overly commercialized products. Virtually all toys were sold on television—and Warner liked the idea of Beanie Babies being special and staying special, something apart from the rest of the industry.

Edstrom's two-year tenure at Ty consisted almost entirely of saying no. Every month, hundreds of phone calls came in from companies wanting to license the Beanie Babies brand. Mattel CEO Jill Barad called personally to see about making a deal to package

Beanie Babies to be sold with Barbie dolls; Warner wouldn't take the call. Ty turned down repeated calls from Steven Spielberg's office seeking to use Beanie Babies in movies. He turned down deals for breakfast cereal, apparel, children's books, and pretty much every other consumer good for which you could possibly imagine a marketing tie-in with a Beanie Baby—and a bunch that you couldn't imagine, including perfume.

McGowan pushed Warner to introduce a line of plastic tag protectors after she saw customers in a store upset over bent hangtags, but Warner demurred. When the opportunists took over and introduced their own tag protectors, Warner eventually did create an official one—but the licensed protectors never took off.

Most would-be partners couldn't even get a response. The New York City Hawks, an Arena Football League team, wanted to distribute ten thousand Beanie Babies to attendees at a July 25, 1998, game. John Hall, the team's vice president and general manager, had trouble finding someone to reject his request: "We kept faxing requests to Ty, because their phone number and address are unlisted. It's like *The X-Files.* We faxed them every day or two for three weeks. Finally, I got the person in charge of the Beanie Baby sales. She told me they get five hundred faxes a day, and they're not opening up to any football league."

"He didn't want to prostitute the brand," says Edstrom—and in an industry where creating a brand that could be prostituted was the goal of nearly every product launch, it was hard not to admire him.

Eventually, Edstrom became concerned that her role at Ty would destroy her long-term career. "I'm getting a reputation as the person who handles licensing who doesn't do any licensing," she told him. Edstrom and Ty parted ways amicably, though she was somewhat puzzled. Why had Warner hired her to do licensing if he wasn't going to license anything? It seemed to reflect ambivalence about his business instincts and how they conflicted with his desire for purity and control. Yes, licensing would bring in no-risk, no-capital-needed cash—and if done right, help to spread the brand. That's what every other brand with a hot toy did, but the same obsession that had Warner turning down Toys "R" Us also had him turning down T-shirt deals.

Before Edstrom left, though, there was one licensing deal that Warner couldn't say no to: McDonald's wouldn't stop calling.

20

Peak

McDonald's pursued Warner for months before they got him to engage with the idea of a Teenie Beanie Babies promotion. Part of this was logistics. In late 1996 and early 1997 he was spending much of his time in China, focused on the enormous task of finding factories that could ramp up manufacturing to meet demand that was increasing tenfold per month.

The cut-and-sew nature of plush creates quality-control problems as volume increases: there is little room for standardization. It costs Lego between $50,000 and $80,000 to create a mold that will produce a single standardized brick, but that one mold can create sixty million perfectly identical Legos before it wears out. An entrepreneur can start making stuffed animals with no money down, and Warner was printing cash by late 1996: the company was buying Beanie Babies from the overseas factories for twenty-five to sixty-five cents apiece, selling them at a wholesale price of $2.50, and paying a 10 percent commission on the sales. Customers paid for UPS shipping, and Warner ran a super-lean operation with no staff anywhere in the United States other than at the company's headquarters in Oak Brook, Illinois, and at a call center in Texas. He offered no bulk discounts to anyone, ever—a deal breaker with bigger accounts, but it kept anyone from undercutting the mom-and-pops on which he was building his business.

It was easy money except that clones can't just be stamped out. Some in the toy industry say it's that cost differential that helps plush attract the strangest characters: people with little money but a willingness to risk it all based on a belief that they can create something with a pair of eyes that will call to a child from a store's shelf. It's funny and almost sad to think about someone as persnickety as Ty Warner trying to manage exponentially increasing production on something that had to be sewn by hand each time. That task, combined with his desire to keep Beanie Babies exclusive, deflected his focus from McDonald's.

Still, Warner knew that McDonald's could offer him something no one else could. As hot as they were, Beanie Babies were primarily a phenomenon of middle- and upper-middle-class suburban women. McDonald's could get the Ty logo in front of lower-income consumers who never set foot inside specialty stores and drive them to the gift shops in search of the larger Babies, which were made with better fabric than any Happy Meal giveaway would be and came in more varieties. There was really no other way to bring the mass market to Beanies without messing up the entire distribution strategy that was fueling the craze.

In her unpublished memoir, Faith McGowan writes of another problem with the deal McDonald's was proposing: "McDonald's didn't want to pay anything for it. And, if McDonald's flooded the market with Teenie Beanies, it might kill the market for Beanie Babies.

"Still, anything with McDonald's was big money, and Ty and I figured there had to be a way to make it pay. Through a brilliant set of maneuvers and negotiations," McGowan reports, they made a deal. "The business deal we pulled off would net Ty, Inc. more than $100 million. At the time, we had a hard time comprehending such a sum. But it was only a small fraction of the profits that the Beaniestalk would produce." The consummation of the McDonald's deal marked one of the few times McGowan could remember Warner ever visibly expressing enjoyment of his success. They danced around his Oak Brook house and made champagne toasts.

Expectations were enormous. McDonald's reported production of one hundred million Teenie Beanie Babies, enough to fill the largest Happy Meal order in history. It was a prediction that there would be enough demand to sell one for every household in America within a span of just a few weeks. The expectation was that the cult following of speculators surrounding a specialty toy could drive greater demand than the Teenie Beanies McDonald's produced to coincide with the release of mega-budget Disney movies. That should have warned consumers that these were unlikely to be scarce enough to appreciate in value, but it didn't. Warner had complained to McDonald's that their production plans would be insufficient, but McDonald's insisted that, either way, its restaurants were simply not staffed to hand out more Happy Meals than that.

With the mass promotion of Teenie Beanies and the TV advertising that McDonald's was planning on the way, the obvious strategy was to ramp up distribution for Beanie Babies. That would bring the toy to the masses while McDonald's brought the masses to a smaller version of the toy. The big-box stores were banging down Warner's door with enormous orders, but he decided to keep everything the same. "They won't give us any," Toys "R" Us's main buyer for plush toys told a reporter. "I have not been able to get them to return my phone calls. We're extremely concerned. We've been shut out by Ty."

Bill Harlow, the president of Ty Canada, remembers the incredulous calls from the Canadian heads of major retailers: some screamed at him and most of them swore, but his hands were tied. Warner had decided he didn't want his product in bins, and that was that. Harlow knew that if he did sell to chains, Ty would somehow find out. And when he did find out he'd stop shipping to Harlow, and Harlow would be out of business.

On April 11, 1997, the first Teenie Beanies landed at McDonald's stores nationwide. "We're getting fifteen to twenty, sometimes twenty-five calls every half hour since six o'clock this morning: 'Do you have the Beanie Babies? Which ones do you have? What time are you going to start selling them?' " the franchise owner of a McDonald's in Elmhurst, Illinois, told CNN. Some customers ordered a hundred Happy Meals and asked the cashier to keep the food. Stores received hundreds of calls per hour and set up automated recordings for anyone who called. "Good morning. McDonald's. We have the moose and the lamb," one Ohio franchisee instructed employees to answer the phone.

When the restaurants started posting per-customer limits, collectors headed to message boards to swap tips on disguises that could be shuffled in the car between runs. Initially, demand in California had been weak, but as people from the rest of the country asked friends to pick them up and curious Californians browsed eBay, West Coast locations sold out within a few days, too. And as the Teenie Beanie demand spread to California, it brought with it demand for the full-size ones. The craze became truly national—and, not surprisingly, more rife with criminality than ever. An eighteen-year-old in Riviera Beach, Florida, was arrested for stealing $6,000 worth of Teenie Beanie Babies from the McDonald's where she worked and then selling three hundred of them to a coworker.

Two weeks into a planned five-week promotion, McDonald's took out ads to apologize and announce that it was ending the giveaway early because it had run out of product. As for the TV commercials promoting Teenie Beanies, the company canceled those after just a couple of days, worried that massive crowds were putting employees' safety in jeopardy. "The stores were just devastated by it," one former executive remembers. "It really created a frenzy. The customers become deranged." McDonald's employees were given pins that read "I survived the attack of the Teenie Beanie Babies."

"When I talk to my former colleagues, all I have to do is just say, 'Teenie Beanie Babies,' and we all just go, 'Oh my God, shoot me,'" says Jane Hulbert, who by then was running public relations for McDonald's after her initial sighting of the Beanies at the Wellness House. "There were reporters who, for ethical reasons, would not let me take them for lunch in New York City who were calling me and saying 'Don't tell anybody, but do you think you can send me a press kit with them?'" She wasn't sure why they wanted the press kits. At first she assumed the reporters were acting on behalf of their kids, but then it occurred to her that at least some of the requests were being made with an eye toward resale.

Miraculous as it was, the speculators were proven right. In the short term, at least, one hundred million pieces was a limited-enough edition to leave anyone who'd spent two weeks staking out drive-throughs with a tidy profit. The hoarding was driving up prices. Everyone thought their values would keep rising, so there were too few sellers to accommodate the buyers. Oxford Bank of Chicago bought one thousand Teenie Beanies on the secondary market to bait people into opening savings accounts. The pitch was simple: open an account with at least $1,000 in it and you get a Teenie Beanie. A penalty was added if you withdrew the money in less than a year: "We didn't want people opening the account just to get the Teenie Beanie Baby and then closing it," the company's vice president of retail banking and marketing told a reporter.

The McDonald's promotion brought massive mainstream buzz to a product with distribution only outside the mainstream. It's a combination that hardly ever happens, and it amplified an already enormous imbalance between demand and supply—the equivalent of buying Super Bowl ads to promote a church bake sale. Most products that are on the receiving end of large-scale publicity are also part of a large-scale distribution system. Yet

Warner hadn't changed his distribution even a little bit in anticipation of the response.

Media coverage of Beanie Babies soared, bringing in still more new collectors. That made the toys harder than ever to find at retail, which only increased their perceived value. Zany Brainy, now defunct but then the largest of the national specialty-toy chain stores, had its clerks answering the phones this way: "Thank you for calling Zany Brainy. We do not have any Beanie Babies in stock right now." The McDonald's promotion and ensuing publicity also marked the beginning of a true frenzy in Canada—monthly wholesale orders soared from a little over $1 million to $7 million.

As new collectors entered the market in the United States and abroad, secondary-market prices skyrocketed—and anyone who had gotten into the Beanie game pre-McDonald's was sitting pretty. On May 11, 1997, just after the Happy Meal promotion ended, Ty posted a new retirement announcement on its Web site. Flash the Dolphin and Splash the Whale instantly shot up to $25 to $50 each on eBay, and as collectors scrambled to find the last remaining Flashes and Splashes on store shelves, the company introduced ten new Beanie Babies. The new releases instantly sold online for five or more times their retail value.

Warner was on top of the world and decided to make an exception to his ban on partnerships for one more entity: Major League Baseball.

Warner had been a great outfielder in high school, but the connection ran deeper. His father had named him after Ty Cobb, the early-twentieth-century Detroit Tigers star. While Cobb still holds the major league record for career batting average, his off-the-field conduct earned him a reputation as the meanest man in baseball. Violently racist and with a reputation for injuring competitors on purpose, he wasn't an obvious choice for a namesake, but so it was: Ty's full name was H. Ty Warner—the *H*, an initial that didn't stand for anything, was an affectation his mother had insisted on.

On May 18, three days after the McDonald's giveaway ended, the Chicago Cubs were in the midst of one of the worst seasons in team history. They'd lost their first fourteen games, with average attendance well below 20,000, but they had a special event that day: a Beanie Baby giveaway that 37,958 paying spectators showed up for. It was the first sellout crowd the team had had in a long time, making Cubbie the Bear, the Beanie given to the first ten thousand fans, a bigger draw for the team than Sammy Sosa. "Beanie Babies Sure Winner for Hapless Cubs," ran the *Chicago Tribune* headline. Aside from the Cubs' first home night game in 1988, the team said, the giveaway had done more to drive ticket sales than any event in its history.

Other teams followed. Major League Baseball took in $2.5 billion in revenue in 1998, the year Sammy Sosa and Mark McGwire broke Roger Maris's all-time home run record in the midst of a chemically fueled bubble that had taken over baseball—just as Internet stocks and Beanie Babies were doing their work on the rest of the culture. Yet steroid-enhanced sluggers weren't even the league's most exciting draw that year. At games that included a Beanie Baby giveaway, attendance rose by an average of 37.4 percent. *Sporting News* named Glory the Bear, given out at the 1998 All-Star Game on July 7, the one-hundredth-biggest person in sports, just below Don King.

————

As Ty's sales grew, Warner sometimes neglected the operational side of the business. His lack of focus on logistics hampered distribution—which inadvertently helped the craze grow by exacerbating supply shortages and driving up secondary-market prices. As the market heated up and the company's facilities became inadequate for the sales volume, Warner resisted the idea of expanding his warehouse beyond the one he had attached to his office. Faith McGowan remembers that Warner "could not separate himself from his office and his distribution. He couldn't fathom that in his mind." Even though it was obvious that a company doing Ty's volume couldn't function with a small distribution center tacked on to a corporate headquarters, Warner dismissed the idea of expansion as "goofy." McGowan scouted locations by herself, and eventually Warner agreed to shell out $1 million per year for 270,000 square feet of off-site distribution in Bolingbrook, Illinois.

He also broke ground on a new 75,000-square-foot, $14 million headquarters just down the road from the old office—with plans that there was to be no signage of any kind and certainly no colorful allusions to Beanie Babies. The company's mailing address remained a post office box in Oak Brook; the mystique was preserved. Warner had a giant fish tank installed in his office but then had it removed when he decided he didn't like it. The CEO's suite was under constant renovations for years after the rest of the building was complete, but Warner never used it. He preferred to work in a conference room where he could see everything that was going on in his building.

Finally, in November 1997 he hired Bob Ricciardi, a gift industry veteran, to serve as president and focus on the management tasks Warner wasn't interested in. Prior to meeting with Ricciardi to indoctrinate him into the Ty Warner method of business, Warner made notes on a legal pad—beginning, as he always did, with what he'd learned from his days at Dakin. "Be a company that predominantly has classics such as Teddy Bears, cats, dogs, [and] bunnies," he wrote. "Stick to smaller stores . . . Don't sell to stores where shoppers are price checking (mass merchants). The WORST mistakes in business are made in good times, not in bad times. Run a TIGHT SHIP—hold down OVERHEAD. Keep [Beanie Babies] on tight supply to keep them in demand. You want kids fighting for them."

One of Ricciardi's first tasks was to inform the sales force that the commission on Beanie Babies was being cut from 10 percent to 6 percent. In 1997 the account executives earned an average of more than $120,000 ($170,000 in 2012 dollars), with many of them working part time. Even for full-timers, little talent was required. Retailers were having as many Beanies delivered as possible, and Ty saw the account executives as glorified order takers. "I didn't start my own business to make other people rich!" he once bellowed at them.

The increasing delegation at Ty also created problems for Internet guru Lina Trivedi, the company's twelfth employee. She was used to reporting to Warner and his information technology head. When another layer of management was added, she clashed with her new supervisor. Trivedi approached Ricciardi with her request for a salaried position following years of making no more than $12 per hour; she now wanted $120,000 plus $60,000 for her younger brother. Ricciardi, however, felt that her demands were excessive. Warner had wanted her to stay, she says, and had promised her a plush office at the new headquarters, but he didn't intervene when the negotiations broke down. Trivedi and her brother walked. At the age of twenty-five, she sold ten thousand dollars' worth of rare Beanie Babies she'd accumulated and started her own business. "We're going to be the Microsoft of Web design," she told a reporter.

Ricciardi left after less than six months of being limited to little more than slashing commissions and hunting for minor cost-saving measures. Warner wasn't ready to relinquish any serious control; he hadn't even shown Ricciardi the company's financial statements. Ricciardi had left a secure career at Enesco for the job, and while he bears no ill will toward Warner, others say that his stint at Ty torpedoed his career. "The Ricciardi events had an effect on my perception of Ty," McGowan wrote. "I began to see that he could be ruthless and callous in his dealings with the people who were helping him. The thought crossed my mind that it could happen to me."

———————

By 1998 a *USA Weekend* poll found that 64 percent of Americans owned at least one Beanie Baby. The second McDonald's giveaway in May 1998 was even more successful than the first— partly because by that point, complete sets of the 1997 Teenie Beanies were selling for close to $200, or about ten times the total cost of the Happy Meals it took to acquire them. Warner was ambivalent about all this: he knew the secondary market was making him rich, and he knew that keeping it going was important. However, Beanie Babies were supposed to be a toy; if children could no longer buy them, the craze's days were numbered. It was a delicate balancing act: fuel the secondary market while still keeping it popular with kids—two goals that were intrinsically at odds with each other.

"We firmly believe that the recommended $5 'magic' retail price point has contributed to the success of the BEANIE BABIES phenomenon," he wrote in an April 1998 letter to retailers. "BEANIES are cute, limited, well-made and affordable. Well, guess what, now in far too many cases, they're not affordable." Warner said that he would discontinue sales to retailers who weren't marketing his products in accordance with his "pricing philosophy," and he set up a hotline for consumers to report price gouging. Yet it was like the arcade game Whac-A-Mole: Warner was largely helpless to police the more than ten thousand gift shops selling his toys.

Emblematic of the conflict between Beanie Babies as toys and Beanie Babies as investments is the story of what happened to Nancee Biank's therapy group at the Wellness House. Once the Teenie Beanie promotion she'd inspired began and the speculative market continued to soar, there was a problem. When the eight-week programs came to an end and each child had a chance to bring home a Beanie Baby, they arrived for the last meeting armed with instructions. "My mom told me to make sure I take Squealer the Pig because it's going to be worth a lot of money," a boy might tell her—and then another kid would explain that he had received the same instructions from his father. Arguments about Beanie Babies shattered the therapeutic atmosphere that Beanie Babies had once been central to creating. "The parents," Biank says, "actually ruined the whole thing."

As popular as Beanie Babies were, Biank had to stop using them for therapy. These particular stuffed animals were now too valuable to be given to children whose parents were dying of cancer. It had gone from cute to heinous, and there was no good way for it to end.

21

The Feedback Loop Spins Out of Control

The collectors had joined the craze in waves: early adopters in 1996, a national spread in early 1997, then an influx driven by the McDonald's promotion and accompanying media wave that started in April of that year. The increasing demand led to ever-rising secondary-market prices; Beanie Babies that were selling between $25 and $35 in March 1997 jumped to between $50 and $70 by May, and the market continued to go up. The trio of Beanies released for the 1996 presidential election, Lefty, Righty, and Libearty, were all retired on January 1, 1997. They were selling for $50 each by October of that year. By December 1997 they were up to $125 each, and by March 1998 they were selling for $625 each.

John Kenneth Galbraith writes of the price increases during the seventeenth-century tulip mania, "In keeping with the immutable rules governing such episodes, each upsurge in prices persuaded more speculators to participate. This justified the hopes of those already participating, paving the way for yet further action and increase, and so assuring yet more and ever-continued enrichment." The continuing escalating demand and prices were driven by one of the most fundamental fallacies identified by behavioral economists: humans extrapolate trends and assume that historical price-appreciation patterns will continue even when it is future demand, not past returns, that will impact prices in the long term.

In *Irrational Exuberance*, economist Robert Shiller writes of how, far from eliciting skepticism about an overheating market, inflated prices serve to lure more investors in. That is, he says, the very definition of a bubble: "I define a speculative bubble as a situation in which news of price increases spurs investor enthusiasm, which spreads by psychological contagion from person to person, in the process amplifying stories that might justify the price increases and bringing in a larger and larger class of investors, who, despite doubts about the real value of an investment, are drawn to it partly through envy of others' successes, and partly through a gambler's excitement."

A few commentators were warning about the risks. Harry Rinker, the antiques expert, frequently devoted his syndicated column to blasting Beanie Babies. He earned the nickname Beanie Meanie during his TV and radio debates with the experts who insisted that the run-up in values was sustainable. In honor of Rinker's steadfast skepticism, a group of antiques dealers presented him with a crucified Stinky the Skunk Beanie Baby. It was inscribed: "King of the Fools. Presented to Harry L. Rinker, Speaker of the Truth, from the Dealers in Central Indiana Who Refuse to Sell Ty Items."

"Hoarding is a major issue," he wrote in mid-1998. "There is no way of knowing the hoarded number of each Beanie Baby. The safest assumption is pick a number and multiply it by 10." But just like the mutual fund managers who resisted Internet stocks until the worst possible moment, some of the flea market vendors who had been smart enough to avoid Beanies in the early days jumped on the bandwagon as the craze peaked.

Manias are often remembered for the peak—the most spectacular period of a frenzy that seemed to have come out of nowhere. Yet in every case it's the slow growth in the beginning, from a tiny base, which ignites the stories that spread the excitement. The year after most outside experts predicted the Beanie Baby fad had already peaked, Ty's wholesale shipments doubled again—and prices on the secondary market continued to climb. It was too late to get any of the really rare Beanies at bargain prices; the Chicago women, whose credibility had increased as the doubters' had diminished, already had those. The ones collectors were clamoring to buy in gift shops were arriving from China by the tens of millions. Monthly circulation of *Mary Beth's Beanie World* had reached over one million copies—and the page count was increasing with every issue as entrepreneurs bid up the rates for ad space.

Brian Wallos, in his midtwenties with a degree in finance from SUNY–Binghamton, was taking out full-color, multipage ads in all the Beanie collecting magazines to promote his Wallos.com site—one of the largest secondary-market dealers for Beanie Babies. He sold dozens of royal blue Peanut the Elephants for $5,000 each and once bought one thousand of the Princess Diana bears with a single cashier's check for $100,000. Wallos went to England regularly in search of undiscovered stashes, and he had at least one thousand of all but the rarest Beanies in stock at all times. He was also flying high on his own supply—keeping an inventory but also hoarding some pieces for himself for long-term investment.

In 1998 he had twenty-five employees, a huge warehouse, and an advertising budget of close to seven figures per year. "PLEASE NOTE," read the fine print at the bottom of every ad, "Prices may change up or down due to the extremely volatile nature of the Beanie business." Buyers were advised to call or go online for up-to-the-minute pricing. As Rinker was warning, it was the worst possible time to start collecting Beanie Babies, so naturally, more people than ever started collecting Beanie Babies.

Chris Robinson, who'd starred as Dr. Rick Webber on *General Hospital* from 1978 until 1986, began collecting in 1998 when his son pointed Beanie Babies out to him on a trip to Boston. The store owner told Robinson that retired Beanie Babies were soaring in value, and Robinson started researching it. "They had these books that were out, and they would project the value in ten years," his son remembers. "My dad was reading these books, and he was taking them to heart. We thought we were going to pay for our college with them. It consumed every part of our lives."

The family spent each day compiling lists of local stores, following UPS trucks, and making calls to keep track of shipments. They built relationships with store owners and bought five of each animal from each store each month, claiming to have five kids. When stores placed limits on the number of Beanies each family could buy, Robinson instructed his kids to pretend they didn't know him. During the second McDonald's giveaway, a friend threw up in their car after eating too many Happy Meals as the family bought them by the dozen. Weekends were devoted to inventory management: putting each Beanie's tag in a protector, then storing them in plastic bins categorized by "species." Robinson spent more than $100,000 on Beanie Babies at a time when he was not working steadily.

Oversupply and hype weren't the only threats to the secondary market. Collectors estimated that roughly one-quarter of Beanies on the market for $1,000 or more were fakes. Knockoffs of rare pieces like the royal blue Peanut the Elephant, the Old Face Teddy the Bear, and the spotless Spot the Dog burned high-ticket collectors, leaving them reluctant to pay up for more rare Beanies. In a weird way, though, the presence of counterfeits—and the endless warnings in magazines, books, and local news shows—also seemed to legitimize the collectability of real Beanie Babies. Peggy Gallagher and the two Beckys, three of the first collectors who'd chased Beanies by phone, started authenticating pieces by mail—for $20 each. That business alone gave Gallagher a six-figure income: Beanie Babies were an investment, and serious collectors didn't blink at paying up to legitimize their rarest pieces.

In July 1998 U.S. Trade Representative Charlene Barshefsky traveled to China with President Clinton and purchased about forty Beanie Babies to take home. She was stopped at Customs and told that her loot was illegal because of trade restrictions Ty had pushed for. Republican National Committee chairman Jim Nicholson denounced her: "Instead of trying to reduce our $50 billion trade deficit with China, our trade representative was scouring the street markets of Beijing grabbing up every illegal, black-market Beanie Baby she could get her hands on."

On May 1, 1998, Ty announced the retirement of twenty-eight Beanie Babies—double the number in the company's previous largest retirement announcement. *Beanie Mania Bulletin*, a popular biweekly newsletter for collectors, reported, "Equally surprising was that no new Beanie Babies were announced at the same time, although Daisy, the Ty 'Info Beanie' is presently hinting at some changes in the Ty nursery."

Mary Beth's two cents: "When 24 Beanies are retired on May 1, they literally disappear off store shelves. The hoarding of retired Ty product by collectors, secondary-market dealers and even retailers becomes the norm rather than the exception. Everyone is a Beanie dealer. Children clean out their toy boxes to make a profit. It is not uncommon to hear about Beanie dealers making enough to go on vacations, purchase vehicles and even put down payments on houses. . . . Beanie Collectors are turning into the equivalent of Wall Street speculators."

By June of 1998, the royal blue Peanut the Elephant was selling for $5,200, the brown Old Face Teddy the Bear was $3,500, and many other Beanies sold in the $1,000 range. The baseball card business was declining and many card stores were rebranding themselves as outposts for rare Beanie Babies: the Texas Sportcard Company in Deer Park, Texas, reported that it was now making more from Beanie Babies than it was from cards.

"There's never been a product in the history of collectibles that has had the impact of Beanies," a Connecticut store owner told one magazine. "Nothing compares to it." As 1998 came to a close, collectors eagerly awaited the latest retirement announcement; seven Beanies had been retired on December 31, 1997, and rumors of a similar event circulated on message boards and at flea markets. On December 1 Ty.com posted a poem:

> *Surprise! Guess What? We're letting you know*
> *One month in advance, so your collection can grow.*
> *The countdown's begun so don't hesitate*
> *Get out to the store before you're too late*
> *This is our promise, our guarantee*
> *Never again, in stores they will be.*
> *Our final goodbye to our retirees,*
> *Will be on December 31st, New Year's Eve.*

Over the next twelve days Ty announced retiring pieces one by one—discontinuing twenty-six Beanie Babies, along with seven Attic Treasures and one Beanie Buddy, although collectors had limited interest in those two lines. Traffic soared, and collectors stripped the soon-to-be retiring Beanies off store shelves.

At the end of 1998, 48 percent of *Mary Beth's* readers said they'd started collecting within the past year—which the recently renamed *Mary Beth's Bean Bag World Monthly* interpreted as a sign that the craze was still on the ascent. In December 1998 the Home Shopping Network announced its best month of sales in company history—buoyed by the sale of 550,000 Beanie Babies at prices far higher than the prevailing values on online auction sites. Ty's sales for 1998 came in at $1,348,418,778—and Warner's pretax income surpassed $700 million. Still, there was enough talk about a peaking market that the experts needed to reassure collectors.

Claudia Dunne, one of the early experts, wrote at the time, "Attending Beanie shows around the country, I see the panic in people's eyes, and I want to say, 'Relax, Beanies are here to stay.' " Jessica Benuzzi, a staff writer for *Mary Beth's Bean Bag World Monthly*, explained that low interest rates would continue to drive Beanie sales. Brian Devany, a Beanie dealer, wrote that "the Beanie market has consistently bucked the odds, and evidence of this continues as 1998 nears a close. The demand in the market for current and retired Beanies almost always exceeds supply, making a mockery of those calling the Beanie phenomenon a fad." The promoters pointed—with some justification—to the collectible categories that had endured for decades: Hummel figurines had been popular since World War II, and Barbie had been a hit since 1959, with values for rare examples rising each year. *Why not Beanie Babies?* the speculators asked.

Signs of trouble came with the new year. In mid-1998 all retired Beanie Babies were worth more than they had retailed for; that high-wire act had fueled the continuing growth of the market. Yet when the pieces that had been announced for retirement stopped shipping in January 1999, the expected price increases didn't happen. There were now only forty current Beanie Babies out of a total collection of two hundred. However, the calculus had changed. The hoarders were stunned to see that the notion of Beanies going up in value upon retirement was not an immutable law of nature.

There were a few reasons for this. First, the rising volume of listings on eBay, which had initially contributed to the excitement of Beanie collecting, was now making it easier for collectors to find the Beanies they were missing. The market had become more transparent, and price guide publishers had lost their ability to impact prices. Now you could see values in real time, and any slowdown in growth could instantly stoke pessimism.

More important, the secondary market for Beanie Babies had become a victim of its own success. Soaring prices had led to intensifying demand on the primary market, and Ty's skyrocketing sales were starting to satiate that demand. The imbalance had been corrected, and people were starting to see that the new issues had no hope of ever producing the returns that Old Face Teddy, Brownie the Brown Bear, Humphrey the Camel, and Slither the Snake had.

The dream of Beanie Babies as a long-term investment was unraveling. So was Faith McGowan's dream of a life with Ty Warner.

22

Money Changes People

On Christmas Eve, 1998, Faith McGowan's daughters went to stay with their father. Faith chilled a bottle of wine and prepared a filet while she waited for Warner's return from an afternoon meeting with a printing company. When he still hadn't arrived at six thirty, Faith was worried. She drove by the office; he wasn't there.

Her worry turned to suspicion when she remembered that Patricia Roche, living in England and running Ty UK, was in town for the holidays with her family. Faith called Patricia's parents' home posing as an old friend and asked whether she was around. She was told Patricia was staying at the Embassy Suites Hotel in Oak Brook—not far from Ty's office.

Faith drove her Porsche through the snow and when she reached the hotel, she saw Warner's black Mercedes in the parking lot. She went to the desk and asked for Roche's room number. The clerk, initially reluctant, dialed the room and handed her the phone. Patricia picked up.

"I want to speak to Ty," Faith said. "I know he's there."

"Leave us alone!" Roche screamed. "You have the house. You have the car. You have him. What more do you want?"

"I want to speak to Ty," she said. "Now!"

Warner took the phone and calmly explained that he had just stopped by to show Roche the new catalog. He hung up, and Roche told him to go out the side entrance and drive home—deal with it later, she told him. Do not under any circumstances take the elevator downstairs to have a Christmas Eve brawl with your girlfriend, who just caught you cheating, in the echo-filled atrium of a hotel ten minutes from the office where your stuffed-animal company employs hundreds of people.

Not surprisingly, Warner chose the latter option. As he emerged from the elevator a few minutes later, McGowan punched him in the face and was promptly grabbed by the police officers the marginally clairvoyant manager had summoned right as McGowan had arrived. The police wanted to file a report, but Warner shooed them away and he and Faith went home.

"That was funny to him. 'Oh boy, look at her go,'" Roche remembers of the incident. "'She really cares about me.'

"If you didn't scream at him, you didn't care about him," she adds. "You would think a billionaire with his unbelievable brain would not need to be chastised twenty-four-seven by women. But he does."

McGowan forgave Warner for the infidelity, but their relationship had other problems. He bought her an engagement ring and showed it off to her father, but she never really believed that he was on the brink of marrying her. He'd never asked her to marry him, but he did tell her that they were engaged—and sometimes he told other people that, too. The first time she told him that she loved him his response had been, "For how long?" When Faith's daughters asked Ty why he wouldn't marry their mother or do something to give her a sense of financial security, his response was, "Because then your mother will leave me."

Faith McGowan wasn't a gold digger. She'd been with Ty before he was especially wealthy, and by all accounts she loved him more than anyone else ever had. However, in 1999 Faith was living with a billionaire and not earning any money. She was terrified at the prospect of being reduced to poverty the moment he decided he was done with her.

"Relax," he said. "You're on the big paycheck."

She wasn't reassured.

On January 8, 1999, the *Wall Street Journal* reported on Warner's decision to reward his employees with bonuses unheard of in the industry: "After working all year to keep small-time retailers stocked with Beanie Babies, Ty's 300 employees received cash bonuses equal to their entire 1998 income. Some wept. No company fixated on annual results would ever do that—but neither would it inspire such gratitude."

It was exactly the kind of good-guy publicity that Warner liked ("He did it for ego," remembers Sharon Altier, the company's general manager at the time), but he wasn't entirely thrilled with it. Here was the central conflict for Warner from a PR perspective: he wanted to be seen as the biggest, smartest, most successful toy company out there—it had his name on it, after all. McGowan said that Warner's driving force in life was the desire to make other people jealous, and showing his capacity for generosity was one way of doing that. Yet he'd also worked diligently to make sure that the company's sales volume was hard to trace: that was the only way the product could work as a collectible.

The *Wall Street Journal*'s assertion that Ty Inc. was not a "company fixated on annual results" wasn't quite in line with the image Ty wanted to project. He decided to open the kimono and show everyone just how successful he was. He responded to the story with a full-page ad—his first mainstream one—in the *Wall Street Journal*: "By reading the single paragraph, as it has appeared on many web sites, one might conclude that Ty Inc. does not concern itself with profitability. For the record, Ty Inc. earnings, before interest and taxes, exceeded Mattel during 1998. In fact, in 1998, Ty Inc. was more prosperous than any other toy company, and on an annual basis, is the most successful and profitable company in the history of the toy industry. Bonuses inspire gratitude and loyalty from employees, and hopefully profit margins can inspire publicly held toy companies to question both short and long-term marketing strategies."

Warner's awarding of bonuses coincided perfectly with the complete end of Beanie Babies as a popular toy for children. Pokémon had emerged as the toy craze for the middle school set, and when it came to Beanie Babies, there was no longer any market other than the speculative one. It had begun as a popular children's toy; over the previous two years the share of Beanies being sold to speculators had steadily risen from 10 percent to 30 percent, then to 70 percent. By 1999 it was nearing 100 percent, and the only thing that seemed to bring Beanie collectors together was greed. One former Ty sales rep, who once traded a single rare Beanie Baby for a set of braces for her daughter, recalls that as much money as she was making, her visits to retailers had become dark and depressing by 1999. "I was in a store in South Bend, Indiana, and there were these women who could not afford shoes for their children, but they were carting wheelbarrows full of Beanie Babies." The "warm and fuzzy" feeling Mary Beth remembered from the early days was gone.

Two Las Vegas divorcees, unable to agree on how to divide up their Beanie collection, were ordered to make their picks one by one under the supervision of Family Court judge Gerald Hardcastle, who rested his head on the bench in agony. "This isn't about toys. It's about control," he told them. "Because you folks can't solve it, it takes the services of a District Court judge, a bailiff, and a court reporter." Maple, a bear released only in Canada who became the subject of Customs drama as prices soared in the United States, was the first one drafted.

In Sherman Oaks, California, a masked man walked into a gift shop with a gun, ordered everybody to the ground, and broke a display case to steal forty Beanie Babies valued at a total of $5,000, escaping into the alley through a back door. "He didn't want the cash register," a detective told the *Los Angeles Times*. "All he wanted was the Beanie Babies. With the amount of money these are getting on the market, it was bound to happen sometime."

One story above all others shows just how little the Beanie Baby market of late 1998 and all of 1999 had to do with the sentimentality and play value of toys.

I drove to Moundsville, West Virginia, to visit the Northern Correctional Facility. I knew I was close when I saw the CORRECTIONAL FACILITY AHEAD; BEWARE OF HITCHHIKERS sign. I was there to come face-to-face—in an unsupervised interview room with nothing but a badly chipped blue Formica table between us—with the man who, according to a detective who'd investigated the case, had killed someone over a "Beanie Baby deal gone bad."

Jeff White was twenty-nine years old when he murdered Harry Simmons; he's forty-two now, with a shaved head, and he sports the yellowed "prison pallor" most Caucasian inmates acquire. He's spent close to one-third of his life in maximum security prison. When he was escorted into the room he had one question for me before we got started: "So, them Beanie Babies. Are those still hot?"

No, they aren't, I told him as I shook his hand. The Millennium Bear—a Beanie Baby released to commemorate the approaching year 2000—had been his introduction to the world of plush toys. The bear was one of Ty's more volatile releases: first sold on January 1, 1999, it was so scarce that it instantly traded at over $100 online. However, a few months after its release, Ty's shipping caught up, and they were more readily available in stores. Prices at collector shows slipped to $15. But White had timed it well. He bought the bear for $60 and sold it for $80. He was all of a sudden interested in Beanie Babies.

It wasn't as if Jeff White had been unlikely ever to end up in prison. He had a long rap sheet that began with an AWOL-related dishonorable discharge from the army in 1989, a string of convictions for writing bad checks, and a grand theft auto conviction. He comes from a long run of Whites who've had encounters with the West Virginia penal system. His brother is in prison, his uncle killed a U.S. Marshal, and his son did a year on a weapons charge. A corrections officer told me that he thought Mr. White might be a member of the infamous White family of criminals chronicled in the 2009 documentary *The Wild and Wonderful Whites of West Virginia*, but White dismissed that family as a "novelty act. My family is more vicious." That a guy like this was ever running around West Virginia staking out Hallmark stores waiting for Beanie shipments speaks to just how far the craze penetrated.

In 1999 Jeff White was working as a boilerman at the Elkins Hardwood sawmill in Elkins, West Virginia. White had also started his own business of sorts out of his trailer. He called it Half Court Cards, and he bought and sold everything from sports cards and stereos to guns. After he'd bought and sold the Millennium Bear, a friend called with a problem. She'd run up $5,000 in credit card debt buying Beanie Babies and told White she was concerned her husband would be upset, possibly even divorce her, if he found out. White started selling them for her via word of mouth. Even in a trailer park in Elkins, West Virginia, people wanted Beanie Babies. Without the wealth to speculate in the stock market, spending $50 on plush was their connection to the so-called new economy. White had Beanies in boxes and bags in his trailer—mostly in the kitchen, which he didn't use because he and his son ate all their meals at Hardee's—and he was selling them when he could. It wasn't much, but it was steady and supplemented his sawmill work and drug dealing.

While all this was going on, White, who is something of a firearms aficionado, invited the sawmill's night shift supervisor,

Harry Simmons, to his trailer to show him the nineteenth-century prison-issue riot gun Simmons was looking to get rid of. Simmons pointed to the Beanie Babies and said to White, "You know, my daughter collects them Beanie Babies."

The deal was struck: five retired Beanie Babies in exchange for one riot gun. A few weeks later White called Harry Simmons and asked to borrow some money. This was not unusual, and Harry agreed to lend him $200 to finance the purchase of some Beanie Babies that White hoped to flip for a quick profit.

Meanwhile, White was also caught in the throes of binge alcoholism. He stopped showing up for work; his boss there phoned to advise him to get his "head right" and that he could have his job back once he'd dealt with his substance abuse issues.

What exactly happened to the $200 that Simmons lent White was lost in the haze of inebriation. He vaguely recalls that the Beanie Baby deal "fell through," and witnesses later told police that they had heard the two argue about Beanie Babies on several occasions. The loan coincided with the decline of the Beanie mania, so that might have had something to do with it. When Simmons called to find out what had happened to the money, White assured him that everything was fine and that he'd repay him soon. Simmons knew he was lying and was sick of it. He called White's home, spoke with his cousin and, White says, told him that he wanted his money back and that if he didn't get it, he was going to make sure that White didn't get his job back.

White told his cousin that he was "done with Harry"—a comment that was later used by prosecutors to suggest that the murder was premeditated, something that White steadfastly denied even as he pled guilty.

On October 5, 1999, Jeff White and his cousins began their day at a Denny's at 7:00 a.m. where they had egg sandwiches and biscuits and washed it all down with Bud Light. They spent the day cruising around, then White took his cousins to a local carnival. To this day he insists that when he showed up at the sawmill at two in the morning, he did so without any intention of hurting anyone. He had just been passing through the neighborhood and thought it would be a good time to stop by and try to smooth things over with Harry.

Fair enough, I said, but why did you bring a gun with you?

"The people I was with at that time in my life were not the bedrock of mental health," he said, smiling through his mostly missing teeth. White, ever the responsible adult, said he brought the gun in with him rather than leaving it in the car because there were two gun-curious future criminals waiting in the car, and he feared one of them would get shot. White parked outside the sawmill, noted that Harry Simmons's truck was in the lot, and entered the building through a back door.

He found Simmons in the break room—sprawled out, half-asleep on a table.

"When we have a break, we lie on the table and stretch out," White said in his confession. "We had a joke we played on each other when one was lying on the table and that one would [throw] a board to scare the one on the table so I went and found a board and threw it."

"How the hell did you get in here?" Simmons asked him.

An argument about Beanie Babies ensued—White says Simmons pulled a knife, but police found the knife in its case on Simmons's corpse—and White shot Simmons three times in the chest with a Smith & Wesson 9mm semiautomatic he'd paid $410 for. Then he took Simmons's wallet—to make it look like a robbery, he says—and turned his face away before shooting him one last time in the head. He was apprehended shortly thereafter.

White began his time in prison as a wild child—never turning down a fight and spending weeks in solitary confinement. This was at least in part a response to the ribbing he was taking for the nature of his crime.

"I cannot go into prison as the Beanie Baby Killer," the twenty-nine-year-old told his mother over the phone while he awaited sentencing. "I'm gonna have to kill someone else just to get my credibility back." His ex-wife had called him too, after she saw the headline in the *National Examiner*. Friends told him there were jokes about the murder on *The Late Show*.

After a few years in prison, White settled down. He was certified in hospice care at the recommendation of an associate warden; he has since taken care of forty-five men as they died.

23

The P. T. Barnum of Plush

At midnight on January 1, 1999, Ty released twenty-four new Beanie Babies—the largest product introduction in the company's history. It was a mistake. Collectors of all things tend to be focused on building complete sets, and as the size of the Ty product line became unmanageably large, collectors were discouraged. With twenty-four new releases at an average retail price of around $5 each, Ty was asking enthusiasts to come up with $120. Many collectors simply gave up. It was the same mistake—oversaturation of too many new styles—that had tanked the baseball card craze of the 1980s and early 1990s. "Ty was introducing so many new product lines and so many new Beanie Babies that general collector psychology started working against him," says Leon Schlossberg, one of the last and largest remaining obsessive Beanie Baby collectors. "Collectors collect because they hope to acquire 'all' or 'most' of some particular item. It had become virtually impossible to collect 'all' of the Beanie Babies. Through sheer production and new introductions [Warner] inadvertently forced them to look for new, alternate opportunities to collect 'all' of something. That's just the way collectors are."

Ty's wholesale shipments for January slipped by about 20 percent compared with the previous year—still the second-greatest pace of sales for a plush company in history, behind only Ty's 1998 results, but a sign that the run was nearing its end.

Some of the new releases were still in short supply, and

collectors wrote in to magazines to complain about retailers trying to charge $30 to $40 for Beanies that were supposed to be in
stores for $5. Yet some overproduced "commons"—Beanies that
had been in production for more than a year without being
retired—were stacking up and selling below retail. At flea markets some sellers offered them at two for $6—a once unheard-of
price. Few dealers could remember the last time they'd seen a
child buy a Beanie Baby. "We're selling the ones we have on
shelves, but after that, we're done," one retailer told a reporter.
"I think there's still interest in a secondary market, but the retail
fad is over." On eBay Beanie volume had continued to surge; on
May 9, 1999, there were more than seventy-nine thousand items
listed in its beanbag plush category—triple-digit growth over
the past couple of years that was rapidly outpacing the growth in
sales of Beanies on the primary market. At last there were more
sellers than buyers. The strategy at Ty headquarters was basically
this: keep some Beanies in limited supply to help foment the
secondary market, then make money by overproducing other
ones in the hope that the stories spread by the rare pieces will
lift demand for the entire line. When the overproduced pieces
were retired, they still lingered on shelves at $5 each. The collec-
tors and promoters noticed it, and they weren't happy.

Mary Beth Sobolewski wrote in the May issue of her *Bean
Bag World Monthly*, "On a recent trip, I noticed an overabun-
dance of Bruno, Snort, and Ants packed into the O'Hare International Airport's 30 W.H. Smith gift stores. I returned four days
later and saw the same shelves overflowing with the same retired
Beanies. It's quite ironic that not too long ago, one would feel
exceptionally blessed to find a Beanie retired months before just
sitting on a shelf." Claudia Dunne, one of the first collectors
trading Beanies online before they were a national craze, now
blames the oversupply of commons in 1999 for the end of the
craze: "I don't know why [Warner] decided to flood the market

and kill it. Instead of limiting the number like he did before, [he was] putting out hundreds in every store of the same one." The third McDonald's promotion, which ran from May 21 to June 18, 1999, was something of a flop. "[T]he lines were easily manageable, and in many cases there were no lines," reported *Beanie Mania*.

By August the tone of the mavens had become frantic. Sobolewski wrote, "[R]etirement does not necessarily mean great investment potential anymore; it appears that most Ty items are now overproduced by the time they reach the retirement stage." In the September 1999 issue of her magazine, Sobolewski followed up with, "Ty Warner, if you are listening, there is one thing that collectors want to tell you. There are simply too many Beanie Babies on store shelves everywhere!" Collectors had previously lamented shortages and price gouging, but now, desperate to keep the craze going and maintain the value of the collections they'd already built, they were demanding that Warner curb production to stoke demand.

Warner's main goal at the time was planning his company for life after Beanie Babies, which constituted around 90 percent of his sales. In the late 1990s mom-and-pop retailers were struggling: big-box stores accounted for nearly all the growth in retailing, and for many small gift and toy stores, the Beanie craze was a lifeline. Warner knew that and took advantage of it. "Your mission is to use your talents and take everything that we offer you into your accounts and make Ty the dominant (if not only) plush vendor in your territory," the handbook provided to all salespeople admonished. The salespeople were told that their goal was to "eliminate the need for competition."

"Ty Warner totally believed that every store should have a minimum order of every single plush he sold," says Irene Plummer, a former sales rep for the company. "And if you didn't, you'd better have a darn good excuse why not." The policy of leaning hard on retailers to stock non-hit items was not unique to Ty; executives from other companies describe similar antics surrounding other such products. It was, as Patricia Roche puts it, about "survival"—and a recognition that the mania would not last forever. However, Ty seemed to take the pushing of unpopular items to heights most manufacturers did not. A Connecticut toy store owner told the *Los Angeles Times* about a visit he'd received from a Ty Inc. regional manager. They went to lunch together and the manager congratulated him on the volume of Beanie Babies he was moving. Then the manager informed him that if he wanted to continue receiving shipments of Beanies, he should place a $10,000 order for some of the company's less-coveted product lines. "I felt like the Mafia was leaning on me," the toy store owner told the reporter—but he placed the order for fear of losing his cash cow.

While his sales force was pushing retailers for orders to diversify away from Beanie Babies, Warner was also diversifying his assets. On March 16, 1999, he acquired the Four Seasons Hotel in New York City for $275 million and started to retreat from his day-to-day role at Ty Inc. to manage an $86 million renovation. By that point, Warner was unwilling to listen to anyone about anything, Faith McGowan recalls. Faith suggested that he might want to find someone who could teach him the basics of the hotel business, and Ty responded with hostility. He owned a hotel, and that made him an expert.

The *New Yorker* ran a story, "Beanie Babies Take East Fifty-seventh Street." I. M. Pei, the hotel's architect, noted that he'd used the same French limestone at the Four Seasons that he'd used in his work on the Louvre. "I've never met them, and they've not paid me any visit," he said of Warner. "I guess they'll keep it nice. My guess is they will. Since the room rates are so high." Asked about the possibility of Beanie giveaways to be included with the rooms, which cost $600 per night, Pei was quiet and then replied, "I hope not." Perhaps in response to that interview, Warner introduced Issy the Bear, named for Four Seasons founder Isadore Sharp, as a Four Seasons New York exclusive Beanie Baby.

At Ty Inc.'s annual picnic, held on September 12, 1999, at the Oak Brook Polo Club, Warner gave his employees Billionaire 2—the second bear celebrating a year of $1 billion in sales and stronger profitability than his entrenched competitors. The poem was cocky: "Ty is the company that can't be beat/Mattel and Hasbro can take a back seat/We did it again and it was fun/ In the toy biz, we're #1." Beanie dealers camped out near the picnic, cash in hand, ready to pay thousands for the bears that would come with an impeccable provenance. The authenticators were there alongside the dealers, ready to slap their seals of approval on the Beanies that were selling for $5,000 each online the following day.

Even as Warner turned down interviews and cultivated a mysterious image, he still wanted to make sure everyone knew that the "Ty" in Ty Inc. was Ty Warner. Beginning in 1999, Ty issued an annual Signature Bear with a heart on its chest featuring a sewn facsimile of his signature. As Patricia Roche had put it, he wanted "everyone talking about him without knowing anything."

Patricia and Ty continued to bicker constantly, as they had for the previous fifteen years. But, for now at least, Warner was also making Patricia Roche rich.

Running the company's UK operations had landed her on a list of the highest-paid female executives in England. In the first six months of operation, beginning in January 1996, Ty UK ran up $2.8 million in sales. Sales for the last six months of the year came in at $4.2 million; 1998 brought in $47 million; and in 1999 Roche did $67 million in sales. Warner waxed enthusiastic about her success to everyone he knew, although she says she found his praise condescending. She still asked him for advice now and then—especially about what to do with the piles of money that were flowing in. "Whatever you do," he told her, "don't go offshore with it. You'll regret it."

In Canada Bill Harlow had seen similar growth. When he'd signed on with Ty Inc. in 1992, his pie-in-the-sky dream was to sell more than Gund—which, at $10 million in sales, was the top plush brand in Canada. Starting from nothing, Harlow had built to $2.3 million in sales in 1996. Sales in 1997 went up to $23 million, and 1998's total was $55 million. In 1999, a year when Ty Inc.'s sales fell 25 percent, Harlow pulled in $83 million—his best year yet, and more than eight times the sales of what had been the country's longtime plush leader.

Warner knew that things were coming to an end. He had always said that as long as kids were fighting over Beanie Babies his business would be fine, but now there were enough Beanies being shipped to eliminate the need for fighting—and it was only adults who cared about Beanie Babies anymore anyway.

Speculative bubbles rely on constant upward movement; once the momentum slows, the bubble collapses. By 1999 every single person who could become a Beanie Baby collector already was one. With no prospects for an influx of increased demand, prices stagnated because there was nothing else for them to do. Once casual collectors could no longer count on quick price appreciation on recently retired pieces, they dropped out—and then prices fell as the market contracted, driving out still more collectors. "How did you go bankrupt?" Mike Campbell is asked in Ernest Hemingway's *The Sun Also Rises.* Campbell replies, "Two ways. . . . Gradually and then suddenly." So it is with bubbles: a pause in a market that relied on momentum had led to an irreversible slide, as the lack of continued growth helped the public to come to its senses—slowly at first and then suddenly.

Collectors held out hope that smaller production runs on

some new pieces and quicker retirements might reignite the mania, but Warner had other plans. First he called Faith McGowan, whose relationship with Warner was in the late stages of its bitter end, and money—and a dispute about how much she'd contributed to the business—was at the heart of their conflict. "All you did was pick colors!" Ty screamed at her once, but Faith always believed that she played a pivotal role in the business—a claim others at the company dispute.

Illinois was not a palimony state, she had no employment agreement with the company, and while a lawyer told her she could pursue a *quantum meruit* lawsuit—a claim for reasonable compensation even without a formal agreement—it would be an uphill battle and also mean the end of her relationship with the man she loved. Warner had told her that they would get married "when the time is right," but the time never seemed to be right. McGowan's desire to have some assets in her name further damaged their relationship. "You're a bitch!" he once screamed at her. "You're not getting a dime from me!" However, with his biggest publicity stunt ever in the pipeline, she was still the first person he called.

"Look, I've designed a black bear with gold fireworks on its chest, and I need you to give it a name and write a poem for it," he said. "This will be the last Beanie Baby."

"Why?" she asked, not understanding. "I was almost afraid of him at that point," remembers McGowan.

When Warner talked to Patricia Roche, the conversation was equally abrupt.

"We're shutting it down," he told her.

"What do you mean, 'We're shutting it down'?" she replied.

"I'm not going to do Beanies anymore. We're going to do Beanie Kids." This was to be a line of Cabbage Patch Kids–like plush toddlers that Ty was planning to release in January 2000.

"He believed his own publicity," Roche says slowly now,

enunciating every syllable at the memory of the conversation. "He thought he controlled it." Warner was determined to assert his power over the market that everyone around him could see was running and then stopping of its own momentum. "He thought he would retire Beanie Babies and come out with a new line."

"Ty, they're ugly," she told him at the mention of the Beanie Kids.

Warner's previously exacting standards of quality, however, seemed to have disappeared. "They'll buy it, Patricia!" he told her, excitement in his voice. "I could put the Ty heart on manure and they'd buy it!"

Just as he had adamantly insisted that he was the designer on pieces he'd pilfered from competitors, Warner seemed genuinely to believe that he had been solely responsible for the mania that surrounded Beanie Babies. He seemed to think that he could end it at will and then duplicate it with a new line. In her unpublished memoir, McGowan describes how Warner's personality was changed by his success: "Ty began to believe that he was a genius, and that every idea he had was brilliant. . . . [A]fter the Beanie mania had produced huge financial results, he focused on the money rather than the people."

When anyone disagreed with him, his response was: "Who's the billionaire here? I am!" When he first appeared on the 1999 *Forbes* list of the four hundred richest Americans, he gave a copy of the magazine to every employee, a gesture McGowan thought tacky. He also handed out copies of a motivational management book written by Jack Welch. He'd done that, he conceded to McGowan, because he wanted his employees to see him as Welch-like.

McGowan thought about Warner's idea for a last Beanie Baby, and they went back and forth with possibilities. She puzzled over names: Fini, Ending, Midnight, Forever, Bye, or possibly Never. Finally, Warner settled on The End, and Faith suggested a poem:

Are they a fad, were they a trend?
A way to show love to a friend
Wishes for happiness, Ty continues to send
From the beginning to whenever . . . The End

A few weeks later, back at his house in Oak Brook, Warner startled McGowan when she came out of the bathroom: he'd changed his plan for getting rid of Beanie Babies (perhaps after taking note of the tepid interest in Beanie Kids from retailers who'd seen the prototypes).

"Faith, I have a good idea," he said. "First I'm going to retire all the Beanie Babies. Then we can hold an election on the Web site and let everyone vote on whether people will want us to bring them back. Of course, millions of people will and then we can introduce our new Millennium Beanie Baby line in January 2000." Faith told him it was a stupid idea; so did Patricia Roche and others. They told him it would come across as an obvious gimmick, that people wouldn't fall for it, and that it would make him look manipulative and desperate.

While he was planning a new-millennium end to Beanie Babies, Warner capitulated in his battle with McGowan and gave her some of the money she'd asked for. During their time together Warner had gone from small-time toy mogul to billionaire. "The Deal," as the two called it, left McGowan with about $6 million—mostly tied up in a Santa Barbara mansion he signed over to her. "It was like pulling teeth . . . to even get that," remembers a friend of McGowan's. What Faith didn't realize was that the $6 million gift was Ty's way of marking the end of their relationship.

On Tuesday, August 31, 1999, Ty.com posted a list of new Beanie Babies, followed by a cryptic announcement: "VERY IMPORTANT NOTICE: On December 31, 1999—11:59 p.m. (CST) All Beanies will be retired . . . including the above!" One of the new releases was The End—the black bear with fireworks on his chest and a hangtag featuring this poem:

> *All good things come to an end*
> *It's been fun for everyone*
> *Peace and hope are never gone*
> *Love you all and say, "So long!"*

24

Lights Out

Traffic to the site soared, and the media pounced. Ty Warner declined to offer any comment, and bidding activity shot up 75 percent in one day on the leading Beanie-only auction site. Reporters who tracked down Ty Inc. employees turned up no answers; customer-service representatives told them that they had found out about the mass retirement half an hour before it went live on Ty.com. Annie Nickels, Warner's secretary, told the *Atlanta Journal-Constitution* that "the news flash is what it was. We have nothing further to add to it." Michael Kanzler, then Ty Inc.'s CFO, told the *Wall Street Journal* that "what we have on the web site is all the information we're prepared to give out." Stores reported a rush of sales, and the announcement of The End Bear sparked a frenzy of its own for a Beanie that was current but still nearly impossible to find.

"It has been crazy to say the least," Dee McKnight, assistant manager at Toys Unique in Fort Worth, Texas, told a reporter. "It almost makes you think of the runs on the banks in the 1920s. Most people, honest to goodness, are in a panic." On October 18, the cartoon feature *Nancy* parodied the publicity stunt with a strip featuring a girl pondering a school assignment to write a persuasive letter about a topic of historical significance: "Dear Mr. Ty, You can NOT stop making Beanie Babies!" she writes.

Beanie dealer Brian Wallos told the *Chicago Sun-Times*, "Our whole business has increased since the Ty announcement, and all

Ty and plush products are picking up." By then, however, Wallos was putting on a brave face. Wholesalers were underpricing him at shows, and he complained to other dealers that he could never sell his inventory for what he'd paid for it. Every day the spread between his costs and current values was widening. Dealers at first blamed the new show attendees who, armed with bags of inventory, were driving down prices—but it quickly became clear that the game was over. Beanie Babies had spent close to three years defying all rules of intrinsic value, and those who hadn't realized it would end were about to give back most of the profits they'd made.

In the past Warner had passed on the short-term philosophy that most entrepreneurs embraced. He had turned down massive orders from chain retailers because he knew that having Beanie Babies in bins would kill the demand. He had turned down licensing opportunities that guaranteed huge checks because he didn't want to prostitute his brand. And he never wavered from the $2.50 wholesale price even as retailers were gouging shoppers.

The announcement seemed out of character. Bob Ricciardi, who had left the company by then, followed it through the media with puzzlement. He told me he thought it seemed like trying to turn a battleship in the Panama Canal. If Warner wanted to stoke demand for styles that were in oversupply, Ricciardi thought, there were ways to do that; collectibles manufacturers had been thinking of creative ways to manipulate consumers for decades. That's what the industry was: a giant manipulation. He might have tried releasing some limited-edition Beanies or perhaps cutting back sales to lower-end stores. But a surprise online announcement that on December 31 an entire product line would be completely retired, including a bunch of Beanies introduced in the same post? That was a new one.

On the other hand, Ty might just have been delusional. Mc-Gowan remembers that Warner had recently begun taking a new antidepressant in the weeks leading up to the retirement announcement. Between that and the looming end of his relationship with Faith, he certainly had a lot on his mind. When the announcement went out, McGowan remembers, Warner expected a throng of reporters to descend on his headquarters. He put on a caramel-and-gold-colored Armani suit jacket and rode to work in his Ferrari with the top down—adopting the persona of the movie star he had once hoped to become. He strolled without comment past the few local news trucks that had arrived. His executives and lawyers had told him that he was the new P. T. Barnum, and Warner seemed to have come under the sway of his own reputation—a personalized version of the delusional bubble that had surrounded his product.

"I don't know what he was trying to create. I think he was losing his mind," says McGowan.

Fellow giftware mogul Russ Berrie was watching, as he had throughout the entire mania, with wistful memories of the millions he'd made during the troll craze (which was similarly weird, but smaller and lacked a speculative component). He told a reporter that he was skeptical. "I would think that what they might be saying is, OK, look, let's call them something else . . . and let's make it in a little different size and let's maybe use a little bit different material and we'll repeat the success of the Beanie Babies." Retailers surveyed by reporters also didn't think much of the stunt. Store owner John Gagaoudakis told one reporter that Ty Warner was "not going to stop making" toys: "He doesn't want to be in *The Guinness Book of World Records* under Stupid People."

A poll on *Mary Beth's* Web site found that more than half of collectors had been inspired by the announcement to start selling off their collections. Fewer than one-quarter of respondents said that the announcement had encouraged them to buy Beanies. One-eighth of respondents clicked on the option "Stop collecting—this is just too much."

Analyst Sean McGowan seemed to take the announcement at face value: "With any other company I would expect this is nothing more than a clever or perhaps even cynical ploy to artificially create debate over a new product launch. But very much of what Ty has done and achieved with Beanie Babies has been unorthodox and unprecedented, including no TV advertising. I would expect they would have some new Beanie Baby product on the market in early 2000 and it will be sufficiently different from what they've had in the past so it won't look so cynical."

Advertising Age wrote that the announcement was "over the top and smacks of the desperation of a company whose star product is about to be obliterated by the Pokémon craze. The lack of follow-up information of any kind resulted in a flood of media exposure but showed a complete lack of respect for consumers who have already been manipulated by artificial scarcity and other tricks of the trade."

The discontinuation announcement stimulated one last run on stores, goosing sales of some of the styles that had been in plentiful supply and getting the national media focused on Beanie Babies once again. The problem was that while before everything looked to have happened organically—and in many ways had happened organically—this was an extremely transparent market manipulation. It couldn't possibly last. On December 25, 1999, Warner, as planned, reversed course with a posting on Ty.com: "After much thought, I am willing to put the fate of Beanie Babies in your hands," he wrote. "You make the decision. You have inspired the Beanie Babies line through your devotion to them."

Warner announced a forty-eight-hour period during which people could call in and pay fifty cents to vote on whether Beanie Babies should be continued, with the proceeds going to the Elizabeth Glaser Pediatric AIDS Foundation—although the question of what kind of psycho would spend fifty cents to vote to discontinue a stuffed animal was left unanswered. Predictably, in a vote that ended on January 2, 2000, at 6:00 a.m. Central Time, 91 percent of the reported 209,763 votes cast went in favor of more Beanie Babies. Ty Inc. announced that it would contribute three times the amount raised by voters to the charity. McGowan says that the actual number of votes cast was closer to one-tenth the number Warner reported and that the whole stunt was a flop.

The announcement that Beanie Babies were coming back barely made a ripple. The media had gotten bored with Ty and his Beanie Babies. Worse, during the nearly four months when no new Beanie Babies were released, prices and sales did not rise—other than that momentary, media-driven blip. Former Ty rep Irene Plummer pegs the end of the Beanie bubble to the day Warner announced the end of Beanie Babies.

"In that three and a half months that there were no new Beanie Babies, all these people that had been buying all of a sudden were thinking, *Oh my God, look at how much money I was spending on Beanie Babies*," Plummer says. "When he announced that he was shutting them off, the value did not escalate. They started thinking, *Whoa, maybe I'm not thinking right on this*. And so sales didn't go back up, never went back up. Suddenly, every single month, you could see the sales going further and further down." Within less than a year Plummer's $250,000-per-year sales job was no longer bringing in a living wage.

Nearly all of the Beanie collectors, gurus, dealers, and Ty employees say the craze died with the announcement that all Beanie Babies would be retired, and chronologically that's true. Yet few of the participants seem able to acknowledge the inherent time limit on a speculative episode. That's always what happens after a mania ends. There is some cause that everyone points to (although few are as clearly delineated as the Beanie bubble was), and the intrinsic impermanence is cast aside.

As John Kenneth Galbraith explains in *A Short History of*

Financial Euphoria, "[I]n the aftermath of speculation, the reality will be all but ignored. . . . So there is a need to find some cause for the crash, however farfetched, that is external to the market itself. Or some abuse of the market that has inhibited its normal performance." The same capacity for delusion that fueled the bubble at its height allowed its participants both to maintain their self-esteem after it was over and fail to learn anything from it. Few of the craze's acolytes acknowledge its insanity even in hindsight. If the mass retirement announcement just had not happened, they all seem to believe, the Beanie craze might still be on.

Ty Inc. announced the release of 71 products on January 5, 2000: 21 Ty Classics, 12 Attic Treasures, 6 Baby Ty pastel animals, and 31 Beanie Buddies. On January 8, 2000, the Beanie Kids were unveiled—and *Mary Beth's* speculated that they would be "undoubtedly . . . attractive as collectibles." Instead they were the most spectacular flop of Ty's career. Kids didn't like them, collectors didn't care, and, for the first time anyone could remember, Warner's instincts about what people would buy had cost him money. They had weird stitching on the faces, and unfortunate hair placement gave them a receded look—the appearance of baby-faced Joe Biden rag dolls. Shortly after their release and likely in response to poor sales, the company sent a memo to retailers urging them to carefully groom and style the Beanie Kids' hair prior to display. "Want to sell more Beanie Kids? Make sure they're having a good hair day!" It didn't work.

On March 1, 2000, Ty introduced twenty new Beanie Babies, with some of the best detail and most varied fabrics in the company's history. However, by that point there were already several hundred Beanies in circulation, and some of the animals were at odds with the company's history of cuddly: Swoop the Pterodactyl, Wiggly the Octopus, Scurry the Beetle, and Glow the Lightning Bug. Also in 2000, Ty introduced the Zodiac Beanie

Babies—a collection of twelve brilliantly colorful pieces, each representing an animal from the Chinese zodiac. The line was promoted with billboards in major cities—the company's first nontrade advertising ever—but failed to ignite much of a buzz, even though these Beanies were more aesthetically pleasing than all but a few of the ones from the craze's height.

Even *Mary Beth's Bean Bag World Monthly* had to concede that the Beanie investment craze had passed. In February 2000, just a month after the announcement that Beanies were to continue, the magazine reported, "The Beanie Baby market has softened. . . . Most Beanies are selling for $5. Some large discount chains have purchased newer retired Beanies on the secondary market and are reselling them for as low as $3.99 each or three for $10."

On November 25, 2000, Ty Inc. noted on its Web site that retired Beanie Babies were showing up in chain dollar stores. Ty had nothing to do with the sales; the dealers and speculators who'd been hoarding plush had finally capitulated. Ty suggested that the Beanies might be counterfeit or sold by a charitable group that had received a donation from the company. It didn't really matter, though: once Beanie Babies were in Dollar Tree, the fantasy was gone. Just as Ty's distribution exclusively through gift shops and high-end toy stores had enabled Beanie Babies to become a collectible, their arrival at discounters announced the end.

Of the remaining collectors, *Mary Beth's* noted, "Collecting more for fun and satisfaction than investment potential, they are frustrated because of the oversupply of newer retired Beanie Babies on the market. Now they can walk into any gift store and have their pick of 20 or more retired Beanie styles for $5 each. Although children can again afford to buy the majority of Beanies with their allowance money, their interest now lies elsewhere. . . . The problem is over-abundance. Many of the dealers from 1998 are now 'dumping' their inventory, causing prices to plummet. Beanie collecting has waned significantly."

The market for truly rare pieces—the royal blue Peanut the Elephant, Humphrey the Camel, and the early bears—had evaporated. The original brown teddy that had sold reliably for $3,500 a year earlier was by mid-2000 said to be worth $1,800. Realistically though, there was almost no market left for the scarcest Beanies.

In one of the more prescient market predictions in the history of children's picture books, *The Berenstain Bears' Mad, Mad, Mad Toy Craze* was published in March 1999—even as the craze was still mostly going strong. In the book Brother and Sister, the two children, come running home and announce to Mama and Papa Bear that they absolutely must have an advance on their allowances because "if we don't get it, Herb's Hobby Shop is gonna run out" of Beary Bubbies. Cousin Fred already had six of them, Lizzy had eight, and Queenie had ten. Papa Bear gives the cubs the money, and he and Mama Bear reflect on how silly it is that "otherwise sensible cubs can get pulled into any silly thing that comes along." The next day, after the cubs show the Beary Bubbies to their parents, Mama Bear reads an article in the paper about a man who had acquired a bunch of Bubbies before they were popular and sold his collection for a lot of money. Pretty soon, Papa Bear is driving all over in search of the Beary Bubbies that seem like a path to riches.

"Of course, not many things are forever—and Beary Bubbies certainly weren't," the book explains. "Pretty soon, Beary Bubbies were everywhere. They came in Krinkly Krumbles cereal boxes. You could get them with a Krazy Meal at the Burger Bear. After a while, just about everybody in Bear Country had so many Beary Bubbies that they didn't know what to do with them.

"All you could do was look at them—except they had a way of looking back at you and making you think about all the money you had spent on them. The only thing you could really do with them is brag about how many you had. And no matter how many you had, there was always somebody who had more."

The book reads like most Berenstain Bears books—light and fun with great, cartoony illustrations—but according to several Amazon reviewers who gave it some of the worst reviews of any title in the series, there was one problem with it. "True to life story but where's the ending?" went one review. "The story is true to the Beanie Baby craze but there is no solution or even an understanding at the end. My children and myself were for the first time truly confused and disappointed with an ending of a Berenstain Bear book."

The critics had a point. The last page features Mama, Papa, Sister, and Brother sitting in the living room surrounded by dozens of Beary Bubbies.

"Now, what do you suppose that was all about?" Papa Bear asks.

"I don't really know," says Brother Bear.

25

Limping into the New Millennium

In the early 2000s Warner was forced to pump his own money back into the business as sales declined by more than 90 percent from the boom years. McGowan's relationship with Warner was mostly over after she'd moved out. After she'd taken some of the furniture from her daughters' bedrooms, Ty ordered exact reproductions of the pieces made in Europe. But Ty and Faith still talked occasionally. She asked him how the business was doing. "It's below a hundred million, isn't it Ty?" He wouldn't answer.

At first he tried to win back the sense of scarcity by ceasing sales to florists and some mall-based stores. That was a lost cause. The mom-and-pop retailers Warner had courted in his early years and mistreated during the boom started ordering plush from other manufacturers—if they were able to stay in business at all without the flow of Beanie money. In 2004, Warner claimed losses of more than $39 million on his tax return. The oversupply, both to retailers who had overordered during the good days and collectors who had stocked up on what they thought was an investment, was filtering back into the marketplace through jobbers. Web sites like BuyingBeanies.com sprang up to buy pieces at a flat rate, no price guide needed: forty cents each. That site sells them to carnies, claw machine operators, and retailers Ty would never have imagined selling to in the halcyon days. The recirculated Beanies land in grocery stores, drugstores, convenience stores, and, worst of all, big-box discounters. Once they started turning up there, the exclusive aura Ty had worked so hard to cultivate was gone. Ty started selling to chain stores, too. Now you can buy newly released Beanie Babies at CVS, and Ty has created pieces available only at Walgreens.

As sales collapsed Warner focused on his hotel investments. A year after buying the Four Seasons in New York, he bought the Biltmore Santa Barbara and the Coral Casino Beach and Cabana Club for a combined $150 million. In September 2000 he bought the San Ysidro Ranch, where John and Jackie Kennedy honeymooned, for a reported $30 million. In June 2003 he added the Sandpiper Golf Course in Goleta for $25 million. In 2004 he acquired the Kona Village Resort on Hawaii's Big Island for $60 million and the Montecito Country Club for $40 million, followed by a $100 million deal for the resort Las Ventanas al Paraiso in Los Cabos, Mexico—along with several multimillion-dollar homes. He reportedly offered $100 million for enigmatic heiress Huguette Clark's empty Santa Barbara mansion but was rebuffed.

H&S Media, the company behind *Mary Beth's Bean Bag World Monthly,* filed for bankruptcy in mid-2001, and the magazine ceased publication. In 2002, perhaps recognizing the value of courting the expert whose magazine he'd once sued, Warner partnered with Sobolewski to produce a collector magazine. *Mary Beth's Beanies & More* ran less than a hundred pages, with emphasis on new Ty products, Beanie-related crafts and activities, and generalist coverage of other collectibles. The market analysis and predictions, once the centerpiece of any Beanie publication, were reduced to a few pages at the back. Even with Beanies selling (and mostly not selling) at yard sales and flea markets for fifty cents each, Warner wouldn't allow any of them to be valued at less than $5 to $7. The magazine lasted less than two years as the collector's market continued to shrivel.

————

The Beanie experts who'd made careers out of the craze moved on to other things. Peggy Gallagher became a special-education teacher and is currently trying to sell a handbook for managing children with autism. Becky Phillips went into real estate as an agent for Coldwell Banker in Naperville, Illinois. Becky Estenssoro has tried a few entrepreneurial ventures—so far without the success that Beanie Babies brought her. Mary Beth Sobolewski went back to being a homemaker; her son Dave is a star basketball player at Northwestern, but occasionally hecklers for opposing teams bring up his mother and her starring role in the Beanie craze. "[I'm] glad that's the biggest dirt they could dig up on him," she told me. Most of the women, who at one time spoke daily about the gyrating market, haven't seen each other in years.

Brian Wallos, now in his midforties, was probably the biggest and most successful of the secondary-market dealers. He gave back a large chunk of his profits in the postcrash years, and plowed what he had left into launching Bench Warmer International, a line of trading cards featuring porn stars. He says he modeled the marketing behind the line after Warner's success with Beanie Babies. He figured he'd either make a comparable fortune or be broke in two years. Ten years into the line, Wallos is somewhere in between. He's his company's only full-time employee, but he's eking out a living. He lives in Los Angeles and is working on a memoir on his career in the collectibles industry, along with a screenplay about baseball cards. In 2011 he appeared on Bravo's *The Millionaire Matchmaker*—but, like most things on reality TV, that millionaire label doesn't exactly fit with the reality of Wallos's life.

Ty's sales reps who became millionaires mostly blew through the money on cars, boats, and Internet stocks—profiting from a bubble while oblivious to its inability to last. In the nearly fifteen years since the craze ended, few have come close to the incomes they achieved then. "I look at most people now, and I think we had a hard time landing on our feet afterwards," remembers one former Ty salesperson who, at her peak in her midtwenties, earned more than $500,000 in a single year.

————————

Warner's girlfriend in recent years has been a woman nearly a decade his senior. It's difficult to find anyone with anything nice to say about her. A former finance executive refers to her as "not a nice person." Faith McGowan says she has a "little weasel face," and Patricia Roche says she "looks at you like you're something she just peeled off the bottom of her shoe." Warner's sister thinks she must be "blackmailing him with something." Those who have been close to them say that Warner mostly just sits quietly while she berates him over things like reading the newspaper during breakfast. "She has Ty where Ty had everyone else," explains Roche.

She had some involvement in the business. A former designer for American Greetings, she helped Ty create an old-fashioned-looking doll named Angeline. The doll came with a small children's book that told the story of an angel with small wings who, after several tries at making her wings look bigger, realizes that she's beautiful just the way she is. The Angeline doll was released in March 2005, and word came down from the top: sell it *hard*. "When I took it out to the retailers everybody hated it," one former sales rep remembers. "No one wanted to buy it." The doll had a retail price of $7.99, making it 60 percent more expensive than the similarly sized and far cuter Beanie Babies line, in an era when gift shop buyers were focused on value. That didn't matter. All Ty reps were told to sell at least a $100 order of Angeline to *all* of their accounts or face termination.

"There were several months there where there was incredible pressure," one rep remembers. "The economy was bad, and retailers were struggling, and you wanted to help them. To push Angeline when you knew it was not going to sell because it already was not selling in the other stores . . . I chose to leave at that time."

A few months later, Angeline went away quietly, without any mass firings. The company no longer had a hot product it could use to beat retailers into ordering stuff they didn't want, and eventually Warner realized that. Huge piles of Angelines were donated to charity.

Ty tried to stabilize sales with new lines. The Ty Girlz series, released in 2007, was modeled after the Bratz fashion doll craze. He discontinued them in 2012. In February 2008, by which time Ganz had taken over the plush industry with the Web-interactive Webkinz line, Ty unveiled the Beanie Babies 2.0 line—a copycat product with an online component. "My intention was to take the original concept of Beanie Babies and reintroduce it to a new generation of children," he told the *New York Times.* However, the product was too late and too "me-too." Warner, who knew nothing about technology, micromanaged the Web developers, and Beanie Babies 2.0 never achieved the functionality of Webkinz. They sold poorly and in May 2009, Ty quietly canned the line and accompanying Web site and reverted to the original Beanie Babies.

Following the 2008 presidential election, Ty captured the media's attention again ever so briefly—and an inflated secondary market for his products reemerged. On January 1, 2009, two new dolls were added to the Ty Girlz line: Marvelous Malia and Sweet Sasha, both of which were produced without approval from the First Family. Scott Wehrs, the company's president and COO, was reportedly adamantly opposed to the idea and thought it would backfire badly. He left Ty Inc. in January 2009; sources say that the feud over the Sasha and Malia Ty Girlz might have led to the end of his nearly eleven-year run at the company.

The publicity stunt did backfire—at least for public relations.

A spokesman for the First Lady commented, "We believe it is inappropriate to use young private citizens for marketing purposes," even as Warner's spokesperson, Tania Lundeen—the company's VP of sales and my sole official point of contact with Ty Inc.—implausibly refused even to acknowledge that the dolls were named after the president's daughters. "Information concerning the development of our products and how we come up with names, how we select them, how we trademark—that's considered as proprietary. I can't go any further with that question," she told CNN.

Less than a month after their release, the dolls were renamed Sweet Sydney and Marvelous Mariah "in deference to the wishes of the first family," Warner himself said in a statement. Warner then announced that all proceeds from the dolls were to be donated to the Andre Agassi Foundation for Education. The original, opportunistically named dolls were soon selling for $200 each on eBay—twenty times their retail price.

Over the past few years the rise and rebirth of Ty Inc. has continued, but it's a very different company. In its prime Warner resisted the advice of executives who told him that there was money to be made as a licensee for leading entertainment brands. With Ty's brand power and distribution, they told him, he could make a ton of money, even after paying out the royalties, by producing branded plush based on cartoon characters, movies, and sports teams. Warner refused. Part of it was that he didn't want to split the money with another company when he thought he could sell just as many beanbag animals on his own; but he also wasn't much interested in giving up creative control over his plush toys. However, changes in the industry made it impossible for Warner to carry on with his original business model at anything like the sales volume he was accustomed to—and so licensing it was.

In 2004, Ty Inc. signed its first character licensing deal,

which gave the company the right to produce Garfield products—the cartoon cat that, twenty-five years earlier, had launched Dakin into the most successful period of its existence and precipitated the end of Warner's career there. According to a source with knowledge of Ty Inc.'s affairs, brands such as Disney and Hello Kitty, along with professional baseball, hockey, football, and basketball teams, and TV shows like *SpongeBob SquarePants* and *Dora the Explorer* now contribute at least 40 percent of the company's sales. Ty's sales of around $60 million per year, according to an industry source, make it the most successful plush company there is—but at a volume of less than 5 percent of its late-1990s peak. Sales remain strong in Europe, with Ty Europe recording revenues of 11.2 million pounds (18.1 million U.S. dollars) for the year 2013.

Warner's day-to-day involvement in Ty Inc. has varied in recent years, but it now seems to be on an upswing. In 2006 he was spending about 80 percent of his time in Santa Barbara, mostly involved in his hotel empire. Yet by 2009 at least 75 percent of his focus was back in Chicago with the plush business. That year, Ty introduced Beanie Boos—a line of beanbag plush similar in size to Beanie Babies, but each animal in the collection features comically large eyes. The company recently started announcing retirements for pieces online, something it hadn't done in years. Rare Beanie Boos retired just a couple of years ago occasionally sell for hundreds of dollars on eBay, but they show no signs of a transformation into a broader phenomenon. Ty.com no longer has an interactive, community-building component. Although the company does sell its animals directly to the consumer at Ty .com (a sore point with retailers and something Ty Inc. never did during the glory days), the site is buggy and dated. The Web designers have pushed for a redesign, but sources say that these days Warner isn't interested in making the site anything other than a place to buy plush. The company that pioneered the use of the Internet to engage consumers and encourage them to interact with one another has totally given up on that idea at a time when it's all most companies can think about. Lina Trivedi says that looking at the Web site makes her "sad." That is a common word among people who were once a big part of Ty Inc. and the life of Ty Warner.

26

Faith's Problem

After her split with Ty Warner at the turn of the millennium, Faith McGowan sank into a depression that was followed by a desire for vengeance. Like thousands of jilted lovers of public figures before her, McGowan's bloodlust took the form of a revenge memoir. In 2004 she and Robert Keck, an attorney she knew through a friend, created a Web site with the header "Soon to Be Released: Ty and the Beanie Stalk: Faith McGowan's personal story of how she and Ty Warner turned bean bags into billions and lost each other." Their blurb for the memoir, whose tone combined a Harlequin Romance novel with *The Wolf of Wall Street*, read:

> *Faith, Warner's power partner and lover, retained attorney/ author Robert Keck to write the inside story revealing how Warner's personal demons prevented him from ever marrying; how they made Beanies the first great product sold through e-commerce; how work consumed them and the avalanche of money changed them; and how, in the end, Warner made the fatal mistake which killed the goose that laid the golden egg.*
>
> *It's all there in fascinating detail in* Ty and the Beanie Stalk, *a soon to be released 300 page non-fiction book with 16 pages of personal photos and personal handwritten letters. It is the writing and the consummate blending of a business story and a love story which distinguishes* Ty and the Beanie Stalk.

They secured a literary agent but failed to attract a major publisher. Keck set up a deal with a vanity publishing outfit, but McGowan recalls that he wanted her to pay him a fee for negotiating it—and indemnify him from any legal liability in the extremely likely event that Warner responded to the book's publication with a lawsuit.

That wouldn't be necessary: when the announcement went up on their Web site and buzz started building on the few remaining Beanie-collecting message boards, Warner called her and they talked for ten hours. McGowan put the manuscript in her closet and stopped talking to Robert Keck. By the time I met McGowan in the summer of 2012, she was living in a $2,400 per month rental a few miles from the home Warner bought her as part of their split. That home, which is worth something like $5 million and owned free and clear, was rented out; the proceeds finance McGowan's living expenses. Any financial adviser would have told her to sell it, but she couldn't bear to. Once, while checking on the house between tenants, she found a stuffed Ty cat the previous tenant had found in a closet and perched on a mantel in the living room. She ran from the house in tears.

McGowan, tall and lean and with somewhat unruly red hair, was friendly as she shushed her two large dogs and finished making a meal-replacement smoothie. Her home was a museum to her time with Ty Warner, and she seemed to live in a state of suspended reality—surrounded by memories, waiting for the day when Warner would come back to her, just as the most optimistic speculators hope that Beanie Babies themselves will soon make a comeback. The first thing I noticed upon entering was a built-in, glass-fronted bookcase filled with Ty prototypes, early Ty cats, and a Steiff dog that Ty had bought her. There was also Kaleidoscope the Cat—a beautiful rainbow-colored Beanie Baby that Faith's sister, at one time a creative director at Ty Inc., designed. Faith showed me a photo of her then preteen daughters at the beach in the mid-1990s; it was, she said, the first time they had been to Santa Barbara, where Ty was having cheek implants removed.

The house and the money were nice, but it was clear that what McGowan really wanted, more than a decade later, was Ty Warner. She'd had other relationships since him but nothing serious. Faith and I drove around Santa Barbara in her Jeep SUV and she showed me the homes and hotels Ty had built and bought with the money he'd made when they were together. She showed me the landscaping at his Biltmore hotel—which, she said, Warner was constantly having ripped up. She made the connection between the landscaping and the constant changes to Beanie Babies that had led, entirely accidentally, to the first of the rare pieces. "Nothing is ever enough and nothing is ever good enough," she told me, "because his soul is empty."

She cried several times, and after a few hours she told me that she couldn't talk about him any more in one day. The hardest part of having a relationship with Warner end, Patricia Roche once told me, "is realizing that he didn't care about you—not even a little bit." McGowan, Roche says, had never recognized that her relationship with Warner hadn't been the fairy tale she'd once thought it was. Ten years after Faith last had any meaningful contact with him, she stayed in Santa Barbara—with few friends and no family.

Faith and I continued talking by phone regularly. A few months after we first met, I was visiting my mother on Cape Cod and had given Faith the landline number. I was out when she called; my mother answered. Faith seemed in no hurry to get off the phone: she talked about her day, her plans to see Norah Jones in concert, and the weather in Santa Barbara. My mother, a psychotherapist, could tell that Faith was lonely. She thought about staying on and chatting with her but didn't.

In June 2013 Faith McGowan died suddenly.

Ty Warner was distraught over the news. He called his sister and described their time together as the best years of his life. He told her that he had left McGowan with plenty of money. Joy replied that for some people it wasn't all about money.

Faith's daughters, Lauren and Jenna, tried to get in touch with Warner after their mother's death. However, they didn't hear from him until he surprised them with an appearance at her funeral. They'd remembered him as having been paranoid; that was also their experience with his reemergence in their lives. He'd been looking at Faith's Facebook page, he explained, and was concerned about the people she'd been associating with. He suspected foul play and told them that he wanted to hire a private investigator. They declined the offer. A week after the funeral, he invited Lauren and Jenna to his Oak Brook home for lunch. "You know," he said. "I should have married your mother." "Don't you ever say that again!" Lauren screamed at him. Warner apologized.

His sister, Joy, posted this comment on the obituary the funeral home posted: "Faith, I was so lucky to have met you and your beautiful daughters. Ty knows you were the best thing in his life. I'm so sorry he threw all of you away. But now his time is coming . . ."

27

Ty's Problem

On September 18, 2013, Warner was charged with tax evasion related to a secret Swiss bank account where he'd been holding more than $100 million—the largest balance of any of the seventy taxpayers pursued by the government over such accounts. The income the federal government alleged Warner "went to great lengths to hide from his accountants and the IRS" was just over $3 million, and the total taxes evaded amounted to less than $1 million—although the tax loss for the entire period of conduct was far higher. Warner agreed to pay a $53.5 million civil penalty and the government announced that he would plead guilty at his arraignment in October. Federal sentencing guidelines called for forty-six to fifty-seven months in federal prison.

Public reaction to Warner's legal plight was swift and negative. It was also intermingled with the memory of the Beanie Babies that hadn't lived up to the expectations for great value. Jimmy Fallon joked, "The Beanie Babies creator owes $53 million for tax evasion. If he sells them all, he'll just owe . . . $53 million."

Faith McGowan had made vague reference to the account when I spoke with her, suggesting that it had been part of Warner's contingency plan—if things in the United States were to somehow go bust with all his hotel deals, he had squirreled away $100 million in judgment-proof wealth in Europe. When I called Joy Warner to talk about it, the sixty-four-year-old was on lunch break at her landscaping job. The account had been opened in

1996—the year, Joy remembers, that Ty had reneged on his promise to build her a $100,000 house because, he said, he couldn't afford it.

Two days before Ty's sentencing, I went to visit his sister for a second time at her home in Camano Island, Washington. When I'd first called her, she'd spoken negatively of "my famous brother," dismissing him as selfish, narcissistic, and obsessed with an opulent lifestyle that didn't interest her. When I'd first met her, Joy was preparing for a hip replacement surgery in a few weeks—surgery that her brother had declined to help pay for, instead advising her to turn to the seven children she'd raised with a former husband, none of whom Warner had ever met. When she asked him for a $1,000 loan, he'd refused via text message. He'd helped her out briefly in the wake of her divorce more than a decade earlier, but for the most part Warner's tremendous wealth has not eased her struggles.

Joy has lived in the same home for twenty-seven years—with old carpets, Native American tourist-grade art, two and a half acres of land, a National Rifle Association sticker on the door, and the scent of the four dogs that live with her, all of whom she adopted or rescued. There are also three horses, including two miniature ponies. "This is the first time I've ever had mini horses because you can't ride 'em, you can't do anything with them, but they needed a home, and I probably have this sign SUCKER written on my head," she says. Two of the adopted dogs are blind. Recently, when one of the dogs had to be put down, Joy brought the body home to show the other dogs where she was burying it. Previously, when one of her dogs died, she had left the body at the vet's—and she says the other dogs spent months looking for him.

The house was a two-story building when she bought it, but Joy had it downsized to reduce maintenance and give her time for gardening—putting her at odds with the general trend of homeowners in America and even more at odds with her brother's penchant for the palatial. She works two jobs in patient care and reflexology to complement the landscaping income, and she keeps the spare bedroom in her house outfitted for patients. She says it's easy for her to relax in her "purple space" where she can meditate and that her greatest joy comes from helping others relax and trust her. "People fall asleep when I'm working on them," she says. "And I can get their body balanced because they are that relaxed."

She showed me her father's will, along with his letters to her and some family photos—including an especially handsome one of Ty when he was in high school. Then she told me more about the childhood in La Grange, Illinois, that she'd like to forget.

Hal Warner began molesting his daughter in 1955 when Joy was six years old. Ty, who knew nothing of the abuse, was eleven. When Hal was home, Joy often ran away. When the police picked her up and asked why she ran away (again), she told them—but they didn't believe her. When she was nine, she told her mother, who responded by disowning her. Georgia refused to speak to or interact with the girl who was, as she saw it, sleeping with her husband. That was the state of the household Ty and Joy lived in through high school. Decades later, Hal apologized to Joy; he told her that molesting her had been his way of resisting the need to cheat on his wife, who was unavailable. Joy once mentioned that explanation to Ty, who was puzzled by it; "Dad cheated on Mom all the time," Joy says Ty told her.

In the middle of this family dynamic, Ty acted out in his own ways. During his freshman year of high school, Joy says she followed him and his friends one day and discovered a trove of televisions and stereos that she thought they must have been stealing and selling. She told Hal. Terrified that his son would end up in jail, Hal, over Georgia's objections, dispatched Ty to St. John's

Northwestern Military Academy in Delafield, Wisconsin. After Ty was dropped off at the train station, his parents separated; the divorce was acrimonious. The legal battle dragged on for more than a decade until their marriage was officially dissolved on April 1, 1971.

St. John's is an elite prep school offering military-style structure to students who often come from wealthy families. Warner excelled: he was placed in Company A, the group that comprised the biggest, strongest, most athletic boys. The divisions ensured fairness in the intracompany tackle football games, which were played without pads. Warner played tennis and basketball and participated in the school's Stars & Circle Club, an elite academic honor society. He graduated with the rank of Fly Sergeant with five silver stars and stars in choir, football, basketball, and baseball, where he was a memorably good defensive center fielder.

Every hour of every day at St. John's was tightly regimented, and the new boy–old boy system exposed students to abuse from upperclassmen. For their first three months at the school, students were new boys and, as one classmate puts it, "completely stripped of all your authority and pride and arrogance and everything." They ran to all their meals and had their personal appearance inspected by a squad leader three times a day. James Novak, Warner's roommate at St. John's, remembers him as intelligent, popular, and preoccupied with concerns about his skin. Warner often got up at 5:00 a.m. to play a round of golf, rushing back to the dorms in time for morning reveille. Warner was an excellent marcher with perfect posture—and he had a fondness for Chubby Checker's fad hit "The Twist."

St. John's sought to instill militaristic toughness in its students. As one former cadet puts it, "They wanted you to be respectful to authority and to women, and tough as hell." He remembered changing the words to the cadences they marched to. ("If I die on the Russian front, box me up with a Russian cunt!" he bellowed into the phone when I asked him for an example.) Joy says Ty hated the school and that he was bullied there. Former students remember hazing that went beyond what would be tolerated today, and Joy recalls Ty calling home in tears after he'd been knifed in a fight.

A spokesman for the school told *People* magazine that Warner has asked St. Johns not to comment at all on his time there. One classmate who coordinates the school's reunions said that Warner "actually doesn't want anything to do with the school"— and said he knew the reason. But he declined to be more specific.

"I've had contact with him three or four times. But he's very elusive, very standoffish," says Gary Richert, St. John's director of alumni relations.

In the fall of 1962, Warner entered Kalamazoo College, a private liberal arts school with a freshman class of 250, and his only yearbook photo shows him with a military-school crew cut, which makes him look more formal than any of his classmates. He majored in theater, and the *Kalamazoo College Index*'s December 7, 1962, edition includes a review of the student production of *Antigone*. The critic praises Warner's performance as Creon, the ruler of Thebes who orders that Polynices's corpse be left to rot and then commands that Antigone be buried alive as punishment for defying him.

"A new face in the cast was that of Ty Warner, as Creon; with his lack of previous theatre experience, he is to be complimented for his success," the review notes. "Playing a role very difficult to make live, because of the necessity of acting Creon's [*sic*] some fifty years, he is to be praised for his near and sometimes completely successful acting. His voice was a bit tiring, but with more work in the theatre he should improve and move to even more successful accomplishments."

Warner dropped out of college after one year and never returned. His sister and one former classmate say he got a girl pregnant and brought her home to his father. Joy says Hal paid the girl off and sent Ty packing. Warner seems to have left Kalamazoo without a trace. As the school's most successful former student (but not graduate—a distinction that is awkward for the college's marketing purposes), he is the topic of conversation at every reunion, but no one seems to remember much about him.

In a sentencing memorandum arguing for probation rather than incarceration, Ty's lawyers referred obliquely to these early years of his life as "unhappy." The details, however, were fictionalized. Just as Warner has always told his life story, the memo neglected to mention that it had been Hal who got Ty his first job in the toy industry. It referred to his childhood, which included three years of private school, as "devoid of any educational advantages" and attributed his decision to drop out of college to the difficulty he had in paying for it. Ty's sister, however, says their father paid for college. The horrors of Ty's childhood were, in his telling of it, mostly reduced to a tale of poverty—perhaps the only bad thing that it wasn't.

———————

In October 2013 Warner appeared in federal court in Chicago for his arraignment. He wore a loose-fitting pin-striped suit. He sat in the front row, talking quietly with his team of attorneys while he waited for his case to be called. Outside the courtroom a PR person he'd hired to handle the reporters seemed as uninformed as anyone else: he wasn't sure whether Warner had a girlfriend or wife; he had no kids as far he knew. The only thing he was certain about was that Warner wouldn't be available to answer questions.

As he stood before the bench, Warner seemed old and broken. His long, styled hair had been recut in a more boyish style but its artificial coloring, combined with his extremely visible plastic surgery and expensive tortoiseshell glasses, made him appear meek. "He looks like he should be in a wax museum," someone whispered, according to a *Chicago* magazine story. He repeatedly asked the judge to speak louder, citing his failing hearing. The judge explained his right to a trial, and the gallery snickered when he said, "If you couldn't afford a lawyer, which I think doesn't apply to you . . ."

Asked about his education, Warner described one year at Kalamazoo College; when he was asked to explain what his crime was, he started by saying that he had opened a Swiss bank account and hadn't told anyone about it.

"I apologize for my conduct," he said while crying. "I had great success with my company, and I had so much to be thankful for." (When I mentioned that he'd cried to Patricia Roche, she said, "Did the jury stand up and applaud his performance?" On Twitter, @philvettel joked that while tearfully pleading guilty, "[Warner] also announced the release of Blubber, the repentant whale.")

The judge cut him off with, "You'll have a chance to bare your soul at sentencing." Warner agreed to reappear for sentencing in three months, and when his lawyer explained that Ty's business obligations required extensive foreign travel, the prosecutor and the judge quickly agreed that he could keep his passport. The prosecutor even volunteered that he wouldn't require Warner to report his travels to the court. Then it was over. Warner and his entourage struggled past a throng of media to a waiting car. "Mr. Warner, was this just about greed?" one local reporter asked.

28

Departures

When I first met Lina Trivedi, the college student who'd had the idea to put Beanie Babies on the Internet in 1996, she was living modestly in Beaver Dam, Wisconsin, with her two-and-a-half-year-old daughter. Trivedi shuffles appointments with the twelve doctors it takes to treat the child's illness: Goltz syndrome, a rare skin condition that has cost her a leg and covered her body with skin lesions. Older Beanie Babies are scattered throughout their apartment. Sometimes Lina tells her daughter that Mommy wrote the poems, but she's not sure she believes her.

The Web development business she and her brother started when they left Ty Inc. never got off the ground. She landed a short-term contract working on a Web site for the rock band Mötley Crüe and did some work for the Spice Girls—but the company quickly fell behind on its bills, and Trivedi was desperate.

A public records search shows nineteen liens and judgments against Trivedi from creditors, including electric companies, Discover Bank, and several payday lenders—most of it dating back to her failed start-up. In late 2001 she was charged with a string of felonies. According to the indictment, the charges stemmed from Trivedi's having passed dozens of forged postal money orders—made on a color printer—over a period of nine months, each in the amount of $614.70. In a motion for a departure from sentencing guidelines, her attorney argued that the crime had been committed as she tried to keep a failing business afloat.

When Trivedi got out of jail, she was homeless. She went to the Chicago Urban League in search of help finding a job. The caseworkers were skeptical when Trivedi described her background: she claimed that she had great sales and customer-service experience, was an experienced Web developer, and had written the poems for all the Beanie Babies. She started working for the Urban League, counseling less-skilled felons and helping with outreach and multimedia projects. In her free time she sang and danced in Chicago clubs as part of a Euro-trance group while wearing a monitoring ankle bracelet as part of her house arrest. Sometimes she had to race home from clubs to avoid breaking curfew.

She neither contacted Warner during the bad times nor begrudged him the money she never made. "There probably were days that I would sort of daydream about what I would have done if I did get a small sliver of the pie," she says. "But you know, it was not meant for me to have."

For all the creativity that came out of Ty Inc. and all that the people who worked there learned, success at the company has rarely been a stepping-stone to an illustrious career. For most people who worked at Ty, it seems, their time there represented the peak of their earnings. These days, Trivedi supports herself through freelance Web development work; a Google search for Lina Trivedi mostly yields mug shots.

By 2004 Bill Harlow was deeply in debt to Ty Inc. as a result of the failure of the Beanie Kids line and the excess inventory he was choking on. One of Ty's executives came to visit. They discussed Ty Canada's dwindling cash flow and the trouble the company was having paying down its line of credit. "The ride on Ty's coattails is over," the man explained—and then the company called the loan and shut down Harlow's business. Harlow hasn't spoken with Warner since. "The downside to Ty was there was always a little bit of a feeling like everything is a sale. He's the ultimate sales guy. *The ultimate sales guy.* He was making a sale with everything that he did. When there isn't a pitch to make or there isn't something to be gained, there's no time in his life for you." Harlow had considered Warner a friend for a decade; they'd talked weekly, and when he was in Chicago, Warner had let him drive his collection of luxury cars. But once it was over, it was over. Harlow still occasionally has dreams about Warner.

Next it was Patricia Roche's turn. The pair had spent two decades bickering endlessly while getting rich together, but things had finally reached a point of no return. They agreed, at Warner's insistence, to part ways in 2004. "I told Ty's CFO, who is still a good friend, that I wanted Ty to be there for the final meeting," Roche remembers. "Not like the way he treated everyone he got rid of, by sending someone else to do the job."

She flew to New York City and went to Warner's Four Seasons Hotel, where they had arranged to finalize the details ending her involvement with the company as the head of Ty Europe— the company that had been Ty UK when she started, but had since expanded its distribution to a much larger area. When she got to the suite at the Four Seasons, she was told Warner wasn't yet available. "I'll wait," she responded. She was told that that might not be a good idea and that perhaps they should get on with it without him. Roche was insistent: she'd met Ty when he was depressed after Dakin fired him, and she'd sat in his apartment stuffing the first Himalayan cats he ordered from Korea. She'd been there for everything as he went from rags to riches, and she wasn't leaving until he came to talk to her. She plopped her purse down next to her and waited.

Finally, Ty Warner walked in—nervous and conflict avoidant but probably unsurprised. He'd been a billionaire for five years, but there was still one person left who would talk to him however the hell she wanted to talk to him.

"Thank you for twenty years," she told him, as she stood up and shook his hand. "You're a bastard, and I hope to God I never see you again." It was the last time she saw him. At her wedding in Chicago three years later, a messenger arrived with a note from Warner telling her how proud he was of everything she'd accomplished. The newly marrieds stood in front of their friends, shaking the envelope in the hope that money would fall out. It did not.

Retired soap-opera-star-turned-Beanie-hoarder Chris Robinson started his collection in 1998, at the absolute height of the market. During the decline in 1999 and early 2000, he'd doubled down on his gamble: when local gift shops went out of business, Robinson bought out their Beanie Baby inventories at wholesale prices, fancying himself a value investor. Between that and his earlier days lining up at stores as they unloaded shipments, his investment in Beanies stretched well past the $100,000 mark. Today, much like the stock speculators who simply stopped logging in to their brokerage accounts post-2000, he can't bring himself to go online and check the current values.

"Before I die, I guess I have to find out what they're currently worth," Robinson, now in his midseventies, says. "If it takes twenty years, the kids will all have them. They can split them up—and play with Beanie Babies. Or sell them. . . .

"You wanna forget it. Did I really do that? But it was fun, it was exciting," he adds. At least some good came of the investment: his son Chris Robinson Jr. majored in film at the University of Arizona and took a class on documentary filmmaking.

Robinson decided to tell the story of his family's "sordid history with Beanie Babies." The visuals were aided by the fact that the elder Robinson still lives with the horde of nearly twenty thousand Beanie Babies he acquired at a cost of about $100,000—all meticulously packed away in bookcases, plastic display cases, and cartons with labels like "6 Beanie Buddies, ALL PEANUT."

The video was just a class project, but Robinson posted it online in 2009. It received few views at first. I interviewed father and son about it in late 2011 while I was working on the proposal for this book. Then in July 2013, out of nowhere, the video went viral. It received hundreds of thousands of views and was the subject of stories on National Public Radio, ABC News, the *Huffington Post*, *Gawker*, and *Entertainment Weekly*, among many others. The Beanies might not have paid for college, but for a new grad looking for his first film industry job in a tough economy, the cautionary tale that went viral was an invaluable addition to his résumé.

29

Endurance

The world of plush collecting was in decline before Beanie Babies came along, but the craze gave the entire industry a reprieve. When Beanies collapsed, however, stuffed-animal fatigue followed, and most of the teddy bear collecting magazines and museums shuttered over the next few years. As the role of teddy bears in the lives of children is crowded out by the ubiquitous miniscreens that entertain them at ever-younger ages, the number of adults with a nostalgic connection to plush declines, too. "Kids used to want plush up to age twelve. Now you can't sell it to a kid who's older than five," says Steven Greenfield, CEO of Commonwealth Toy & Novelty Co., Inc., which recently scored a hit with the license for Angry Birds plush—a rare breakout seller but, in a sign of the times, one that came as a result of the success of a smartphone game.

The implosion of Beanie Babies and the rise of eBay brought the broader collectibles industry to its knees. Many of the collectibles market's former stars say that eBay was responsible for its demise. "Ten years earlier, it was difficult to connect with people and find pieces," remembers Dean Griff, the artist behind the Charming Tails figurines that were popular in the late 1990s. "There was a perceived value because it was so hard to find that piece. But then people could go on eBay and find five hundred of that piece. That's what killed it."

Many of the major manufacturers went into bankruptcy, and none of them have anywhere close to the sales they had in the late 1990s. Precious Moments, one of the most popular figurine lines, saw its sales plunge from $206 million at its 1996 height to $55.7 million in 2004—and Precious Moments fared better than most. There was an evaporation of the entire industry that began with Joseph Segel and his National Commemorative Society and climaxed with Beanie Babies.

A few Beanie collectors remain, however, and I went to Fayetteville, North Carolina, to meet the most fanatical of them.

———————

When my friend Ryan dropped me off at the house, he thought it would be the last time he'd see me. All that either of us really knew about the trip was that I was there to meet with a sixty-four-year-old man who owned a collection of sixteen thousand Ty products and lived with his thirty-two-year-old daughter, who made a full-time job of cataloging her father's Beanie Babies. The first thing we saw when we pulled up in front of the house was that the windows in one of the rooms on the second floor were covered in tinfoil. "I am not," Ryan said, "dropping you off at the home of an obsessive Beanie Baby collector who covers his windows with tinfoil." But he did.

You could be forgiven for thinking Leon and Sondra Schlossberg were married; she's his daughter, not his wife, but he assured me that lots of people think they're a couple.

"People are like, 'Hey, nice going,' when they see us together," Leon says and looks at Sondra, who is thin and attractive. Their Web site is called leonandsondra.com and, Sondra writes, "As the site's name may suggest, and I hope it does, we have been a close team for a long time. Leon is my father, the biggest inspiration in my life and my best friend." On his biography page Leon writes that "Sondra and I are the greatest team imaginable. She is my best friend, my partner in a variety of business endeavors and the inspiration for almost everything I do or write." When

Sondra studied for her undergraduate degree at the University of Maryland, Leon went to the same school to finish his degree. Their diplomas are together in one frame in the house they share. It's a reminder of their seemingly permanent status as a singular unit.

Sondra generally calls her father Leon rather than Dad. Leon is something of an illeist, dropping his own name into conversations more than anyone over age five I've ever met, but he is not without charm. He's tall, portly around the midsection, and was wearing an untucked, oversize Dickies button-down shirt. He's extremely talkative, especially when the topic is Beanie Babies. After our meeting he e-mailed me to apologize: "I do feel obligated to apologize for interrupting you so many times. Sondra says I tend to get over-animated and talkative when it comes to the topic of Ty or Beanie Babies. She normally steps in to calm me down a little when I start in with wild hand gesturing."

Their house is a 2,400-square-foot white elephant, and it would be roomy inside if it weren't for all the Beanie Babies— which, as is the case when you have sixteen thousand of them, are everywhere. Leon has to remove hundreds of Beanies from the bed each night before sleeping in it. The tinfoil, it turned out, is in the room they use exclusively as a studio for taking professional-quality photographs of every Ty product they acquire.

Two oversize display-bear Beanies (with X and O lipstick prints) sit on chairs in the living room. There are also stacks of large plastic bins filled with Ty products and boxes with an almost complete collection of Beanie-related magazines.

"Did you pull all this stuff out for me?" I asked—but as soon as I said it, I was afraid I knew the answer: there was no way they had the closet space for all this stuff.

"No, this is how it is," the pro-gun Republican with twenty

years of service in the army and seventeen years in civil service told me.

The home has the look of many houses on the reality TV show *Hoarders* except that it isn't dirty and the clutter is intensely focused—it is virtually *all* Ty products. Leon says he devotes about sixty hours per week to his Ty collection, and his daughter is similarly absorbed. When Ty's line of squeeze-them-and-they-shout-gibberish Monstaz was released, Leon digitally recorded the sounds and then played them back at slower speeds to see whether there was any kind of hidden message. There wasn't, but the whole exercise is a nice summation of how Leon combines his obsession with a children's toy with his military-honed affection for technology and order. Sondra spends time trying to connect with dealers and traders in countries like France and Israel, where special versions of Ty products not sold in the United States are available.

Leon assures me that Ty products are not the driving force behind his life. The driving force, he explains, is the Ty Museum he will build.

"Huh?" I respond.

Leon talks about the museum quickly, easily, and in great detail. He describes the pricing rubric for admissions—discounts for senior citizens and kids and a free gift included with admission. Next he tells me about the Mobile Museum, a trailer stocked with rare Beanie Babies that will travel to schools to raise awareness for the Ty Museum, whose location will be determined by tax credits and taxpayer matching funds. He's drawn plans for the museum, but he wouldn't show them to me (they're not ready yet, he says).

He ushers me into a spare bedroom with stacks and stacks and boxes and boxes of hundreds of Color Me Beanies—a white bear Ty produced in 2002 that came with markers that could be used to color it and make it one's own.

"You might be wondering," Leon says, "why you can't buy Color Me Beanies on eBay for less than five dollars or so these days."

Actually, I admit, I hadn't been wondering about that.

"Well," he continues, "this is going to be the official Beanie Baby of the museum."

He explains that the museum will also have a McDonald's annexed to it—a food court and homage to the record-breaking Teenie Beanie promotion. The only problem—Leon says he's still working on a solution to this—will be making sure that the smell of fast food doesn't waft into the museum galleries.

Leon's museum, like stuffed animals and speculation in general, brings him happiness, optimism, and the comfort of a finely elaborated dream. Leon's descent into Beanie fixation—accompanied by his daughter—came after a tough divorce. While I was at his home, two more boxes of Ty products arrived, including more than a dozen different variations of SpongeBob and Hello Kitty Beanie Babies that Ty had recently released.

It's these variations, not the rare pieces, Leon says, that will make his museum an entertaining experience.

"You see one Hello Kitty Beanie Baby and it doesn't really look like much. But you see a hundred different ones and all of a sudden, that's something," he says.

When I e-mailed Leon to ask him if he could try to articulate what it was about Beanie Babies that so captivated him, his response lacked deep psychological reasoning.

"OK . . . why the Beanie Babies?" he wrote. "I'm speaking for myself here . . . They are incredibly cute/adorable/precious/endearing/etc. Does that sound strange coming from a guy? Probably a little, but that's just the way it is. They appeal to children and they probably appeal to me in the same way.

"[T]here are so many Ty collectibles, there's no reason to go looking elsewhere. Ty made an impact that far exceeds that of any other plush manufacturer. We enjoy documenting that and I look forward to watching the looks of awe when visitors enter the main exhibit hall of our museum to discover just how many thousands of collectibles Ty produced. Bottom line, we needed something to do after I retire and nobody appeared to be doing the 'Ty Museum' thing. What a great niche.

"We're not thin-skinned. We know we have a lot of planning, coordination, purchasing and fund-raising ahead of us but it's an enjoyable challenge that will translate into a lot of smiles from children and adults who will be able to visit our museum."

In a follow-up e-mail, he attached a photo of Burrows the Meerkat—a late-model Beanie Baby that came after Ty had worked his way through all the common animals. Burrows, Leon told me, "decided to volunteer as my keyboard guard."

"Try to convince me these critters don't have personalities," he wrote.

———————

The allure of plush is also irresistible for some within the industry. Few people who experience success here are ever able to extricate themselves, even long after anyone from the outside can see that they should have moved on.

Robert Solomon built Applause into a worldwide leader in stuffed toys and then used it to acquire Dakin in 1995 before selling the whole thing for a fat payday. Other than Ty Warner, he was the most successful stuffed-animal impresario of his generation. He took over Dakin once again in 2001, with backing from Prudential Life Insurance. It was a small acquisition and one that, in his prime, Solomon easily would have been able to fund on his own. But he'd lost his entire net worth in the stock market and was starting over—with his reputation as a onetime wunderkind as his only asset following a long battle with bipolar disorder. "The money was wired about an hour ago," he told cheering employees as they assembled in the company's cafeteria, according to a *Fortune* Small Business profile. "The documents have been signed, and it's our company."

In interviews after the acquisition Solomon was frank in his assessment of industry challenges: "Over the years what's changed in the stuffed animal or plush business is that, with all of the direct importing coming out of Asia, plush in many ways has become a commodity, and price is what matters to many major retailers."

Solomon, a charismatic visionary, had a plan to escape the cost-driven rat race: revive Dream Pets, the line of velveteen toys that had launched the Dakin brand prior to the plane crash that killed its founding family. It was the line that Harold Nizamian had sold while speeding around California, accumulating tickets on his way back to his MBA classes, and the line that had transformed Ty Warner from a layabout college dropout into a superstar salesman. Solomon hoped that Dream Pets also had the power to revive him and relaunch him to the top of the toy industry. In early 2004 Solomon decided that Dream Pets would be the next Beanie Baby. He told everyone he knew that it was going to happen. It made a certain sense: Warner had learned the plush business at Dakin, and with their small size and endless, whimsical variety, Dream Pets were one of the lines whose success had inspired Beanie Babies.

Solomon designed them painstakingly. First he pulled the original drawings and production samples from the company archives. These were the drawings that Virginia Benes-Kemp, the Dakin product chief in the 1960s, had been working on when Warner, clad in a camel hair coat, knocked on her door to talk about his product ideas. Next Solomon spent endless hours trying to replicate the exact feel of the original Dream Pets that had been introduced in 1957. In a heavy-handed effort to capture the Beanie Baby magic, he also hand numbered each piece to promote collectability.

Then, just as Warner had done forty years ago, he went out

to sell them. When Solomon met with the buyer for Cracker Barrel Old Country Store (the first chain to carry Ty products), he offered, without notes, detailed biographical sketches for each of the twelve samples he'd brought. Cracker Barrel responded with a huge order for the five hundred stores it operated in forty-one states. Beanie Babies had begun as a toy inspired by Dream Pets and then had become a collectible; now Dream Pets were relaunching as a collectible inspired by Beanie Babies.

"I know that our Dream Pets will find a place in so many hearts just as they have in mine," Solomon said in a press release. "Phenomenon's [sic] happen because they're supposed to, not because they are planned.

"I'm sure that everyone will find a Dream Pet that they will want to call their own, because the Pets are so much more than stuffed animals—like all of us, they're individuals."

On March 15, 2004, the first one million pieces were shipped to stores all over America. However, consumers weren't interested, and the Dream Pets reorders Solomon had been counting on didn't materialize. His company's balance sheet deteriorated, and he lost the license to produce Disney products. His focus on the specialty retailers that had made Ty Warner so rich failed at a time when the industry was contracting. Just over five months after the Dream Pets launch, Solomon died of a self-inflicted gunshot wound to the head.

"He bet the farm on Dream Pets," one consultant told a reporter. A line that had brought so much happiness to its creators and customers but had been tinged with tragedy almost from the beginning was gone forever. Post-Solomon, Dakin went into bankruptcy, and in late 2005 the brand's intellectual property was acquired for $835,000 by Big Lots, the discount retail chain. But Big Lots has done little with the name: the only Dakin-branded product listed on the company's Web site is a fourteen-ounce bottle of baby oil with the teddy bear of Ty Warner's dream emblazoned on the label. It's the first time the Dakin logo has ever been on baby oil, and it sells for $1.50.

———————

One of Warner's many lawsuits reunited him with his former boss, Harold Nizamian. In 2000 Ty sued a start-up, Softbelly's, over its marketing of Screenie Beanies, a line of plush toys for cleaning computer monitor screens. Warner's legal strategy, as usual, was to assert an exclusive right to the term "beanie" when it came to the marketing of toys, and the defense's task was to show that the word "beanie" was generic. To help make that case, Softbelly's hired Nizamian as an expert witness to testify that, for as long as he'd been in the business, beanbag toys had been called beanies. They had been called that at Dakin, Nizamian remembered, and that's what he was prepared to tell the court.

Warner wasn't pleased. He called Nizamian the day before his scheduled deposition, and in a seventeen-minute phone conversation, asked him not to testify. Nizamian says Warner also dangled the possibility of a job working for Ty in Europe, where he'd finally be able to use his foreign-language skills.

"I realized after speaking to Ty that it was a very important matter to him, and even though I didn't understand all of the particulars, I felt if he felt that strongly about it . . . maybe it would be best if I did not go," Nizamian told the court. "Because of the seriousness in his voice and the importance to him . . . I figured I'd just rather not get involved." Nizamian then declined to testify. Based on the witness-tampering issue, in 2005 a judge ordered Ty Inc. to forfeit the $716,046 it had won in the case— but that was reversed on appeal in 2008. Warner never did give the struggling toymaker a job, and they haven't spoken since.

Right after Warner's tax evasion case made news, I logged on to Nizamian's Timeless-Toys Inc. company Web site to order Bart, the stuffed bear puppet he'd shown me at Toy Fair the first time we met. A few minutes after I placed the order, Nizamian called to thank me for my $11.99 purchase and to promise that he'd drop it at the post office in the morning. Not surprisingly, we also talked about the Ty Warner indictment news.

Of everyone who has known Warner, only Nizamian seemed especially sympathetic to his plight. For all his gifts and talents, the best plush peddler Nizamian had ever known was never able to overcome the worst parts of his personality. "It was never going to be enough," Nizamian says. "It's like a Greek tragedy." When I met Nizamian in person he was in the process of moving his office closer to home, and that move was complete by the time we talked about Warner's legal problems. The official Web site for Timeless-Toys lists a new address in San Mateo, California—but a quick search reveals that it's just a virtual office: rates start at $130 per month, conference rooms are available for $25 to $45 per hour, and Nizamian keeps his inventory in a self-storage unit. Still, the toymaker is in business—and if you log on to Timeless-Toys.com and place an order (payment is via PayPal), the former CEO of what was at one time the top plush company in the world will mail it to you himself. He might even, as he did for me, toss in an extra lamb puppet as a special gift.

————————

In December 2013, less than a month before Ty Warner was scheduled to be sentenced, I sat in a Starbucks near Wrigley Field, discussing Warner's life with a former high-level executive at the company. He said Warner had told him to think of him as a second father. (When I mention this to Patricia Roche, she laughs. "If you were older than him, he said you were like his father. If you were younger than him, he said you were like his son. If you were approximately his age, you were like brothers.")

"So," the former Ty Inc. executive told me, "Ty will probably go to prison—probably for a few years. And then he'll get out.

And sometime in the next twenty years, he'll die. And that'll be that. It will have been a pretty sad life."

For all of Warner's gifts, talents, and luck, success was never fulfilling. The speculative craze for Beanie Babies had left most buyers out however much they'd spent on the toys, and those dashed dreams made Warner one of the richest people in the world. On balance, though, he was probably far less content than the average failed Beanie speculator. Once I had some understanding of Warner's character, I started asking everyone who had known him whether he was happy. Some laughed at the question. Roche quipped that Ty couldn't be happy unless he was miserable. His sister said she'd asked him that the last time they'd spoken and that he hadn't answered. One former employee said, "Mental health isn't his strong suit." Among a group of former Ty employees who get together every couple of years, Warner's capacity for happiness is a frequent topic of conversation. Even before the tax evasion case, the consensus was that no one wanted to trade places with him.

At Warner's sentencing in January 2014, the judge opted for a surprisingly light sentence. Although federal sentencing guidelines called for him to serve four to five years in prison, Judge Charles Kocoras opted for two years' probation and five hundred hours of community service. Kocoras explained his decision by citing the seventy letters from current and former Ty employees, business associates (including Warner's own lawyer), and heads of charitable organizations who attested to Warner's good character and philanthropy.

The U.S. government, which is appealing the sentence, noted that in the context of Warner's wealth, his total of $35.7 million in charitable contributions was unremarkable. "Charitable donations over the course of fourteen years that equal approximately 2 percent of current net worth are not extraordinary," the prosecution argued. "The median household net worth was

$68,828 in 2011; if that household gave 2 percent of its net worth, or $1,377, over fourteen years (less than $100 per year), it would not be deemed an 'exceptional' amount. Given Warner's net worth, to qualify as extraordinary, he would have had to donate a much greater percentage of his wealth to charity. Additionally, in no sense did [the] defendant's charitable contributions cause him any deprivation or sacrifice, as his assets include a $153 million residence, numerous luxury automobiles, and art valued at over $41 million."

When I texted Warner's sister about the sentence, she wrote back to say that her prayers had been answered; their relationship has had its ups and downs, but she says he's her brother, and she loves him.

Columnists and bloggers, especially in Chicago, mocked the sentence. Writing in the *Chicago Sun-Times*, Mark Brown explained that "to fulfill his community service, Kocoras ordered Warner to work with three Chicago schools where the billionaire says he can organize a curriculum to teach students how to manufacture and sell a product such as a school mascot modeled after his Beanie Baby success. That's cool, and maybe on the side, he could help them put on a school play. I'd recommend the 1959 musical, 'Never Steal Anything Small,' starring Jimmy Cagney. These are my favorite lyrics: 'Steal $100 and they put you in stir; Steal $100 million they address you as sir.'"

A month after his sentencing, Warner was back at Toy Fair— in unusually but understandably good spirits. He invited a few dozen industry leaders to his Ty Warner Penthouse at his Four Seasons Hotel, two and a half miles from the Javits Center. The cocktail party was scheduled for 6:00 p.m. to 8:00 p.m., and his guests listened to the pianist he'd hired, drank, ate the hors d'oeuvres offered by the uniformed staff, and ogled the apartment. For $45,000 a night, it doesn't even have a kitchen, but it does have 360-degree views of Manhattan from seven hundred feet high. Warner was involved in every design decision. He personally visited a quarry in France to buy $500,000 worth of marble for the bathroom, and the bed cost $65,000, including the twenty-two-carat gold woven into the bedspread. He spent $500,000 on gilded bronze for the bookcase.

However, he didn't show up to his own party until around 7:55—five minutes before it was scheduled to end, and long after most of his guests had left. He chatted briefly, mostly about Beanie Boos, and left.

After Toy Fair, it was time to get started on the community-service requirements.

I called another former high-level Ty executive to ask about Warner's prospects as a mentor in an inner-city school. How could a reclusive billionaire who'd lived inside a bubble for the past seventeen years—and a partial bubble for close to seventy—all of a sudden drop everything and start mentoring underprivileged children?

"I think he's going to do fantastic," he said. "Ty Warner is one of the best actors out there. Whether he likes it or not, it won't show in the way he handles the kids. Hopefully in the time he's faking it or not faking it, he'll genuinely feel something. That's what you hope for.

"I truly believe that he has the heart of a kid who was harmed by his mom's psycho crap," he added. "That's where I always thought that he had a soft spot. He never really had a childhood. He's got that, like, Michael Jackson syndrome. He's a really sensitive guy, but he's got so much damage."

Dan McGrath, president of the Leo Catholic High School, an academically rigorous all-boys school on Chicago's South Side, where Warner is doing some of his community service, met with him and his lawyer in early April of 2014 to start planning for the program. He was instantly impressed. "The visit went quite well," he told me. "Ty was very engaged, and engaging.

He's not just putting in his time. He really wants our kids to get something from this. He's giving them ownership of the project and he expects accountability. He wants to be hands-on, but he wants the kids to be doing the actual work."

Later that month, Warner met with the twelve members of the school's Entrepreneurs Club to discuss ideas for his community service. In a quiet voice he answered all the questions the enthusiastic students had about business. "How did you come up with the idea for Beanie Babies?" someone asked. "I tried to think like a kid," he said. Next he talked about the importance of his tactile, almost visceral response to a new product: "How does it feel when you grab it? Is it fun?"

McGrath says that Warner is "very comfortable and accessible. He has a very easygoing manner, and the kids are not at all put off by the fact that he's very well-to-do."

In May Warner came back with an idea he'd been discussing with McGrath. The Leo School has an eighty-eight-year history and many proud alumni. Its football team just had an exceptionally good year, and the school had sold out of all its hats, T-shirts, and sweatshirts. The idea: to stop buying logo merchandise from a national company and turn the process over to the Entrepreneurs Club—with Warner there to help them with the product design, sourcing, and marketing.

Warner, wearing jeans and a blazer over a black sweater, announced the plan to the students and then told them to start working on designs. He wandered the room, shedding his blazer as the building grew warmer, and he quizzed them on their ideas: Had they thought about who their target market was? That V-neck sweater design you're working on, he said to one student: Is that something for a grandfather or a younger person? Always remember, he explained: stay focused on who you're selling to. He talked about different kinds of materials, and he suggested tweaks to their designs. He collected the students' drawings and left.

In mid-June he arrived for his third meeting with the Entrepreneurs Club, but this time he had a surprise: several bags of prototypes that he'd personally gone to the factories in China to have made. There were baseball hats, the V-neck sweater, plush footballs, and more. "A full product line," McGrath marvels. The goal is to have the merchandise ready for the alumni golf outing in August. "We could sell three tables' worth of those V-necks," McGrath says. "When the kids saw the product line today, they were really, really thrilled. These were their own designs. It was the fruit of their labors."

School was out for the summer, but the Leo School remained open daily—a new policy. "Last year," McGrath tells me, "kids came back from summer vacation, and I asked them what they did, and they would say, 'I didn't go out of the house, Mr. McGrath. I don't live in a neighborhood where you can.'" And so the school remains open. "Most of it is organized," McGrath says, "but it's also just saying 'Hey, we're open. Come sit in the library or come shoot hoops.'" Or, on some days, come learn about business from the richest man in the history of toys.

30

Exit Strategy

The life and career of Ty Warner and his toys is probably best summarized by the logo that is such a ubiquitous symbol of a 1990s childhood that it's now a popular costume at retro-themed Halloween parties. The Beanie Baby hangtag, whose every detail collectors fussed over before securing it in a plastic shell to protect it from age and mishandling, is a heart, with room in it only for the name "Ty." That was how he'd always wanted it, and he dispatched anyone who threatened what he wanted with a zeal matched only by the dedication he brought to the design and manufacture of the animals his name was attached to. A child who has known no healthy love can grow up to be an adult too damaged to love. The women who loved Ty Warner—Patricia Roche, Faith McGowan, and his sister, Joy—would ultimately take no more comfort from him than he did from his abusive father or his mentally ill mother. Warner found himself no happier than the people he abandoned. The Beanie Babies brought him, as the Norwegian playwright Henrik Ibsen wrote of money, "the husk of many things but not the kernel . . . food, but not appetite; medicine, but not health; acquaintance, but not friends; servants, but not loyalty; days of joy, but not peace or happiness."

The last time Warner saw his sister, in the mid-2000s, he took her on a tour of the Montecito, California, estate he was building at a cost of well over $150 million. He showed her the landscaping and the Mediterranean architecture; then he led her into the formal dining room with seating for at least forty people. "And this is where we eat when we have company," he explained.

"Who would you have over?" Joy asked with an edge she quickly regretted, because she could see that it had hurt him.

He was quiet. Then: "Nobody," he said coldly. Then he turned and walked into the next room to continue his tour of one of the most expensive homes in America.

The Internet bubble of the late 1990s is mostly remembered as a force for destruction: massive overinvestment in dubious start-ups stripped Americans of their life savings and jobs and undermined confidence in American industry for years to come. There is, it is often said, a conflict between the real economy and the speculative economy—with the result being wasted resources and ever-rising inequality.

Now, however, some economists and revisionist observers are wondering whether bubbles are really as bad as they so obviously seem. In a column based on his 2007 book, *Pop! Why Bubbles Are Great for the Economy*, financial journalist Daniel Gross argues that speculative manias have enabled the creation of products and services with broad social benefits that otherwise never would have happened:

> *The cheap, pervasive national railroad network led to an integrated market in goods and commodities—and long-lasting businesses such as department stores, mail-order retailers like Sears, and national brands from Coca-Cola to Procter & Gamble. The Internet pop has left us with Web 2.0—Facebook and Skype, MySpace and YouTube, and, most of all, Google. Each of these companies either was started or gained critical mass after the Internet bubble burst. Each gained tremendous scale overnight thanks to all the cheap excess capacity built during the 1990s bubble.*

Speaking of "cheap excess capacity": Whatever happened to all those Beanie Babies people hoarded? Some are still in plastic bags in garages, some were sold for twenty-five cents each to carnies, and some were thrown in Dumpsters in disgust.

In March 2000, shortly after the bubble deflated, a collection of DeWitt, Iowa, Beanie Babies found itself engulfed in flames. As he explained in a deposition, Robert Sager was tired of his wife Ramona's Beanie Baby collection. "She had Beanie Babies everywhere and I was sick of them sons of bitches and I decided I was going to barbecue them," he said. "I had a big brush pile that I was going to burn outside and I had decided I was going to get all her Beanie Babies and take them out and barbecue the sons of bitches and went to get the charcoal lighter . . . [It] flared up a lot faster than I thought it was going to."

Ramona sued the insurance company for denying her claim for $100,000 in damage to their home. In his ruling, which began, "A battalion of Beanie Babies has marched a legal question before us," Iowa Supreme Court justice Michael J. Streit noted that "150 Beanie Babies and Buddies perished in the fire. . . . Not surprisingly, Robert and Ramona later divorced." By the time of the fire, the collection was not a source of significant value: Ramona filed a claim for just $1,100 in destroyed Beanie Babies.

A few Beanie Babies, the ones that were retired prior to the craze's taking off in 1996, are still worth $50 or $100—occasionally a few hundred for the rarest pieces, once supposed to be enough to cover the down payment on a McMansion. At least 99.5 percent of the perfectly preserved Beanie Babies from the late 1990s are today worth significantly less than they retailed for.

Nicholas Walsh, a twenty-nine-year-old social media marketer who grew up in Red Bank, New Jersey, remembers lining up at Hallmark stores after school, jockeying for position with the middle-aged women who were his main competitors in the Beanie hunt. Inspired by the price guides, he preserved each of his three hundred Beanies' hangtags in plastic tag protectors—and added Lucite containers for the bears, some of which he paid as much as $100 for. The collection was worthless by his teens but has since found new life: a few months ago, Walsh started decapitating his Beanie Babies and mounting them on wooden plaques as mini hunting trophies. He calls it "Beanie taxidermy" and he's already sold eighteen at $25 each—giving him, at long last, a tidy return on his Beanie investment. "I make a point to make sure they still have their tags on—and people ask me why. I tell them that if the decapitated Beanie Babies don't have their tags, they're not worth anything."

Usually, though, the speculative dreams of more than a decade ago come to more heartwarming resting places. Every week, small-town newspapers report on the donations of mint-condition Ty products to local children's hospitals, police departments, and American soldiers stationed overseas, who use the toys to connect with children in potentially hostile circumstances. The donations are usually anonymous, because while philanthropy is a source of pride, philanthropy as the exit strategy of last resort from a comically bad investment isn't.

"Thanks to a donor, Spokane police officers have new toys to use to comfort children in traumatic situations," reported the *Spokesman-Review* of Spokane, Washington, in a 2012 story. The piece was accompanied by a photo of a smiling patrolman holding two Beanie Babies in his hand, standing in front of the Beanie-filled open trunk of his cruiser: "A young woman who wishes to remain anonymous recently gave the Spokane Police Department 1,600 Beanie Babies in near perfect condition." The speculative boom for Beanie Babies has resulted in an unsurpassed volume of high-quality, perfectly preserved, monetarily worthless plush animals for children most in need of the comfort of something soft. A few years ago, Warner's sister emptied her closets of the hundreds of Beanie Babies she'd accumulated haphazardly during the craze years—they were made by her brother, after all—and dropped them at the nearest children's hospital. Nancee Biank, the psychotherapist who'd introduced a McDonald's communications executive to the line and had to pull them from her practice when parents became consumed by greed, is once again able to use Beanie Babies in groups with children. Today's kids know them only as toys because they're too young to remember that there was a time when people abandoned their senses over beanbag animals.

As for what will become of the septuagenarian Ty Warner's plush winnings: in a court filing related to his tax case, Warner reported a net worth of more than $1.7 billion—the product of a thirty-year run in plush that included, at last count, more than 2,000 Beanie Babies, just under 1,000 Ty Classics, 487 Beanie Buddies, and enough other pieces for a total of just under 6,000 products, most of which Warner designed himself. Warner will never be able to spend his entire fortune. But when one executive who asked to remain anonymous asked Ty's lawyer about estate planning, the reply was memorable: "That is a question that should never be asked."

Ty Warner poured the best and most focused parts of his powerful mind into creating the soft toys that are the first loves of more children than any other brand's. Whisper the Deer, a Beanie Baby released in May 1998, sits on my desk as I write this. The difference between average and spectacular, Ty knew, is often in the minutest details. It was that knowledge that had him sitting alone at his desk late into the night perseverating over every piece of fabric and examining hundreds of samples for possible eyes. It was that attention to detail that made his first cats popular sellers, and the constant quest for a better product also led to the first "retired" Beanie Babies that collectors fetishized. I've been contemplating Beanie Babies enough to notice, I think, what makes Whisper special: There's a stitch in her back and a little pucker in her belly that gives her attentive, bolt-upright posture—this in spite of the fact that she is under-stuffed and squishy. It's the posture that creates her personality and, as Warner himself describes his toys, "charisma."

At age seventy, Ty has devoted more time to that stitch on Whisper's back than to his estate planning. In his sentencing memorandum his lawyers wrote, "Counsel for Ty was stunned to learn that he does not even have a current will nor any structure designed to minimize estate taxes." His defense team tried to argue, based on the lack of estate planning, that Warner was not the greedy, calculating, tax-dodging tycoon the prosecution had portrayed in its sentencing memorandum arguing in favor of incarceration. Rather, they said, he was a benevolent man who hadn't gone through his life obsessed with money. Most people who know Warner disagree: his lack of a will, they say, was a product of his self-absorption, not a disregard for material concerns.

Unless Ty Warner suddenly gets interested in his estate planning, his mostly estranged younger sister, now sixty-five years old and relying on aid to the indigent for medical bills and part-time jobs to feed her half-dozen adopted animals, will be the sole heir to the largest fortune in the history of stuffed animals.

NOTE ON SOURCES

This is a work of nonfiction. No dialogue has been invented; all dialogue is either lifted from primary sources, like Faith McGowan's unpublished memoir, or from interviews I conducted with people who were present for the conversations. However, please note that remembered dialogue is not necessarily the same as real-time dialogue.

The bulk of the research and reporting for this book consisted of hundreds of interviews—in person and by phone. I also used contemporaneous trade publication and mainstream media accounts of the craze. Where possible, I've simply named the source within the text. Most of these accounts are available online and if you Google the quote "in quotes," you will be able to find the original source. In the note on sources in his most recent (and excellent) book, The Price of Silence: The Duke Lacrosse Scandal, the Power of the Elite, and the Corruption of Our Great Universities, journalist William Cohan writes, "In an era when digital access to documents of all stripes is becoming increasingly ubiquitous, the idea of providing page after page of notes on the sources of my research . . . seems somewhat superfluous." I agree.

To understand the story of Ty Inc., I met and spoke with former Ty executives and employees, freelance designers, sales representatives, personal connections of Ty Warner's, executives at competing plush companies, retailers, and the collectors, authors, and secondary-market dealers who were part of the Beanie mania. Many of the former Ty employees and independent sales representatives I spoke with requested anonymity; in other cases, in the interest of concision I have incorporated their recollections into the story without naming them. Legal and regulatory filings related to the company were also consulted.

There were similar interviews—in person and by phone—with the collectors, dealers, and experts whose lives were consumed by the fortunes they made and lost during the Beanie craze.

For their insight into Warner's life and career and early days of Ty Inc. and its founder, I especially want to thank the volunteers at the La Grange Area Historical Society, Joy Warner, Donald Danald, Gary Richert, Pasquale Capra, Patricia Roche, Faith McGowan, Jenna Boldebuck, Lauren Boldebuck, Bob Ricciardi, Lina Trivedi, Bill Harlow, Harold Nizamian, Paul Roche, and Virginia Benes-Kemp.

For a view into the machinations of the secondary market for Beanie Babies, I want to thank in particular Mary Beth Sobolewski, Becky Phillips, Becky Estenssoro, Brian Wallos, Chris Robinson and his son Chris Robinson Jr., Claudia Dunne, Leon Schlossberg, Sondra Schlossberg, and Jill Finlayson. Their patience in answering endless, persnickety questions from a stranger who phoned more than a decade after the fact to ask about their experiences in the world of Beanie Babies is much appreciated.

For background on the collectibles industry generally, Franklin Mint founder Joseph Segel and Charming Tails creator Dean Griff provided valuable perspectives.

In his entire career Ty Warner has conducted exactly one extensive interview: with Joni Blackman of People magazine in 1996—prior to the height of the Beanie mania. Ms. Blackman was unbelievably helpful in providing her recollections of her time with Mr. Warner at his home and at his office.

As artifacts of the mania, the hundreds of books, VHS tapes, magazines, and cached Beanie Babies fan sites accessed through the Wayback Machine are tremendously helpful. In particular, Mary Beth's Beanie World (changed to Bean Bag World because of litigation from Ty Inc.)

and Beanie Mania *are useful*—Beanie Collector, Hot Toys, Beans! Magazine, *and* ToyFare *were also consulted. For broader perspective on the industry during (and before) the period,* Collecting Figures *and* Collector's Mart *magazines were used. A complete collection of Ty catalogs from 1988 until the present was indispensable in tracking the evolution of the company, its products, and its marketing. A several-hundred-page handbook given to all the company's sales reps in 1998 was also important.*

For background on the history of the toy industry, the definitive source is the tremendous volume of back issues of Playthings *magazine, which has served as the definitive and well-reported trade magazine for the industry since 1903. For a more specific look at the plush industry, and teddy bears in particular, my favorite is the out-of-print* Christie's Century of Teddy Bears *by Leyla Maniera.* The Story of the Steiff Teddy Bear: An Illustrated History from 1902 *by Günther Pfeiffer is helpful for the story of that company, as were several brochures and guides from the Steiff Museum in Germany. There were several teddy bear magazines with strong followings during the 1990s:* Teddy Bear Review *was particularly helpful, as was* Teddy Bear and Friends. *Peter Bull's* The Teddy Bear Book *and Patricia Schoonmaker's* A Collector's History of the Teddy Bear *were also consulted. For details on the design and production of teddy bears, I like Sally Winey's* How to Make and Collect Rainbow Bears.

For contextualizing Beanie Babies in the history of speculative manias—and, in so doing, better understanding how the Beanie mania and other crazes happened—there are two books that stand above all others: John Kenneth Galbraith's A Short History of Financial Euphoria *and Robert Shiller's* Irrational Exuberance. *Edward Chancellor's* Devil Take the Hindmost: A History of Financial Speculation *is also good, as is Charles Kindleberger's* Manias, Panics, and Crashes: A History of Financial Crises.

Understanding how consumer crazes—and fads in general—happen is difficult: there is at the core of every fad something intrinsically inexplicable. That's the gap between rationality and irrationality. Too often, writers attempt to distill phenomena to clever rules and acronyms when that's not really how these things work. However, books that were helpful in at least trying to sort it all out include Malcolm Gladwell's The Tipping Point, *Chip Heath and Dan Heath's* Made to Stick: Why Some Ideas Survive and Others Die, *and Jonah Berger's* Contagious: Why Things Catch On. *Finally, I want to thank Ty Warner. He continues to produce the best, most affordable plush animals in the world. While he might have preferred that nothing be written about him, in no way did he interfere with my reporting for this book.*

ACKNOWLEDGMENTS

Thanks to everyone at Portfolio/Penguin for their belief and involvement in a book on a strange topic: Adrian Zackheim, Brooke Carey, Maria Gagliano, Will Weisser, Rachel Moore, Margot Stamas, Taylor Fleming, Kathy Daneman, Kent Anderson, and Kary Perez.

At Kuhn Projects: David Kuhn, Kate Mack, Jessie Borkan, Nicole Tourtelot, and Grant Ginder.

At Amplify Partners: Elizabeth Hazelton and Allison McLean.

Marc Acito, for his insight on how to make the original manuscript read vaguely like a book.

My family, for accepting my belief that stuffed animals are an appropriate gift for people of all ages on any occasion. As always, Andrew Tobias. And Ryan—a thousand violins begin to play.

INDEX